Teaching in the Primary School

Maurice Galton
Professor of Education
University of Leicester

David Fulton Publishers
London

David Fulton Publishers Ltd
2 Barbon Close London WC1N 3JX

First published in Great Britain by
David Fulton Publishers 1989

British Library Cataloguing in Publication Data

Galton, Maurice, *1937* –
    Teaching in the primary school.
    1. Great Britain. Primary Schools. Teaching
    I. Title
    372.11′02′0941

    ISBN 1-85346-095-8

Typeset by Chapterhouse, Formby
Printed in Great Britain by
St Edmundsbury Press Ltd, Bury St Edmunds, Suffolk

Contents

List of Tables and Figures

Tables

Figures

Preface

When I was asked to write this book by the series editor he told me that I could write about anything that I wanted. Initially, I had thought to write about the difficulties of putting theory into practice, using the extended diary notes I made when I returned for a short period to obtain 'recent and relevant experience' of the classroom. However, the original publisher (previous to David Fulton) said that nobody would wish to read long accounts of my personal triumphs and disasters in the classroom. Neither did he want me to write only about the ORACLE (Observational Research and Classroom Learning Evaluation) research.

In the end, therefore, I compromised. There are two central chapters on ORACLE, since it was the largest observational study of primary classrooms carried out in Britain until the recent ILEA research, and I also include, in the final chapter, descriptions of three incidents that took place when I returned to teaching.

This brief return to the classroom influenced my thinking in many ways and these are reflected in the themes of the book. Like more experienced colleagues, I failed to live up to the Plowden ideal. But I was also able to see frequent occasions when the children prevented the teacher's attempt to encourage them to take responsibility for their learning as the model prescribed. Most teachers have such natural talents and skill when working with young children that one becomes frustrated looking for the key that will release all this creative energy in both the teachers and the pupils. I hope the book is a modest contribution to this search for a means of implementing progressive ideas in a way that is practicable within the current classroom context.

I have many people to thank for their help in the writing of this book: first, the teachers who, over the years, have taken part in successive projects which I have directed and, in particular, the staff and the then headteacher of the school where I returned to teach. I should like to thank Paul Croll for his agreement to release some hitherto unpublished data which he analysed during the original ORACLE project. This is presented in Chapter 2. I have also included unpublished data from the PRISMS project (Curriculum Provision in Small Primary Schools).

I should also like to thank Diana Stroud who has worked as secretary to successive ORACLE projects for the past twelve years and who, because she is the one person who can read my writing, was the only one who could type the book. Lastly, my thanks to my wife, Pam, who put up with me while I was writing the book and did the best she could to improve my English.

Throughout the book, whenever reference is made to a pupil, a teacher or a tutor, the convention has been adopted of using 'they', 'their' and 'them' rather than the singular 's/he', 'his/hers' or 'him/her', in the interests of impartiality with respect to gender.

Maurice Galton
July 1988

Editor's Foreword

Many of us in education are becoming numbed by the numerous proposals for changes to so many aspects of schooling in England and Wales. Some of us have wondered on what evidence this or that imperative and urgent 'innovation' was based. How many of the changes introduced in recent years have been reasonably assured of success because they have been subjected to prior evaluation in some embryonic form?

Twenty years after the publication of the Plowden Report seemed to be a proper and conventional time for some assessment of the state of affairs in Primary Schooling, and the series of which this volume is a member arose from such a consideration. Powerful in its presentation and comprehensive in its coverage, the Plowden Report was also distinctive. Previous reports on education appeared to rely mainly upon their Committee's sampling of presumed informed opinion for their recommendation. In contrast, the Plowden Committee conducted national surveys to obtain answers to some of their questions. Further, the authors of the report attempted to portray the psychological development of the child as a frame of reference to which to relate the curriculum. Alas, the precedent of establishing a sound and appropriate research base on which to found educational decisions has not been the hallmark of subsequent government policies. Neither has there been a systematic review of Plowden's proposals and assumptions.

Which psychological principles in Plowden have been applied and found to be efficient and desirable? Which psychological principles in Plowden have not been applied or have been misapplied? With what consequences? Which principles have been tried and found to be wrong, perhaps making assumptions about children which are just not true? A variety of questions of this kind can be asked, and if we are to follow Plowden's prescriptions we have to 'find out' for ourselves what the most likely answers are.

One major question addressed in this volume is not whether the tactics of teaching proposed in the Plowden Report were implemented, but why they were not implemented much more extensively. Maurice Galton offers various reasons, ranging from the subversive cleverness of cunning children to the simple impossibility and undesirability of the adoption of such tactics for all of the teaching all of the time. Plowden was romantic as well as progressive. Its assumptions about the inherent virtues of children and their development are well in excess of what the evidence permits us to believe. While we have to have faith and aspirations if we are to improve ourselves through our education, the aspirations have to be realistic. The eventual potential of our species is unknown, and fortunately we still have a long way to go. However, and for the present, whilst we should not stifle curiosity that is beneficial, we should not base our teaching on the assumption that all children are chronically curious and anxious to learn, if that is not true. Similarly, whilst there are circumstances in which we can encourage the development of a child's own interests, to presume that these should define the whole curriculum is based on a misunderstanding about the role of culture in development and is inconsistent with anything other than a bizarrely anarchic view of society. We also know that to be most effective the methods of teaching have to be varied according to who is being encouraged to learn what, where and when; learning by guided discovery is not the 'best' method for all learning.

To answer such questions requires evidence rather than opinion, and Maurice Galton provides a succinct and excellent summary of what it is currently reasonable and defensible to believe about teaching in primary classrooms. The critical review of studies of the practice of teaching relies heavily upon the work of the Leicester University School of Education and rightly so, since that department has been the origin of so much of the relevant research. Galton draws our attention to the gaps between what teachers may believe they are doing and what they are actually doing. He refers to the variety of styles among teachers and among pupils and the educational advantages and disadvantages of these. The mixed economy of part-Plowden and part-other approaches which emerges as our best buy at the present is not a sad compromise between what is desirable and what can be done as things are at present. It is a balanced pedagogy that will retain what is sensible, humane, vital and cheerful, and fit the teaching to the learning tasks, the children, and the culture.

Peter Robinson
October 1988

CHAPTER 1

Towards a Pedagogy of Primary Teaching: Vision Impossible

Nine o'clock on a wet morning in October. Twenty-eight children, aged between 9 and 10 years, assemble in Mr Aspin's classroom in a school situated about five miles from the centre of an industrial Midland town. As in most primary schools of this type, the children come from mixed backgrounds. Some are from one-parent families, some live on council estates, others in private housing, a few come from the ethnic minority communities. They sit in groups of five or six around tables, chatting quietly while Mr Aspin calls the register and collects dinner money.

Once the formalities are out of the way, Mr Aspin begins the lesson. He hands out banda sheets on which is set out a mathematical crossword. The actual squares within the crossword, however, are blank and Mr Aspin has produced a replica on the blackboard for the children to copy. He tells them which squares to shade in black and where to write the numbers for the clues. The class quickly settles to the task while Mr Aspin walks round to see that everyone has got the idea. One boy, Darren, makes a mistake and has to start again with a fresh sheet. Mr Aspin makes a joke about it, telling Darren that if the bookmakers allowed him (Mr Aspin) to have a bet on who would always have to start again he could make a fortune. Darren grins. In general, however, the classroom is very relaxed and the mood purposeful.

Gradually, after about twenty minutes, the children begin their attempts to solve the crossword clues. Now the atmosphere changes. Mr Aspin sits at his desk and the children begin to come out for help. Soon there is a queue of waiting children. Some don't understand the question. Some are not able to recognise the appropriate method needed to solve the problem. The noise level in the classroom gradually rises until Mr Aspin finds it unacceptable and has to admonish some of the children, particularly Darren who is no longer grinning. By the end of the lesson about half the children have done three-quarters of the exercise while others, including Darren, have attempted only three or four of the problems.

Afterwards, Mr Aspin talks about the lesson to the observer who was present, for the school is taking part in a research project for the local university and Mr Aspin is one of the teachers involved. He tells the observer that the sequence of events was fairly typical. 'They start off well but some of the pupils, like Darren, have little concentration and find it difficult to do anything useful after the first twenty minutes. I try to give them something easy to do at the start of the day to get them in the mood for work.'

After break, the observer goes to a top infants class taken by Miss Lavine. Here the classroom arrangement is very different. Miss Lavine has the children organised into four colour groups (whites, yellows, blues and greens). The whites, although sitting in groups round the same tables, are all working individually (on their mathematics workbooks). Yellows are engaged in writing their story news. Blues are cutting out pictures from colour magazines and pasting them into a collage. The pictures mostly have to do with things in the home and with fashion – the class is preparing a display showing changes that have taken place during the last twenty years. Greens seem to be engaged in a variety of activities. Some are finishing off previously started paintings, others are reading to Miss Lavine, while others read to themselves. It is clear, from the instructions written on the board, that the groups rotate throughout the day so that each child gets the opportunity to take part in all these activities.

The atmosphere is businesslike and the children appear to understand the system well, although it is only just six weeks into the new school year. When the noise level rises, Miss Lavine just looks up and stares at the offending child. Occasionally she will put her finger to her lips and call 'Shhhhh'. Afterwards, Miss Lavine explains her system to the observer in a manner reminiscent of another teacher reported by Coe.

'I know all my children as individuals. Of course there are times when we come together and share activities like music making, drama, or perhaps just quietly listening to a story. But in basic work I give twenty different lessons. The children work individually, each at their own pace, and I circulate among them, helping, guiding and correcting. Always I have the particular need of the child in mind. Sometimes the children work in groups helping each other. Class lessons? They just wouldn't work ... I never teach a class. I teach children.'

(Coe, 1966, p. 77)

The above descriptions of lessons are in fact an amalgam of various incidents observed during the last ten years (Galton, 1987). Yet they are not untypical of similar incidents reported in other studies at infant and junior level. They raise a number of interesting questions. What, for example, influenced Mr Aspin to organise his class in one way while Miss Lavine chose another, although both of them worked in the same building? Why, as the lesson progressed, did Miss Lavine seem so much more effective in maintaining control, having merely to put her finger to her lips, while Mr Aspin ended up by shouting at the children? More importantly, what were the children learning as a result of these experiences? Why, for example, did the children work so well initially in Mr Aspin's class but seem to lose concentration just at the point where they needed to think more deeply about the tasks that were set?

The Study of Teaching

This book attempts to provide explanations for these and other similar events which make up teaching and learning in the primary classroom. These explanations are based, in part, on the systematic study of the behaviour of primary teachers and their pupils. In the UK such studies have become one of the major growth areas of educational research, beginning with the publication in 1976 of Neville Bennett's book, *Teaching Styles and Pupil Progress*. The principle behind all these investigations is one propounded by Barr as long ago as 1935 when he argued that it was possible to conduct a scientific study of classroom supervision by using criteria to distinguish between successful and unsuccessful teachers and then observing these teachers in order to determine how their practice differed systematically. Until recently, many studies (particularly in the United States where the research has a longer history) have defined success solely in terms of pupil achievement on norm-reference standardised tests of basic skills. The approach, however, does not have to be limited in this way. It is possible to use all kinds of criteria to distinguish between different groups of teachers. We could, for example, divide teachers into successful and unsuccessful questioners or those better able to create conditions whereby children co-operate in groups. The choice of criteria will, in part, reflect the area of interest being studied and the particular philosophical approach to teaching adopted by those carrying out the investigation. All studies, however, whether explicitly or implicitly, make such value judgements whenever they seek to describe and recommend one form of practice as against another. The process has been described by Gage (1978) as the scientific basis of the art of teaching.

There are, of course, those who would dismiss these claims out of hand. Reviewing one early work that attempted to establish a science of teaching (Bennett and McNamara, 1979), a headteacher, admittedly of a secondary school, wrote,

> Penetrating analysis of interactional processes in the classroom has nothing to offer teachers who know when they are teaching effectively. Teachers have their own checks. General class response, individual pupil interest, the work pupils produce, the progress they make, all indicate whether things are going well. By and large, teachers acquire their skills pragmatically. They learn to vary their approach to meet different types of problem.

> (Spooner, 1980, p.554)

Teaching as an Art and as a Science

The view, reflected in Spooner's comments, that, except at the crudest level, the process of teaching is too complex to be subjected to systematic analysis has a long tradition within the British educational system. As Simon (1981) observed, we differ from almost every other Western industrialised society in having no concept of pedagogy, described by Simon as 'a science of teaching embodying both curriculum and methodology' (Simon, 1981, p.125). The rejection of any scientific basis for teaching must inevitably place a great deal of stress on experiential methods for improving practice. Those charged with inducting new recruits into the profession adopt an approach not unlike learning to ride a bicycle (Galton, in press). Learner riders will be given the minimum instruction and then sent off to a *safe* environment to practise. Whenever they fall off the trainer is there as counsellor and guide, to offer support and listen to the riders' explanations for their failure. Eventually, through talking to the trainer and to other competent bicycle riders, learners gradually begin to make sense of their experience and get the 'feel' of what it is like to ride their machines. They are then ready to be launched into the more dangerous environment of the public highway.

In a similar manner, student teachers will be sent to a classroom initially to teach one child, before graduating to groups and then to the whole class – the educational equivalent of the public highway. Teacher training courses will place great emphasis on sharing experiences and learning from each other. At this initial stage students will not be challenged with complex ideas about practice or with research findings because it is argued that they should be first allowed to build up their confidence. This process continues until they are indistinguishable in their attitudes and their practice from more experienced teachers (Manning, 1977), by which time they are sufficiently confident that they no longer feel the need for any theory of pedagogy.

There are, of course, scientific principles that enable one to define the optimum position of a bicycle rider so that the centre of gravity of both the person and the machine affords maximum stability, but no one in their right mind would think of learning to ride in this way. Mr Aspin, in the opening episode, in all probability uses his particular approach because he did his teaching practice in a classroom where similar methods were used by the supervising teacher, while Miss Lavine had an altogether different experience, or perhaps attended a course where rotating children around the curriculum was advocated. Whatever the reasons, the notion of teaching as an art is now a confirmed part of primary ideology in Britain. Many of the current profession were brought up on Gilbert Highet's book, *The Art of Teaching*, which ran into twelve editions in the period 1955–70. Highet's book discusses general principles that should concern all teachers, such as choice of aims, justification for punishment, differences between education and indoctrination, together with advice on the nature of children. He also offers Plato, Aristotle and Jesus Christ as examples of master teachers who intuitively put these principles into practice. They are included as guides for the students as they begin their first encounters with pupils. More recently, Eisner (1977) has developed the notion of 'connoisseurship' as applied in the appreciation of the visual arts, music and literature to the evaluation of teaching. Thus, within a range of different writers or artists from different backgrounds, there will be some fundamental agreements about what constitutes good literature or art although the criteria used by different people may vary. In Eisner's view such definitions can be helpful in improving practice in that, by attempting to elucidate the principles on which judgements are made, key concepts can be further clarified.

Writers who argue for a more systematic approach to the study of teaching do not deny that teaching – because it involves human beings, their emotions and their values – has much in common with other art forms. They claim, however, that it is nevertheless possible to employ scientific methods to gain greater understanding about teaching. According to Gage (1978), artistic activities have an inherent order and lawfulness that make them quite suitable for scientific analysis. Gage denies Highet's (1963) claim that the artistic qualities of the teacher are 'quite outside the grasp of science' and asserts that, even within this scientific analysis, ample scope remains for the artist's subtlety and individuality (Gage, 1964, p.270). Like Gallagher (1970), who compared teaching with surgery and noted how the introduction of scientific processes has improved survival rates, Gage argues that teaching, like medicine, is a practical art rather than one 'dedicated to creation of beauty and aesthetic pleasures as ends in themselves' (Gage, 1978, p.15). Like medicine, therefore, teaching has a strong scientific basis although artistry is required when applying this scientific basis to achieve practical ends. Gage's view goes further than many other writers in that he believes that, ultimately, the nature of the scientific basis of teaching will be 'established relationships between variables in teaching and learning' (1978, p.72). According to Gage, the more these relationships are 'causal' rather than 'correlational' and are established through experimental research, the stronger will be this scientific basis and the better will be the opportunities to improve teaching.

The Systematic Study of Teaching

Most large-scale studies of primary classrooms in Britain and in the United States have made use of structured (systematic) observation methods. These techniques originated, in part, from the creation of a committee of child development by the American National Research Council at the beginning of the 1920s. This committee was particularly interested in research into teaching methods at nursery and kinder-garten stages where more usual data collection methods of question-naire and attitude inventories were inappropriate with children of this age. The first researchers therefore made diaries or narrative logs of all the activities observed in their visits to the kindergarten, but the sheer volume of this descriptive material made the task a very arduous one, in terms of both collection and analysis. Gradually, researchers focused their interest on particular categories of behaviour, and in 1929 Olson introduced the notion of time sampling, whereby these categories were recorded at specific fixed intervals of time.

In the early systems (as, for example, the one developed by Anderson, 1939), an essential theoretical distinction was made between 'direct' and 'indirect' teaching on the basis of the differentiation of categories where teachers instructed pupils about what to do as opposed to situations where they responded to the pupils' initiatives. Anderson's finding that two out of three teachers studied made approximately the same use of direct and indirect categories heralded considerable optimism that such dimensions could yield useful patterns by which teaching might be described. Anderson's work was subsequently developed, after the Second World War, by Flanders, and the Flanders Interaction Analysis Categories (FIAC) observation system became widely used throughout the United States (Flanders, 1964). This system had ten categories, of which the first three characterised *indirect* teaching while the next three (teacher asks questions, teacher lectures and teacher criticises) described *directness*. From early studies, Flanders established what he termed the 'two-thirds rule': two-thirds of classroom activity was talk and two-thirds of that talk was done by the teacher.

Studies of teacher effectiveness using FIAC and comparing the 'indirect–direct' (i/d) ratio of teacher behaviour with pupil performance on standardised tests have been reviewed by Dunkin and Biddle (1974). They criticise much of the research because of the arbitrary way the 'i/d' ratio was often defined; some studies used only two out of the three categories to calculate the direct teaching element. Nevertheless, the findings appear to be consistent in that, although many results produced no 'significant' differences, none of the results indicated a superiority for direct teaching. One puzzling feature, however, was that in experimental studies (the kind advocated by Gage, 1978), where teachers were randomly assigned to use either indirect or direct teaching approaches, no significant differences between the pupils' achievements were obtained.

An interesting explanation of these results is given by Soar and Soar (1972) and is illustrated in Figure 1.1. They suggest that the relationship between indirectness and achievement is curvilinear: most teachers in naturalistic settings are placed towards the maximum of the curve but slightly skewed towards the 'direct' side where there is a positive relationship between indirectness and achievement. Consequently, samples taken from this point (sample A) will provide a significant result in favour of 'indirectness', whereas a sample that straddles the maxima (sample B) will give rise to an insignificant difference. In experimental studies, teachers are artificially forced to the extremes of the curve where the positive relationship at one end is cancelled out by the negative one at the other. Soar and Soar (1972) argue that many teaching variables exhibit curvilinear relationships with pupil achievement; for example, both praise and criticism must be used sparingly, otherwise they begin to have an opposite effect to that intended to that intended.

The Flanders system, however, was designed primarily for use in relatively static classrooms where teachers stood in front of pupils who were arranged before them in rows while all worked on the same subject matter (Silberman, 1970). Such a system was inappropriate for the 'open' or 'informal' approaches to classroom organisation that by the 1970s were prevalent in British primary schools. At the time, review of some forty classroom observation systems in the United Kingdom showed that only two were based on the FIAC system

Figure 1.1 *Curvilinear relationships in teaching*

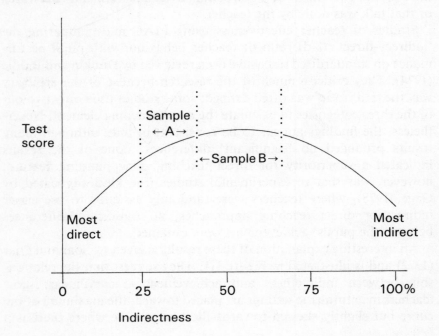

(Galton, 1979). The systems used to study the British classroom, such as that by Boydell (1974, 1975), had more in common with the Personal Record of School Experience (PROSE) developed by Medley *et al.* (1973). In such systems the emphasis was on providing descriptions of individual teacher/pupil contact as well as of ways in which pupils worked together in the absence of the teacher and the proportions of time in which these contacts were devoted to task as opposed to distraction. Such themes can be traced in the work of Bennett (1976), Bennet *et al.* (1980), Galton, Simon and Croll (1980) and, more recently, Mortimore *et al.* (1987). These and other findings to be described in this book begin to make possible similar claims to those made by Good and Brophy (1986) of American research, that we are now at a point where there exists a scientific basis for the study of teaching in the British primary classroom.

The Educational Disciplines and the Development of Pedagogy

Critics of the scientific approach to teaching point to the fact that much of this empirical study is atheoretical in that, according to Edwards and Westgate (1987), systematic observers seem to have 'a remarkable confidence' in their ability to solve the problem of identifying and coding highly problematic situations as they happen in the classroom, a view shared by Scarth and Hammersley (1986). In more extreme form the same points are also made by Barrow (1984) and by Egan (1983), with the latter arguing that empirical studies of the classroom can have nothing to offer to our understanding of teaching. Barrow claims that what holds teachers back from deepening their understanding of the teaching process, and so improving their practice, is the lack of clarity in the language used to define key concepts. Thus it is to philosophers of education rather than to empirical researchers that teachers should turn for help. Empirical researchers, particularly those who have carried out studies of systematic observation, have hindered teachers from attaining a deeper understanding about their practice because of the lack of conceptual clarity that surrounds the definitions of the categories they use to describe the teaching process.

It must be admitted that there is some substance to these charges, in that almost every dimension of behaviour used to describe teaching has to be viewed as highly problematic within the classroom situation. Attempting to classify such behaviours into unambiguous categories will inevitably over-simplify a complex situation. For example, much use has been made in recent studies of the notion of 'time on task' (Denham and Lieberman, 1980). On first inspection, given that the observer is familiar with the classroom, this particular category should cause little problem for anyone seeking to identify and code such behaviour. An observer can, fairly easily, identify when the pupil is talking to their neighbour about what was on television the previous night rather than about work. What will be more difficult, however, is for the observer to decide what is happening when a pupil is working on their own. Pupils may, for example, work continuously but slowly (Galton and Willcocks, 1983) *or they may be responding to internal stimuli*, which can vary from being fast asleep to gazing out of the window. In the latter situation it is very difficult to know whether the pupil is daydreaming or whether they have paused to think about their work. Observers have then to rely on their previous knowledge of the particular child and the context in which such behaviour takes place – for example, if gazing out of the window is immediately followed by rapid writing. The fact that different observers observing the same child can agree about such behaviour does, however, suggest that there exist common understandings about the nature of classrooms that allow such inferences to be made (McIntyre, 1980).

Philosophers such as Dearden (1976) have contributed enormously to the clarification of our ideas about various aspects of primary practice such as discovery learning, the nature of integrated approaches and notions of balance within the curriculum. These ideas have also been useful in better shaping and defining the categories used in various observation systems and in the design of other kinds of empirical studies. We still need to check, however, that our intentions, based upon better understanding, have been translated into action, since in teaching, as in many other instances of human behaviour, the assumption that there is a direct relationship between what we *know* and what we *do* is open to question. Indeed, studies of teaching have repeatedly shown the existence of a 'perception gap' whereby, as teachers, we are often unaware of our actions. Thus John Elliott and the Ford Teaching Project team showed that many teachers were unaware, until they listened to the tape recordings, of the extent to which they guided discussion during discovery lessons, even though they had spent a considerable amount of time clarifying the concept of discovery learning beforehand (Elliott, 1976a,b). As attribution theory predicts, the very fact that teaching is often a stressful experience can almost certainly lead individuals into suppressing the reasons for engaging in certain behaviours and into offering explanations for one's actions that lie beyond one's immediate control. Such explanations provide us with 'safe' reasons for not changing our behaviour – safe because we are not compelled to examine the possibility that the problem lies within ourselves. As with teachers, so with many philosophers. Over the centuries, it would seem that their undoubted capacity for clear thinking has not enabled them to apply these qualities to the conduct of their own personal lives in ways that would seem markedly superior to other human beings.

There is one other limitation to the approach whereby the application of logical analysis to the process of teaching can in itself be a sufficient condition for the improvement of practice. By its very nature such analysis is concerned to abstract ideas so that the discussion takes place outside a historical context. The result at the hands of different authors may lead to confusion rather than conceptual clarity. For example, Kliebard (1986), in his book describing the history of the American curriculum reform movement, notes that

> I was frankly puzzled by what was meant by the innumerable references I had seen to progressive education. The more I studied this the more it seemed to me that the term encompassed such a broad range not just of different but of contradictory ideas on education as to be meaningless. In the end, I came to believe that the term was not only vacuous but mischievous. It was not just the word 'progressive' that I thought was inappropriate but the implication that something deserving of a single name existed and that something could be identified and defined if only we tried.
>
> (Kliebard, 1986, Preface, p.xi)

Kliebard points out how writers, by ignoring the context of much of John Dewey's writing, have succeeded in attributing to him a variety of views and ideas that Dewey himself referred to as 'the more negative aspects of progressivism'. Thus, contrary to popular opinion, Dewey was suspicious of the emphasis placed by other progressives on the 'natural development of the child', with the curriculum chosen by the child rather than imposed by the teacher. Dewey also objected to a curriculum based upon project work because of the prominence it gave to skills training, which he viewed as largely antagonistic to the orderly organisation of subject matter, considered by Dewey to be an essential factor in learning and teaching. The lumping together of such a diverse group of writers as Rousseau, Pestalozzi, Froebel and Montessori with Dewey has helped create a view of progressivism that, to the public at large, appears at its best to be simplistic and at its worst anarchic.

Historical studies of education, besides putting such educational writings into a contextual framework, also enable us to deepen our understanding of how current practice, as described by empirical research, has developed. Without such knowledge we may find it difficult to devise successful innovation strategies that enable such practices to be modified. For example, Bernbaum (1976) has reminded us that the busy nature of the primary classroom has its origins in the dominance of the Church colleges in the training of elementary teachers during the nineteenth century with their inculcation of the 'Protestant ethic' built upon the twin virtues of 'honesty' and 'industry'. Any attempt to change classroom practice so that less time was spent on routine, relatively undemanding tasks, thereby increasing the amount of challenge, and possibly of noise, would need to take this strong tradition in the training of teachers into account.

Both philosophy and history of education therefore have a part to play in deepening our understanding of the central concepts of teaching and of their developing context, but in themselves they cannot supply the means to bring about a transformation of practice. For this to happen we need to explore both the thinking and the emotions of teachers and pupils and also to place this behaviour within the context of the school and the classroom as a social setting. Since the mid-1970s considerable strides have been made by sociologists in their attempts to forge links between what they term the functioning of the school system at the macro level and the finer detail, or micro level, operating within the classroom. Some writers such as Sharp and Green (1975) have made these links within the framework of Marxist interpretations of schooling, while others such as Hargreaves (1978) have interpreted teacher behaviour in terms of coping strategies, an idea expanded by Pollard (1985).

Nearly all these sociologists made use of non-systematic or, as it is more commonly called, participant observation to illuminate this micro structure. In the early 1970s there was considerable argument concerning the respective merits of the two observation methods (Hamilton and Delamont, 1974; McIntyre and MacLeod, 1978). There has since been a considerable rapprochement between classroom researchers working from within the different traditions so that it is now widely recognised that both methods can usefully complement one another (Galton and Delamont, 1985). We now realise that both teachers and pupils often say what they do not mean and mean what they do not say. Sociologists have helped us to interpret classroom discourse in ways that illuminate these hidden meanings within the wider social context, while educational psychologists can better help us to understand why the reasons that participants in classrooms give for their behaviours appear to offer only a partial explanation for their actions. Such understandings serve to deepen our knowledge of how children learn and form an essential element in the development of an effective theory of pedagogy. Pollard (1987) in his introduction to a recent book – an introduction aptly subtitled 'New Perspectives on Children' – makes a similar point when drawing attention to the potential significance of this new 'social constructionist' psychology for children's classroom learning. The paradigm reflects

> An approach to human thought, perception and action through meanings and . . . an acceptance that meanings are created and conveyed through the interaction of people, in particular by using language.
> The study of psychology would thus focus on inter-actions between people and on the 'development of the mind' through intersubjectivity rather than on the thought process of individuals studied in socially artificial settings.

> (Pollard, 1987, p.3)

Pollard is correct in claiming that the study of educational psychology, in particular, has changed rapidly since the mid-1970s. In the 1960s and early 1970s, standard educational psychology textbooks never mentioned teaching. Studies of learning, when they did take place in classrooms, occurred under experimental conditions where the effects of different teaching styles were strictly controlled. More often these experiments were carried out as clinical laboratory studies, such as those that gave rise to Piaget's theories of child development. Typically, whenever studies in natural settings were undertaken, the most convenient populations to hand were used and the results extrapolated to normal classrooms. For example, studies of child development using ESN children (Lovell, 1961) extrapolated the results obtained on tests of mathematical reasoning to 'normal' children of younger chronological age but having the same mental ages as the ESN sample. Wittrock (1963) used college freshmen to conduct experiments on discovery versus didactic teaching and the results have been interpreted in terms of junior age pupils.

According to Simon (1981), such studies have had a detrimental effect on the development of an effective theory of pedagogy because they have served to focus teachers' attention on the analysis of classroom problems in terms of children's difficulties rather than on possible weaknesses in the instructional method. Thus Mr Aspin, in the opening vignette, attributed Darren's failure to lack of concentration rather than to his own teaching methods. Simon (1981) argues that the development of the Piagetian school and its use by the Plowden (1967) committee to place the emphasis on the individual needs of the child has made it impossible to fashion an effective theory of pedagogy because:

> if each child is unique and each requires a specific pedagogical approach appropriate to him or her and to no other, the construction of an all embracing pedagogy or general principles of teaching becomes an impossibility.

> (Simon, 1981, p. 141)

While it has always been recognised that learning is not simply a cognitive but is also a social activity, the two aspects of the process have usually been treated separately, so that teachers have had to cope with conflicting messages about children's behaviour. Developmental psychologists, following Piaget, have emphasised the gradual growth of the child's thinking towards adult maturity. The implied message is that children are different from adults and therefore their behaviour must be interpreted differently. Those concerned with social learning theory, on the other hand, tend to emphasise the similarities between the experiences of children and of adults so that, for example, the behaviour of the pupil when asked a question or when expected to work in a small group is not dissimilar from that of the teacher when the latter takes on the role of learner as a participant on an in-service course.

The 'constructionist' paradigm makes it possible to interpret such classroom events as products of a series of bargains between the teacher and pupils, with each side seeking to manipulate the situation in order to maximise the extent to which their needs can be fulfilled. Formerly, much of this bargaining has simply been relegated to consideration under the broad categorisation of 'the hidden curriculum' and as such has been regarded as outside the control of teachers. Recent developments in social psychology, allied to empirical studies of classrooms, have now begun to change this situation to a point where the developmental and experiential traditions within the primary curriculum can be brought together (Blyth, 1984). This should provide a more coherent explanation of classroom practice so that teachers are in a better position to understand their situation and to alter it in accordance with their aims and purposes.

Some Key Concepts in the Study of Teaching

Throughout this book a key distinction is made between teaching strategies and teaching tactics. Both are used in the sense defined by Taba (1966). Strategies, as used here, relate to the decisions taken about the *curriculum content*, *classroom organisation* and *method of delivery* prior to a lesson. Such decisions concerning *how* to organise the lesson, *what* to teach and *how* to teach it are usually rationally planned and are often justified by teachers in terms of criteria over which they have no control. Thus a curriculum where the emphasis is on the basic skills will be justified in relation to parental or government pressures. The decision to organise the classroom into four 'rotating' curriculum groups, as in the case of Miss Lavine, may be justified as a more effective use of limited resources which current cutbacks in local authority finance have imposed. The use of teacher-directed approaches will be explained, in part, by the claim that children 'need structure' if they are to feel secure.

Once the lesson has begun, however, numerous decisions have to be taken and these 'moment-to-moment' occurrences are largely intuitive and often unrecognised. Few teachers are conscious, for example, of the extent to which they guide discussions, or how their body language offers clues to pupils about approved behaviour. Much research has taken place into the process of questioning during discussion (Rowe, 1974; Dillon, 1982). Teachers may begin by genuinely wishing to explore children's ideas. However, their anxiety to develop some structure may well cause them to emphasise certain replies rather than others or unconsciously to smile at certain responses or to repeat them. Pupils gradually gain clues as to what answers seemed to elicit these more positive responses from the teacher and quickly become adept at developing tactics whereby they avoid answering the questions until another pupil has established the kinds of response that will find favour with the teacher (Holt, 1984). At this tactical level, therefore, the needs of the teacher (e.g. a desire for a structure so that the lesson produces some tangible outcome) and the needs of the pupil (a desire not to be embarrassed by offering an unsuitable answer) combine to create a particular kind of learning environment.

Although most writers seem to use the terms strategy and tactics interchangeably, the distinction is nevertheless an important one because it helps to explain the existence of the 'perception gap' in teaching. Strategic decisions, because they are taken rationally and consciously, are a product of what Hargreaves (1979) and Pollard (1985) call coping behaviour. Psychologists, such as Gordon Allport, however, define behaviour not only as a coping activity but also as an expressive action. The distinction Allport (1966) makes is that coping is largely a rational response to an external situation (we cope with an open door by shutting it) whereas expressive behaviour is largely determined by unconscious motivations based upon strong needs and emotions (we either shut the door quietly or we bang it). In the classroom, both pupils and teachers experience these unconscious motivations as a result of certain needs, mainly concerning possible conflict between one's own view of self and the view of one's peers. Such conflicts can be stressful, and one mechanism for reducing such stress is to minimise the awareness of their existence – hence the 'perception gap' between the teacher's explanations of classroom events and those by outside researchers.

It is for this reason that current emphasis in the research literature on teacher decision-making (Calderhead, 1987) must be treated with a certain degree of caution. While it can be accepted that teachers' actions in the classroom must to a large extent be based upon sets of beliefs about practice, these teacher explanations may not, in themselves, provide a valid analysis of their personal ideology, since teachers may be unaware of some of the reasons for their behaviour. One way out of this dilemma is to give a greater emphasis to pupils' explanations of the same event, so that they may act as a counterpoint to those provided by the teacher. Because these pupil explanations are more difficult to obtain there is a danger of basing theories of pedagogy on only partial explanations of classroom events. This appears, for example, to have happened in the case of Hargreaves (1979) and his explanation of why teachers give guidance during discovery learning. Hargreaves argues that it is the teacher's 'creative attempt to ensure that the pupil achieves some product which is acceptable to his peers and to parents'. These are both reasons outside the teacher's control. There is thus no pressure to change as a result of discovering this failure to let the children 'find out' for themselves. The interactionist's perspective adopted here might interpret the same event as an unconscious response to the teacher's need for a 'safe' predictable framework for the lesson while, from the pupil's point of view, it is a tactic designed to avoid the possibility of failure by getting the teacher to give more and more clues to the 'right' answer.

Outline of Succeeding Chapters

In summary, therefore, it is argued that in seeking explanations of classroom practice it is important to look for different sets of reasons to explain the strategies and tactics that pupils and teachers employ. At the same time it is also necessary to take into account the generally recognised purposes of schooling, particularly those operating within the accepted ideology of primary education since the early 1970s. The next two chapters, therefore, examine the research evidence about the strategies and tactics of primary schooling, largely from the teacher's perspective. Chapter 2 looks at this research evidence during the 'golden age' of educational opportunity, the period up to the 1970s, before economic cutbacks led critics to question whether current provision gave 'value for money'. Chapter 3 looks at the more recent research, based mainly on systematic classroom enquiry, which has identified a gap between the public rhetoric of primary education and the reality of much practice. Chapter 4 then looks at the same data from the pupil's point of view.

Chapter 5 discusses a number of alternative explanations for this failure of current practice to match the prescriptions on which much modern primary teaching is still based. This leads to the second half of the book where some proposed solutions to the problems previously discussed will be explored. Chapter 6 looks at models of teaching where the teacher retains full control over the pupils' learning, while Chapter 7 examines alternative approaches which allow 'ownership' to remain with the pupil. In Chapter 8 the consequences of this latter approach for classroom management are discussed. The final chapter is a 'personal postscript' based on my tentative attempts to put some of these ideas into practice while carrying out a short period of retraining in an 8–12 middle school. This venture, a response to CATE's (Council for Accreditation of Teacher Education) call for trainers to demonstrate 'recent, successful and relevant' experience of the classroom, inevitably leads to some questioning of current training procedures.

This brings the debate about progressive education once more to the fore, so that by the end of the book it should be possible to attempt to reinterpret current theories of primary practice in a way that may make their implementation more practicable for the teacher and more acceptable to the public and to politicians.

CHAPTER 2

Teaching in the Primary Classroom: Reform or Revolution?

The imagery of primary teaching, as Robin Alexander (1988) has observed, is invariably linked with nature and the seasonal cycle. In the Plowden Report (1967), the metaphors are springlike and to do with growth. Writers on informal methods in the 1960s frequently had recourse to horticultural images. A decade later the language had become autumnal in tone. As a result of the oil crises and economic recession, all the talk was of cutbacks and pruning. At different times during the cycle there were brief summer flowerings, particularly in the West Riding, Oxfordshire and Leicestershire, where, 'if one was teaching in a group of particularly adventurous schools, there was a feeling abroad of being at the centre of exciting educational developments' (Jones, 1987). By the mid 1980s, according to some writers (Barker-Lunn, 1984), retrenchment had taken place and testing and streaming were once more on the increase. On this evidence, teaching in the primary school has been subject to cycles of fashion, influenced in part by economic factors. In times of expansion there are calls for new teaching methods to meet new challenges, during periods of economic decline there is a tendency to blame the situation on these same methods with a corresponding call for a return to traditional practice, particularly in the so-called 'basic areas' of the curriculum. Seen in this light, the Conservative government's Great Educational Reform Bill (1988) is but a manifestation of this trend.

Within these cycles of fashion, however, it is worth noting that classroom practice usually lags far behind the public acceptance of the need for change based upon the current theory. Thus, according to Selleck (1972), by the late 1930s progressive theories had become 'the official orthodoxy' in English primary education and were supported by educationalists and officials in the Board of Education. These theories were enshrined in the Hadow Report (1931) with its famous statement that 'the curriculum of the primary school is to be thought of in terms of activity and experience rather than of knowledge to be acquired and facts to be stored' (para. 75). Implementation of some of the principles of Hadow, however, was only accomplished during the Second World War as a result of the 1944 Act. For example, in Leicestershire observable changes in the schools only began after 1947 with the appointment of Stuart Mason as the Chief Education Officer (Jones, 1987). Jones quotes one teacher who describes Mason's influence:

> 'He would call us to meetings for discussion about the future trends in education but he was interested mainly in what you yourself hoped to achieve. For example, I got fed up with children marching into assembly and decided to let them come in and sit with whom they liked, while a teacher played soft music on the piano. The children took part, made up their own prayers appropriate to a particular theme, and made up their own little prayer books. I told Stuart Mason about this and he came and sat on the floor with the children and talked to them. I thought he was excellent. He was never too busy to listen.'

(Jones, 1987, p. 37)

Similar things were happening in the East Riding under Alex Clegg. Both men brought in advisers who were charged with the task of developing the new forms of teaching. Mason, for example, appointed Dorothea Flemming, who was Froebel trained and had been a lecturer at Goldsmith's College. Jones illustrates Miss Flemming's influence by quoting the recollections of one teacher:

> 'I am thinking of when I was at Hinckley. We used to have classes of over fifty in such tight rows that nobody could leave the room until somebody stood up. Then this Flemming came and caused a great deal of consternation among many Heads. She was the catalyst. She would come sweeping into the classroom saying, "Do away with discipline, do away with formality, get freedom, let the children play, to start with." '

(Jones, 1987, p. 35)

Just how far such advice percolated into other primary schools across the nation remains to be considered. American enthusiasts for

these new teaching methods tended to visit schools in Oxfordshire and Leicestershire, not only because of their reputation for excellence but also because they were handy for major tourist centres such as Stratford! These visitors were in no doubt that they had seen a 'primary revolution', one reporting enthusiastically that on 'visiting these schools in Oxfordshire I haven't been quite the same since'
(Rogers, 1970, preface, p.v).

Primary Teaching and the Counter-Revolution

Talk of revolution coupled with the student revolts in the universities during the early 1970s – with some politicians suggesting that the anarchic behaviour of the students was a direct consequence of these new-found freedoms in the primary school – undoubtedly began a backlash. The editors of the *Black Papers*, for example, argued that traditional standards were being rapidly eroded because 'some teachers are taking to extreme the belief that children should not be told anything but must find out for themselves' (Cox and Dyson, 1969a,b). The controversial study on reading standards carried out around this time by the National Foundation for Educational Research (Start and Wells, 1972; Burke and Lewis, 1975) and events at the William Tyndale school in London (Auld, 1976; Gretton and Jackson, 1976) were taken up by the media as an indictment of modern methods. During this period, when standards were thought to have declined and when the country was immersed in the oil crisis, current methods of primary teaching were held responsible, at various times, for indiscipline, for the increase in the crime rate, for vandalism, as well as for the decline in literacy and numeracy. These criticisms led the government to institute a survey of primary schools (HMI, 1978) and to initiate a 'Great Debate'. In the same period some leading Conservatives, including Mrs Thatcher, founded the Centre for Policy Studies which argued that the party's future policy, when it returned to government, should set its sights on deterring the 'half-hearted progressive' and 'curbing the most extreme' (Wilkinson, 1977). Those who hold with the idea of 'cycles of fashion' argue that from there on the continuing emphasis in government policy has been on tighter control over the content and methods of education. This has been accomplished principally through a reform of teacher training procedures, by the setting up of the Council for Accreditation of Teacher Education (CATE) and by the 1988 Act, with its emphasis on monitoring performance standards. It is noticeable, however, that the new Act becomes law during a period of alleged economic resurgence, so that by the time it is fully implemented the pressures for a reversal of existing trends towards traditional methods may once again be all the stronger.

It is, of course, too simplistic to view changes in teaching as, in the main, the result of changes in political and economic conditions. What is perhaps more important is that arguments about teaching methods, once they become linked with the changing needs of society, are likely to be defined in terms that can readily be communicated by the media and by politicians to the public at large. Thus the issue of progressive methods, which has been at the centre of the debate about primary schooling since the mid 1970s, has largely been presented in over-simplified terms whereas, as with most ideas in teaching, the concept itself is complex and not easily defined.

Nevertheless, one benefit of so much public interest in progres-sivism, or more generally in 'modern primary methods', is that it has stimulated funds for research. Since the Second World War a number of studies have been carried out which have attempted to describe and to evaluate the effectiveness of different teaching methods in the primary classroom. I shall now examine this evidence in order to see how far the various approaches to primary teaching have become inte-grated into typical classroom practice.

Research in the Primary School

For the purpose of this survey it is convenient to divide the evidence into three parts. The first part takes us from the end of the Second World War to the publication of the Plowden Report (1967), which has been described as the 'progressives' charter' (Anthony, 1979). The second period, a relatively short one, coincides with the publication of Neville Bennett's highly influential book, *Teaching Styles and Pupil Progress*, which raised serious questions about the use of informal methods in the primary classroom (Bennett, 1976). Bennett's study marks a significant change in the methodology used to conduct this research in that it made use of a limited amount of systematic obser-vation in some of the classrooms studied. The third phase of the research, beginning with the Observational Research and Classroom Learning Evaluation (ORACLE) studies (1975–80) and culminating in the report of the Research and Statistics Branch of the Inner London Education Authority (Mortimore *et al.*, 1987), describes research in which classroom observation was the main method used to investigate differences in teaching methods.

The immediate post-war years

According to Jones, 'One could be forgiven for believing that the progressive movement in the English primary school, that is the movement towards a child-centred education, began and developed in the period after the second world war reaching a climax with the Plowden Report in 1967' (Jones, 1987, p.32). By the time the report was published, a number of research studies (admittedly small scale) had been undertaken and this work must, in part, have influenced the committee to make their famous claim that 'finding out has *proved* to be better for children than being told'.

These early studies are of particular interest in the debate about teaching methods for another reason. In order to study teaching effectiveness, researchers are required to take concepts such as 'progressivism' and to define them operationally so that they can be used to characterise different types of teachers. By studying these definitions we can gain some insight into the ways in which terms such as 'progressive' and 'traditional' were interpreted by practitioners at the time.

Anthony (1979, 1982) has provided us with a critical evaluation of these studies. The first was by Kemp (1955), who reported an investigation into fifty London junior schools. Kemp used a rating scale to define the extent of progressivism in the classroom. One dimension concerned the school organisation – from the formal (children sitting in rows) to the extremely progressive, which, presumably, was not too dissimilar from the kind of classroom described by Jones (1987) earlier in the chapter. A second dimension examined the way the curriculum was organised, with the emphasis in the progressive classroom on activities and experiences related to 'the needs and interests of children', rather than a timetabled series of subjects determined entirely by the teacher. Besides Kemp, an inspector of schools also rated these classrooms and the two sets of judgements were in close agreement. Kemp correlated this 'progressiveness rating' with a large number of variables (including children's height!) and more importantly, in the present context, with a 'comprehension' attainment score (a combination of arithmetic problem-solving and reading comprehension tests) and also a 'rote' attainment score (a combination of mechanical arithmetic, spelling, handwriting and composition). Progressiveness correlated positively with both attainment characteristics although correlations were not statistically significant. Kemp concluded that there was no evidence from the investigation to suggest that 'progressiveness' had a positive or negative effect on pupil performance.

The second study reviewed by Anthony was by Warburton (1964). Again 'progressiveness' was defined in terms of ratings by judges using a scale that varied 'from the very formal, rigid and orthodox to the most informal, free and progressive'. The progressive end of the scale was identified, as in Kemp's study, by the way the curriculum was organised, with activities related to the needs and interests of the children. In this research the children were in the final year of compulsory schooling rather than at primary age, but Warburton reports statistically significant correlations between progressiveness and scores in reading and arithmetic.

A more detailed definition of progressivism was provided by Dorothy Gardener (1950, 1966). Gardener's research, which was interrupted by the Second World War, compared the results of progressive infant schools and a series of 'control' infant schools. The results favoured the experimental schools. When these children were again studied at 9 and 10 years of age, the results of pupils who had previously attended the progressive infant school were still superior (Gardener, 1950). In his analysis, Anthony (1979) concentrates on the 1966 study in which the children of 10–11 years of age whose infant and junior schooling had all been progressive were compared with those whose infant and junior schooling had all been of the 'control' type. Gardener's studies were particularly noteworthy for the variety of test materials that she produced in order to avoid curriculum bias. If all the items on the test had been identical to the tasks set by teachers in the more formal schools, children taught by informal teachers would have been at a disadvantage, since they would have been less familiar with this kind of test item.

The criteria that Gardener used for selecting the progressive schools included the freedom for children to move around the school, the opportunity to exchange with teachers in an informal way and the allocation of 'considerable' amounts of time to activities designed to make full use of the children's interests and purposes. Observers rated the school atmosphere and were asked to note whether the children were interested and whether the interest lasted. The children were also rated on whether they showed initiative, handled materials well and occupied themselves when undirected.

In twelve pairs of junior schools the children were tested in the second or third term of their final year. Except for arithmetic, where Gardener tested both mechanical arithmetic and problem-solving, the results were generally distinctly in favour of progressive schools, relative to the controls.

The final research in this phase of the study of progressivism was that of Barker-Lunn (1970), who carried out a longitudinal study of children in thirty-six streamed and thirty-six non-streamed junior schools. Although Barker-Lunn's study was mainly concerned with the effect of streaming, the teachers were asked about the use they made of different kinds of lessons. These lessons were classified as traditional (writing class-prepared compositions, learning spellings, formal grammar, formal tests of sums, rote learning of tables, etc.) and progressive (story writing, projects, nature work, group work, practical arithmetic, and a choice of what to paint in art). Barker-Lunn classified teachers according to their attitudes and their teaching methods: Type 1 teachers on the whole believed in non-streaming and made less use of traditional lessons, whereas Type 2 teachers generally preferred more traditional lessons and exhibited opposite kinds of attitudes to those of Type 1.

Barker-Lunn tested pupils in the last term of the fourth year of junior school using standardised tests of English and of arithmetic. Anthony's (1979) re-analysis of these data concludes that the Type 1 teachers did marginally better in English, while on arithmetic the Type 2 teachers were more successful. This pattern reflected the trends seen previously in the studies by Warburton and Gardener. Barker-Lunn also scored free writing essays for originality of ideas (mistakes in grammar, spelling and punctuation were ignored). The results appeared to be slightly favourable to progressive teachers.

Anthony (1979) is, however, somewhat critical of these studies. He argues that the comparisons were distinctly favourable to progressivism in that, where observers were asked to rate pupils, they did so on the evidence that the pupils were successfully carrying out the practices used to define progressivism. For example, in the Gardener study, the raters were asked if the pupils occupied themselves reasonably well when undirected. Such classrooms were therefore not simply ones that attempted to use the method but ones where the method could be judged to be working effectively. Anthony argues that in both Warburton's and Kemp's studies judges were likely to determine whether the curriculum was organised through activities related to the needs and interests of children by observing whether the children did indeed appear interested. Similar considerations did not apply when selecting the more traditional schools. Anthony therefore concludes that like was not being compared with like. He points out, however, that in spite of these possible biases in favour of progressivism there was a trend for the more traditional schools to do better on tests of arithmetic and that the comparisons in the other curriculum areas produced very small differences.

The post-Plowden era

In 1976 Neville Bennett, at that time a lecturer at the University of Lancaster, produced a report into teaching methods in primary schools under the title *Teaching Styles and Pupil Progress*. The Lancaster research set out to construct a typology of teaching styles, some of which were later merged and reinterpreted as 'formal', 'informal' or 'mixed styles'. These descriptions of teaching were then used to compare the gains over a year on tests of mathematics and English language made by children who were taught by these different teaching styles. The most controversial finding of this research was that the pupils taught by 'formal' or 'traditional' methods made greater gains than pupils in classes where 'informal' or 'progressive' teaching was used. The children who were taught by a mixture of methods fell between the formal and informal groups when judged by their performance on the tests.

Much public debate followed the publication of the report as well as considerable discussion in academic journals concerning the reliability and validity of the results. It was claimed, for example, that sampling errors and inappropriate statistical analysis gave rise to spurious results and that little account was taken of external variables such as teacher experience or the results of the 11+ (Gray and Satterly, 1976).

Bennett's typology of teaching styles was based on a self-completion questionnaire administered to 1,258 fourth-year primary school teachers from counties in the north-west of England. The original variables in the questionnaire were reduced to nineteen key ones by the use of factor analysis, and the responses of teachers to these key items were used to identify a typology of styles based on twelve groups (or clusters). Bennett then used seven of the twelve clusters to form three 'general teaching styles'. Two clusters from each of the extreme ends of the typology were combined to make up the informal style and the formal style respectively. The clusters in the middle of the range were used to describe the mixed style. Thirty-seven teachers were then selected to represent these three general styles – twelve each for the formal and mixed styles and thirteen for the informal style.

The nineteen variables chosen to describe formal and informal teachers deal, for the most part, with aspects of classroom organisation concerning seating, free movement of children, use of tests and approaches to discipline. Teachers were also requested to indicate whether they made use of integrated subject teaching. Although in some cases teachers were asked to report the relative emphasis placed upon categories (e.g. amounts of class or group teaching) these were eventually reduced to dichotomies by coding the response as either 'above' or 'below' the mean value.

This led to a number of unsatisfactory features because some of the variables were not independent. For example, if the teacher indicated that he or she had made use of an above-average amount of class teaching, then it was logically impossible to do the same for group work. In the same way, teachers who indicated an above-average amount of single-subject teaching must have, by definition, engaged in below-average amounts of integrated subject activities. Since it would be impossible to carry out class teaching while using an integrated approach to the curriculum, an interdependence between different categories was built in. These related variables then tended to dominate the cluster descriptions giving rise to the various styles. In Bennett's study, therefore, although the nineteen variables included most of the elements of 'progressiveness' highlighted in previous surveys (such as freedom, activity and discovery in children's learning), the stress in Bennett's typology was placed upon the forms of classroom and curriculum organisation rather than on the teaching approaches used. Only half the teachers in the informal group, for example, allowed individual work on topics of the pupil's choice.

According to Bennett's analysis, the results formed a coherent pattern, the effects of teaching styles being statistically and educationally significant on all the tests of attainment. In reading, pupils taught by teachers using the formal and mixed style were three to five months in advance of those taught by informal methods. In mathematics, formal pupils were four to five months ahead of both mixed and informal pupils, while in English formal pupils again did better than those taught by informal methods, being approximately three to five months in advance of their equivalent age group. Bennett also asked pupils to write imaginative and descriptive stories which were impression marked by three teachers (one from each of the formal, mixed and informal style) both in terms of their creativity and also for correctness of grammar, punctuation and spelling. Formal and mixed pupils were better at punctuation and no worse at creative or imaginative writing than pupils in informal classrooms. On the basis of these results, Bennett argued that 'informal' or 'progressive' teaching methods did not appear to compensate in creativity for the weaker performance of these pupils on standardised tests of basic skills.

These interpretations have been strongly criticised, however, by Gray and Satterly (1976). They argue that, instead of comparing individual pupils' scores, class means should have been used because the measures that described the teachers were class effects, which applied to all the pupils. The individual scores of pupils were therefore not independent of each other since all of the children in the class had been subject to the same classroom conditions, as defined in Bennett's typology. Using relatively few classes instead of a large number of individual pupils to make these comparisons, however, increases the size of difference between test scores that would be necessary in order to obtain a significant result. Gray and Satterly argue, therefore, that the method of analysis may have given rise to a false interpretation. Perhaps more seriously, they criticise the failure to control for certain important variables, particularly the fact that some of the schools were still taking the 11+ examination and that teachers in these schools would give pupils more practice at the kinds of tests used by Bennett to assess progress. Other possible effects that were not controlled included class size and the age and experience of teachers.

In response to these criticisms, Bennett carried out a reanalysis of the data. Unfortunately, this did little to resolve these controversies. In the reanalysis a new form of aggregating teachers into clusters was used (Aitken *et al.*, 1981). When progress was analysed in terms of class means, differences between the redefined 'formal' and 'informal' styles were reduced, with the pupils taught by the 'mixed' styles performing more poorly by comparison. For this reanalysis, responses to all the items on the original questionnaire, rather than the nineteen variables selected by Bennett, were used. Presumably this helped to reduce the influence of certain interdependent categories on the final cluster solutions, but it also meant that the characteristics of the new styles were very different from those previously used by Bennett. For example, the dominant feature of the new 'mixed' style was that the teachers within it tended to have more pupils who created discipline problems. This, in itself, appeared a questionable method of describing a teacher's style, since the fact that pupils behaved badly in the class would seem to be more a consequence of what the teacher did than a way of defining the teacher's practice. A more serious concern was that, in this new 'mixed' style, teachers from the original 'formal' and 'informal' styles were present in almost equal proportions. The reanalysis concluded, not surprisingly, that in classrooms where there was serious disruption academic progress tended to be slow, but it was unable to demonstrate whether this indiscipline was the result of applying either formal or informal methods. As a result, one of the authors of the report concluded that the descriptions of teachers in these terms had perhaps now outlived their usefulness so that the term 'progressiveness' no longer fulfilled a useful function (*Times Educational Supplement*, 24 July 1981).

Returning to the original Bennett study, a limited amount of observation was carried out in the classrooms of the teachers where the tests had been administered. The behaviour of a sample of pupils in these classes was coded under the subheadings of *work activity* (including preparation, writing, computation, etc.), *interaction with other pupils* (including asking, responding, co-operating), *movement* (including fidgeting or moving from their places), and *other activities* such as watching or task avoidance. From these observations it was concluded that pupils in formal classrooms more frequently engaged in work activity whatever their initial level achievement, especially in areas of computation, writing and reading. In particular, high achievers in progressive classrooms were said to display low levels of on-task behaviour, spending considerable amounts of time either talking about the task or in social gossip. Small differences occurred among average achievers, but the same pattern of increased work activity in formal classrooms was found with low-achieving children. On the basis of these results Bennett drew a clear inference of a strong relationship between the time spent on task and the level of achievement. In mathematics, high achievers engaged in 23 per cent more actual work activity; in English, the figure was 17 per cent. High achievers also interacted less with other children.

Again, there are some problems in the interpretation of these results. In this research, Bennett did not control for curriculum activity. In formal classrooms, with all pupils engaged on the same curriculum at the same time, it is a relatively straightforward task to ensure that different pupils' were sampled under similar conditions. In informal classrooms, using an integrated subject approach, there is a greater possibility of sampling error. The very order in which different pupils were observed could mean, for example, that a proportion of them was seen more often when engaged on tasks that require children to move around more frequently, as when doing art, rather than when sitting in their places completing a worksheet on arithmetical computation. In Bennett's study no attempt was made to check whether the proportion of observations in the different curriculum areas represented the curriculum balance within the particular classroom. It is not, therefore, clear whether the data for the informal classroom where the integrated day was used actually represent the typical behaviour pattern. Nevertheless, it must be admitted that the trend displayed in Bennett's data has been replicated in a number of American studies (Bennett, 1978).

Bennett (1976) also used a specially constructed questionnaire in which pupils were asked to rate their personal characteristics within the classroom context. In general, the different teaching approaches seemed to have little effect on the various attributes examined, except in the case of pupil motivation and anxiety. Informal classrooms appeared to improve pupils' motivation but at the same time they increased some pupils' anxiety. An explanation put forward by Bennett for this finding was that anxious children disliked the loosely structured informal classroom atmosphere and preferred a teacher who made it very clear what was required in terms of both the task and the outcomes.

Both Anthony (1982) and Gray and Satterly (1981) have carried out further reassessments of the British research on progressive teaching on the basis of their own reanalysis of Bennett's (1976) results, including the Aitken et al. (1982) reanalysis and the results of Galton and Simon (1980) to be discussed in the next chapter. Gray and Satterly reject Anthony's (1979) conclusion that the earlier surveys showed a trend in favour of formal education across all subjects. They place greater weight on studies that employed a pre–post test research design and where, unlike Barker-Lunn (1970), teachers or teaching styles were the major focus of interest. They conclude that these studies tend to indicate that there is a trend for pupils taught informally to do better at reading while the formal pupils do marginally better in mathematics and English. Gray and Satterly argue that the question of educational rather than statistical significance is the more important one. While the differences between formal and informal classes do reach a statistically significant level, they seem less important educationally than the differences between different teachers within the same style. They estimate, for example, that in Bennett's study the class mean scores of teachers in the informal cluster differed to the extent of nineteen standardised points.

These same differences are also in evidence across subjects. One teacher, for example, was highly successful at reading and mathematics but only average in English. Given these wide variations, Gray and Satterly (1981, p.193) conclude 'that teaching style, defined in terms of formal/informal dichotomies, is not a central concept in the study of teacher effectiveness'.

Anthony (1982), p.385), in responding to Gray's criticisms, remains unconvinced and argues that 'since teachers will continue to want to provide children with practice in the exercise of "freedom" and "discovery" the question of "how much and how soon" continues to be important whether it is a central concept or not'. Anthony claims that the research findings are consistent once one recognises that the two kinds of research – the earlier surveys such as Kemp's and Gardener's and that of Bennett – attempt to answer different questions. Kemp and Gardener address the question, 'Can progressive teaching work as well as other teaching?', to which the answer appears to be 'Yes', given sufficient pupil interest in the topic. Surveys such as Bennett's ask the question, 'Does progressive teaching *generally* work as well as other teaching?', to which the answer is 'No', from which one might infer, as did the then Prime Minister, Callaghan, that progressive teaching is only suitable for the exceptional, experienced teacher. Gray and Satterly's finding that, within the informal style, different teachers produced markedly different results is therefore explainable on Anthony's (1982) hypothesis. In studies such as Bennett's, which looked at a representative sample of informal teachers, some were better at securing the pupils' interest and maintaining their motivation. This, of course, leaves unanswered the important question of what such teachers did in order to facilitate this behaviour in their pupils. Such questions can most readily be answered by observing teacher and pupil behaviour in the classroom as it happens.

Some new evidence

Some hitherto unpublished data, collected as a by-product of the ORACLE (Observational Research and Classroom Learning Evaluation) research, provide information about this issue. The ORACLE research (Galton and Simon, 1980), which will be discussed in more detail in the next chapter, defined teaching style largely in terms of the tactics used by teachers during lessons rather than as in Bennett's study where aspects of their strategy, particularly their classroom and curriculum organisation, were collected by means of questionnaires. The ORACLE analysis gave rise to a more complex set of descriptions of teaching style, although two of these, *class enquirers* and *individual monitors*, were taken by Gray and Satterly (1981) to correspond loosely to Bennett's formal and informal styles, respectively. However, it was possible for the ORACLE researchers to use some of their observation data to categorise teachers in the same way as Bennett by, for example, comparing individual teachers' use of class teaching with the average for the whole sample. Other indicators, such as the use of integrated subject teaching, could be extracted from the impressionistic accounts of lessons written by observers and from the lesson plans that observers filled out at the beginning of each session.

For this analysis, fifty-nine teachers were observed. Since this smaller number would have been unlikely to give a good replication of the original twelve Bennett styles, the ORACLE teachers were matched on the basis of possessing or not possessing the key characteristics that defined formal and informal teachers in Bennett's studies. This *ad hoc* approach gave correlations between the sets of formal, mixed and informal teachers in the two studies of 0.69, 0.70 and 0.60 respectively. In general, the ORACLE classrooms appeared to be less formal than the Bennett ones and this is consistent with the fact that, in the ORACLE research, the three local authorities chosen had a reputation for progressive education and had abandoned selection at 11, unlike the principal local authority in the Bennett study. In the ORACLE sample there was more freedom of movement and choice of seats and more choice of work, and less homework and grading. On the more academic variables, such as curriculum and testing, there were no differences between the two samples.

Table 2.1 shows some of the differences in pupil behaviour associated with the different styles. The most important differences to emerge were that the pupils spent more time on work activity in formal classrooms than in either mixed or informal ones and that pupils in informal classrooms spent more time in distraction or in other activities, such as watching other pupils or the teacher. These findings replicate Bennett's (1976) small-scale observation study. Pupils interacted with the teacher either individually or in groups for about the same amount of time in all three styles of classroom, but formal teachers provided much more whole-class teaching so that, overall, pupils in the informally organised classes had 50 per cent less contact with the teacher than children in formal classrooms. There were approximately the same number of pupil–pupil exhanges in all three

Table 2.1 *Pupil activities in formal, mixed and informal classrooms*

	Informal %	Mixed %	Formal %
Pupil activity:			
Task work	54.0	57.1	63.0
Routine (preparation, etc.)	10.4	12.3	11.5
Waiting for teacher	2.4	4.6	4.7
Distracted*	20.4	16.6	12.8
Other	12.9	9.4	8.0
Interaction with teacher:			
Individual	1.9	2.4	2.1
Group	1.0	1.7	1.3
Class	6.5	11.1	16.6
All	9.4	15.2	20.0
Pupil–pupil interaction:			
All	19.4	19.1	17.0
% concerned with work	21.4	27.6	33.0

* Included 'disruption' and 'horseplay' (categories of distraction in which there was aggressive behaviour, either verbal or physical, resulting in no work activity).

styles of classroom but formal teachers seemed to ensure that these pupil–pupil contacts were more often concerned with work. In each case, therefore, there is a tendency, from the formal to the informal classroom, for pupils to engage in more task work, less distraction, more interaction with the teacher and more work-oriented interaction with other pupils. If Anthony's (1982) supposition is right, then it would appear that those teachers in informal classrooms who can generate greater pupil interest in the topic ensure higher levels of concentration on task and better results.

The ORACLE researchers also observed the teachers' behaviour so that it is possible to compare the different types of teacher interactions in formal, mixed and informal classrooms. These results are shown in Table 2.2. Whereas the analysis of data derived from the observation of pupils suggested that there were differences in classroom behaviours between the three different styles, particularly with regard to the amount of time spent working on the task, similar differences did not occur when a more detailed analysis of individual pupil–teacher inter- actions was undertaken. All three groups of teachers asked approxi- mately the same proportion of questions, with a slight tendency for

Table 2.2 *Type of teacher interactions in formal, mixed and informal classrooms*

	Informal	Mixed	Formal
	Percentage of all interactions		
Teacher activity:			
Questions	15.3	14.9	15.6
Statements	61.1	55.9	56.8
Other (marking, gesturing, etc.)	23.6	29.2	27.6
	Percentage of all questions		
Questions:			
Asking for facts	27.3	31.2	29.3
Asking for closed solutions	13.2	18.0	20.6
Asking for open solutions	3.2	5.6	5.4
Dealing with task supervision	33.9	31.8	29.6
Dealing with routine	22.4	13.4	15.1
	Percentage of all statements		
Statements:			
Statement of facts	15.9	15.3	15.9
Statement of ideas	4.5	5.7	6.5
Dealing with task supervision	50.8	53.0	49.4
Dealing with routine	28.8	26.0	28.2

informal teachers to make more statements, which was compensated for by the other two styles carrying out more activities, such as marking and demonstrating.

When the different types of questions and statements are examined there were some interesting differences. Contrary to the criticism that informal teachers never told pupils anything but 'left them to find out things for themselves', informal teachers asked almost as many factual questions as formal ones and made an identical number of factual statements. Informal teachers, in fact, asked fewer 'open' questions but showed a greater tendency to question pupils about task supervision or routine matters. Overall, however, the three categories of teaching style were not good predictors of the variation in detailed teaching interactions. If, as it would seem logical to suppose, the tactics teachers use in the classroom have consequences for learning outcomes, then the concept of formal–informal teaching does not help us greatly in identifying these variables. This remains true even though the relationship between pupil progress and teacher style found by Bennett was replicated in this ORACLE analysis.

Progressiveness: A Confusing or a Useful Concept?

To sum up, then, research on progressive and traditional teaching methods in the primary classroom seems to leave many questions unanswered. The first concerns the problem of definition. In the writings of advocates of progressivism such as Dewey, Piaget and Isaacs, 'freedom, activity and discovery in children's learning' were key concepts. In relation to the early surveys, however, Anthony (1979) shows that, when defining 'progressiveness', greater stress was placed on activities related to the needs and interests of children.

Such terms as 'freedom' and 'discovery' are highly problematic when either teachers or observers are asked to rate the extent to which such practices are carried out in a classroom. In Bennett's (1976) questionnaire, for example, freedom seemed to be equated with pupils deciding for themselves where they wished to sit and with the extent to which they were able to choose to work on a topic of their own choice. According to Nathan Isaacs, however, choice has more to do with the question of process than of content. He argues that 'progressive educators have placed the utmost value on the give and take of free discussion' in allowing children to engage in 'testing, making and planning' (Isaacs, 1955, pp.39–40). It is perfectly possible to conceive of classrooms where children are given freedom to choose a topic but where methods of investigation are seriously curtailed by the requirement that the results have to be represented on a side of A4 paper, suitable for display on the classroom wall!

Bennett also introduced other criteria to differentiate formal and informal styles, such as the degree of teacher control, the use of sanctions, the extent of integrated subject teaching, the setting of homework, the use of regular testing and the emphasis placed upon intrinsic rather than extrinsic motivation. In practice, however, as has been seen, it is the amount of whole-class teaching, coupled with the tendency for all pupils to work at the same time on the same subject matter, that emerged as the key characteristic of formal teachers in his study.

A second question relates to the definition, in operational terms, of 'discovery learning' within the primary classroom. Anthony (1979) examined teachers' ratings in a series of vignettes developed by Richards (1975). He concluded that, although there was a range of interpretations, centring on the idea of exploration, experimentation and physical activity, the five descriptions rated nearest the 'definitely discovery learning' end of the scale required the child to infer a generalisation from a set of examples. Greater agreement occurred when the generalisation concerned a mathematical or a scientific problem. Defining discovery learning as the discovery of one or more rules in order to solve the problem (in contrast to a didactic method where the student is told the rule and is not required to find it out for himself) allowed Anthony to examine a considerable body of American experimental research. Most of these studies concluded that if one is told the rule one has a better chance of solving the problem. However, if one has the ability to work out the rule for oneself, there is a likelihood of greater success when confronted with a fresh set of tasks requiring a different solution. Most of the American research involved under-graduate students working under artificial laboratory conditions (artificial in the sense that a laboratory is not very similar to a primary classroom). To link this experimental evidence with that obtained from the surveys it was necessary for Anthony to argue that, 'although discovery methods were ''not prominent'', as such, in the researchers' descriptions discovery in a broad sense is implied by the idea of learning by (relatively) free activity' (Anthony, 1982, p.381). As Dearden (1976) demonstrates, however, discovery learning is not a simple concept to define. All the vignettes presented by Richards (1975) appear to highlight the process of testing one's ideas, as emphasised by Isaacs (1955), as much as finding a solution to a specific problem, as emphasised by Anthony. In the teachers' minds, therefore, there may be a distinction between the process of learning *how* to discover and the process of actually making a discovery.

This distinction is strongly represented in the analysis of the concept of discovery learning undertaken by the Ford Teaching Project (Elliott, 1976a). The Ford Teaching Project team attempted to get teachers to define what they meant by discovery learning. Despairing of making progress after lengthy discussions, even after devoting a two-day conference to the subject, they asked teachers to record a transcript of a 'discovery lesson'. One such lesson, 'Fish in a Tank', was the subject of a demonstration film for the Open University. The film concerns the children's freedom to carry out investigations on topics and in parti-cular to decide on the methods of investigation. It transpires, from the film, that there was considerable discussion in the project about whether or not teachers should give information to pupils. One pupil in the film, while examining some creatures in a jar full of pond water, asks the teacher, 'Is that a slug?' During a playback of this sequence the teacher and the researcher collectively decide that it was legitimate to give the pupil the name of the creature because the information was consistent with the child's line of investigation and did not sidetrack her away from her chosen method. In another part of the film, however, the children are seen examining the various samples of water but the teacher now attempts to direct them towards an investigation of the effects of some local industrial development on the purity of the water by asking factual questions concerning the environment immediately surrounding the pond. This time the researcher argues that this was an inappropriate intervention.

Thus, in the Ford Teaching Project, discovery is mainly concerned with the child's freedom to plan investigations and to carry out testing, based, in particular, on careful observation. The teacher introduces topics through 'open' rather than 'closed' questioning so that the children decide their own ways of doing things. The teacher introduces factual information only when it helps to clarify the pupil's own lines of thought. Thus discovery-oriented classrooms, according to the analysis carried out by the Ford Teaching Project team, should be those where there is a higher incidence of open rather than closed questioning, fewer factual statements, and less tendency for the teacher to initiate statements about the supervision of the task, since the pupils are expected to design and to carry out their own testing procedures. As we have seen, however, in the unpublished comparative analysis of the ORACLE and Bennett data, formal and informal teachers do not seem to differ markedly in the use of these kinds of interactions.

Such categories of teacher behaviour, which are concerned primarily with the acceptance of pupils' ideas, can more readily be identified with the Flanders notion of *indirect* and *direct* teaching discussed in Chapter 1. While, as we have seen, the Flanders Inter-action Analysis Category system (FIAC) is unsuitable for use in informally organised classrooms, since it presupposes an environment where the teacher is generally concerned to address the class rather than move rapidly around individual children, the concept of indi-rectness may provide one alternative dimension upon which it is possible to classify informal teaching styles. This notion can, however, only readily be investigated by the observation of the teacher's behaviour, and it this method that dominates research into primary teaching during the post-Bennett era, to which we now turn.

CHAPTER 3

Inside the Primary Classroom: Teachers in Perpetual Motion

In the previous chapter we saw that the notion of 'progressivism' had to be defined at both a strategic and a tactical level. In the earlier survey research, it was inferred that in classrooms where teachers took a strategic decision to organise their teaching so that pupils were free to choose and to plan tasks, which required active engagement, then such investigations were carried out with relatively little guidance from the teacher. Deciding whether or not to guide pupils can be part of a teacher's general strategic considerations prior to the lesson, but this strategy will obviously be influenced by the particular context in which the pupil and teacher interact in the classroom. These interactions – 'the moment by moment incidents within the lesson' – have been defined as the lesson tactics. In Bennett's (1976) survey, these tactics were not directly observed; instead, teachers were asked whether they tended to favour 'discovery' approaches in their teaching. There was a high degree of correlation between teachers whose organisation was classified by Bennett as informal and those who claimed to make the greatest use of discovery methods.

There is, as we have already seen, a considerable problem in defining the term 'discovery'. Even if we accept that there is a general consensus as to the meaning of the term, there is a further difficulty when asking teachers to report the extent to which they engage in such activity. This is because the teacher in the classroom often experiences what might be termed a 'perception gap' between what takes place in the classroom and what the teacher, as a participant, believes to have occurred. The existence of this 'perception gap' was demonstrated, in no uncertain manner, during the early stages of the Ford Teaching Project when participants were asked to make a tape recording of a lesson in which they were introducing a discovery learning topic for their pupils. Some teachers refused to make a tape but those who did were reluctant to play it back to their colleagues. One teacher dramatically burnt his tape because

> 'The playback of the class discussion was a shattering blow! I had no idea how much discussion was dominated by me, how rarely I allowed children to finish their comments, what leading questions I asked and how much I gave away what I considered to be the "right" answers.'
>
> (Elliott, 1976b, p.62)

Classroom dominated by teacher [handwritten margin note]

Using an observation schedule, the observer might have recorded much of this discussion in terms of factual or closed questions, whereas the teacher would have been under the impression that there was a much greater proportion of 'open-ended' enquiry.

Explanations for the 'Perception Gap' in Teaching

Before examining the observation evidence concerning primary classrooms it is perhaps worth while to consider some of the explanations why the results of such studies appear to be at variance with the teacher's own picture of events in the classroom. The perception gap can be explained by making use of the distinction first put forward by a psychologist, Gordon Allport, a distinction mentioned in Chapter 1, between *coping* and expressive behaviour (Allport, 1966). Allport argued that our actions are a product of our attempts to respond to both external and internal stimuli. If a door is left open a person may go to shut it because there is a draught lowering the temperature within the room. This is a coping action. The individual may, however, also feel annoyance because the last person to leave the room left the door ajar and may then demonstrate this annoyance by violently closing the door so that it makes a loud 'slamming' noise. The importance of Allport's distinction between coping and expressive behaviour is that the former is a conscious rational response to the stimulus whereas when a person acts expressively they are largely unconscious of the link between their feelings and their actions. The individual does not rationally plan to slam the door because they are annoyed.

Whether or not we recognise our expressive actions appears to be linked to the degree to which we accept personal responsibility for our behaviour. When we set out on a course of action we naturally evaluate what subsequently happens as a guide to future decisions. As part of such evaluations we attribute responsibility for success or failure and these attributions then help to determine our subsequent behaviour. Attribution theory has to do with the explanations that we give for our actions. One particularly relevant part of the theory concerns the explanations we give to account for our perceived failure. The theory suggests that we usually attribute reasons for our failure to circumstances over which we have no control (Whitley and Friele, 1985; Weiner, 1986). This ensures that we then have no possibility of overcoming our failure through our own efforts.

In teaching, circumstances that are outside our control will often consist of external factors, such as the attitudes of parents, lack of resources, and either the children's learning or behaviour problems. For example, open-ended questioning of the kind that the Ford Teaching Project sought to encourage may cause us to feel threatened. Left to our own devices, we first try to suppress the awareness that we are heavily guiding the discussion so that we do not feel the dissonance caused by our wish to teach by discovery and our feelings of unease because we no longer appear to be in full control of the classroom. When forced to recognise our failure to conduct the discussion in a manner that is logically contingent upon our original intentions, we then attribute our failure to the pupils' lack of confidence and their seeming need, 'at this age', for guidance and structure. Beckman (1976), for example, in a study of teachers' failure to use open-ended questions, found that none of the respondents mentioned the teacher or teaching as a factor that might have influenced pupil performance. Attributing failure to factors other than teaching decreases our awareness of the events in the classroom for which we feel personal responsibility. We continue to see ourselves wishing to ask open-ended questions but having our intentions thwarted because pupils fail to respond appropriately.

The above discussion serves to make two points. First, teacher intention and action may be very different things, so that it is dangerous to rely solely on surveys of teacher opinion to describe what happens inside the classroom. In the previous chapter, 'progressiveness' was defined on two levels. The first of these had to do with curriculum and classroom organisation. These concerned strategic decisions, made at the coping level, to do with how children were seated, whether there was a choice of curriculum activity and whether the subject matter was to be integrated. Associated with these coping strategies was the use of the discovery teaching method. The implementation of this method involves expressive behaviour, which is subject both to a 'perception gap' and also to attribution effects. Thus reliable evidence about this second level of 'progressiveness' may not always result from the teachers' response to questionnaires and must then be obtained through the use of classroom observation.

The second point to emerge from this discussion is that it puts recent reports of observation studies in a more positive context. In the past, some teachers have responded unfavourably to published descriptions of their classroom practice because they felt it implied criticism. This is particularly true of participant observation methods where the observer tries to give a description of what it is like to be part of the classroom process. As Delamont (1983) observes, however, it is very difficult for such observers to write detailed accounts about the ordinary events in the classroom; they therefore tend to focus on incidents that seem to point to a breakdown in communication or behaviour between the pupils and the teacher. During the 1970s, study after study of this kind was produced, each making strong criticisms of current practice. However, once we introduce a psychological dimension to these perceived failures, with an understanding that many of these behaviours are unintentional and may not even be perceived, it becomes possible to move away from a situation where the individual teacher takes personal responsibility for the disjunction between intention and practice. Instead, research findings can be analysed in terms of *teaching* rather than of *individual teachers*, so that there is less tendency to attribute failure to external factors outside the classroom and a greater chance of using such findings to change existing practice. It is with this purpose that we now examine a number of observational studies, beginning with the ORACLE research.

The ORACLE Research 1975–80: The Background

The ORACLE research (Observational Research and Classroom Learning Evaluation) officially began life in September 1975 as a Social Science Research Council programme entitled 'The Nature of Learning in the Primary Classroom'. Within the first few weeks of the project, this title was converted to Observational Research and Classroom Learning Evaluation – principally, some would have it, to accommodate a postcard picture of the Delphic oracle on the notepaper heading. The programme ended in August 1980 but the Social Science Research Council then agreed to fund further investigation into Effective Group Work in the Primary Classroom. Funding then switched to other sources for the study of Curriculum Provision in Small Primary Schools (the PRISMS project: Department of Education and Science) and to the Leverhulme Trust who sponsored a joint venture with the University of Liverpool for the Primary Science Teaching Action Research Project (the STAR project). This STAR project aimed to define effective practice in science through systematic enquiry in the primary classroom. More recently, funding has returned to the Economic and Social Research Council (the re-christened SSRC) for the DELTA project, the Development of Learning and Teaching in the Arts within the primary school. This last project will ensure that the study of primary classrooms within the framework of systematic observation has continued within the original ORACLE framework over a fifteen-year period. During this time, although nearly all these studies have been designed around the traditional process/product framework (with the implication that what teachers say and do in the classroom has profound effects on what pupils learn), there has been a considerable increase in our understanding of how such effects are achieved.

The origin of these studies, however, went further back to the period of the Plowden Report. As part of their evidence to the Plowden Committee, the magazine *Forum* commissioned a series of articles on the efforts of teachers to change practice as a result of de-streaming in the primary school. The *Forum* observer was, in fact, the magazine's editor, Brian Simon. Simon had played an important part in the campaign for the introduction of comprehensive education, arising out of his opposition to selection at 11+ by means of intelligence style tests (Simon, 1953). Part of the evidence, which the magazine submitted to the Plowden Committee, concerned the ways in which school systems based upon streaming and selection restricted teachers' attempts to introduce 'progressive' practice into the classroom. One of the major arguments at the time in favour of mixed-ability classes was the under-achievement of pupils from the bottom streams.

Unlike many educational reformers who, having achieved change, then assume that what follows must automatically be better than what has gone before, Simon continued to interest himself in the question of how disadvantaged pupils might best be catered for within these new mixed-ability settings. As part of his task as a *Forum* observer, Simon set out to visit three junior classrooms where the teacher was responding, in different ways, to the problem of mixed-ability teaching. One teacher sat at a desk and had pupils come out for attention while the others preferred to move rapidly round the class. In both cases Simon commented on the time that children had to spend waiting for the teacher (*Forum* observer, 1966). He also noted the attempts of teachers to group pupils by ability for subjects such as mathematics, contrary to the practice eventually suggested in the Plowden Report where it was urged that groups should form and then re-form on the basis of children's interests and needs. This raised the question of whether disadvantaged pupils continued to suffer the same handicaps as in previously streamed classes now that there was streaming inside the classroom.

Simon therefore secured funds for a small-scale project to examine this question. With the help of one researcher, Deanne Bealing, he carried out a small-scale survey of classroom organisation in Leicestershire schools to see how far, amongst other things, streaming within the class was commonplace (Bealing, 1972). The study showed that while there had been a large-scale move towards individualisation of learning there appeared to be little enthusiasm for group work of the kind recommended by Plowden. Typically, desks were pushed together to form tables around which sat five or six pupils but these pupils worked on their own tasks individually. The study also raised important questions about the nature of exchanges between teachers and pupils within these informal settings.

Simon and Bealing (now Boydell by marriage) began to look for ways of exploring the interactions of teachers and pupils within these groups, since there were many assertions in the Plowden Report about the advantages of working informally. For example, it had been claimed that, in relation to group work, slow-learning pupils would often 'risk a hypothesis' in the absence of the teacher and that the brighter pupils would themselves become instructors of the slower-learning ones. Systematic observation had already been used in Leicester as part of a Schools' Council Evaluation of Secondary Science Teaching (Eggleston *et al.*, 1976). Boydell therefore went to the United States to talk with researchers who were involved with classroom interaction. On her return, she devised two instruments, one to monitor teacher behaviour and the other to monitor the pupils'. The Teacher Record bore some resemblance to the Science Teaching Observation Schedule (STOS) used in the Schools' Council study (Eggleston *et al.*, 1975), while the Pupil Record was an adaption of an American system, PROSE (Personal Record of School Experience), devised by Medley *et al.* (1973).

Boydell (1974, 1975) reported the findings of two small pilot studies which tested out these observation instruments. Her results raised questions about the extent to which the ideas enshrined in the Plowden

Report – ideas concerning pupil collaboration and the use of 'enquiry' learning approaches – were being used in informally organised classrooms. Using the earlier distinction between strategy and tactics, Boydell's findings could be interpreted by saying that, at the strategic level, teachers had changed both the classroom and the curriculum organisation. But there was no evidence from these results that the classroom tactics differed, to any great extent, from those that one might expect to find in a more traditionally organised classroom where teachers operated a single-subject curriculum and where children sat at their own desks rather than grouped around tables.

The way was therefore clear to propose a larger study that would investigate whether the results of these pilot observations could be generalised. As a result ORACLE was born. The first phase of the research lasted five years and it enabled pupils to be followed, in some cases, for a three-year period so that in the final year they could be observed after transferring to the secondary school. The material from this research has been written up in five volumes: *Inside the Primary Classroom* (Galton *et al.*, 1980), *Progress and Performance in the Primary Classroom* (Galton and Simon, 1980), *Research and Practice in the Primary Classroom* (Simon and Willcocks, 1981), *Moving from the Primary Classroom* (Galton and Willcocks, 1983) and *Inside the Secondary Classroom* (Delamont and Galton, 1986).

The ORACLE Observation Instruments

The ORACLE observation instruments designed by Boydell were later modified for the full-scale study. Both instruments – the Teacher Record and the Pupil Record – used a time-sampling unit of 25 seconds.

When using the Pupil Record the observer was required to track eight previously selected target pupils in a predetermined order. Various safeguards ensured that a representative sample of curriculum activities was observed for each pupil and that pupils were not always observed at the same time of the day on each occasion. The names of target pupils were concealed from the teachers in order to refute the argument that, because a teacher knew the target pupil's identity, additional attention would then be given to that particular child. At the end of the year, when teachers were asked to name the target pupils, none identified more pupils than would have been expected if they had simply randomly chosen names from the class list. As far as possible, therefore, in keeping with observation of this kind, the observer tried to remain like 'a fly on the wall' so as not to interfere with the working of the class.

The main categories of the Pupil Record concerned the frequency of the pupil's interaction with the teacher or with other adults, the target's activity and location, together with the teacher's activity and location if the latter was not interacting with the target pupil at the time the observation was made. Pupil–teacher interaction was concerned, principally, with the nature of the exchange (whether task work or routine) and the setting in which the interaction took place (individual attention, whole class, or group). Whenever interaction took place with other pupils, the observer focused upon whether the target pupil initiated or responded to an interaction, whether such interactions were sustained beyond one time-sampling unit, whether they were related to the task, and whether they were with pupils of the same or opposite sex. The observation data obtained in this way could then be cross-tabulated with the pupil's activity and location. In these latter categories pupils were either co-operating on task or on routine or distracted in some way. They could be waiting for the teacher or moving around the classroom. A typical set of observations, during one time unit, might record that the target pupil had initiated an inter-action with another pupil, these pupils were working on the same table and were of the same sex, they were talking about the same task and the teacher was involved elsewhere in the classroom. At the bottom of the sheet the actual task on which these pupils were engaged was noted.

At other times the observer would follow the teacher using the Teacher Record. Here the emphasis was upon the nature of the conversations in which the teacher engaged during the period of observation. The range of teachers' questions and statements was sub-divided under general categories of task, task supervision and routine. Note was also taken of times when the teacher was showing or marking or reading a story. Again, the teacher's audience (class, group or individual) and the curriculum activity were noted. In this way it was possible to build up two different pictures of the curriculum – one defined by what the teacher was doing and the other by aggregating the pupils' activities from the Pupil Record. A more detailed description of the instruments can be found in Galton *et al*. (1980) and a critical appraisal of their uses and abuses is provided by Croll (1986).

The ORACLE Research: The Findings

ORACLE and classroom organisation

The major findings of the observation study are contained in the first ORACLE volume, *Inside the Primary Classroom* (Galton *et al.*, 1980). Perhaps the most striking result to emerge initially was the 'busyness of the teacher'. In general, these primary teachers were engaged in some form of interaction with pupils for over 78 per cent of the time during which they were under observation. During this period of teacher involvement, over 70 per cent of these interactions were with individual pupils and just under 20 per cent were with the whole class, leaving around 9½ per cent of observed occasions when the teacher talked with a group of pupils.

The consequences of this strategic decision to carry out conversations with pupils largely on a one-to-one basis were many. Most striking was the asymmetric nature of the primary classroom, in that the pupil's pattern of interaction was almost the reverse of that for the teacher. Whereas the teacher was observed interacting with pupils for around 80 per cent of the time, the pupil, in turn, was observed interacting neither with the teacher nor with another pupil for approximately the same proportion of time when they were under observation.

One paradox of this pattern of organisation was that although teachers, typically, talked to the whole class for around 20 per cent of the time, this period accounted for nearly three-quarters of the attention that an individual pupil received from the teacher during which they might be listening or answering a question. Nor did the data show that the pupil compensated by discussing work with other pupils. Of the 80 per cent of the time when the pupil was not involved with the teacher, some 20 per cent was spent interacting with other pupils, but for nearly two-thirds of this period pupils engaged in non-task-related conversations. Less than one-third of these exchanges were sustained into the next time unit and most of these sustained conversations were not about work.

A survey by the observers of the incidence of children working in groups on a common task showed that 69 per cent of the teachers in the sample never used this kind of co-operative group work for either art and craft or topic work and nearly 90 per cent never did so with single-subject teaching such as mathematics and language. Group work was therefore a relatively 'neglected art' in the primary classroom (Galton, 1981).

ORACLE and the primary curriculum

A further consequence of the decision that pupils would largely work individually concerned the nature of the curriculum. Such an individualised strategy obviously requires that the tasks pupils are set can be carried out without making too many demands on the teacher. This, inevitably, leads to the frequent use of worksheets and published schemes of work. One teacher, quoted in *Inside the Primary Classroom*, remarked that she was under so much pressure that she 'had to let the worksheets do her thinking for her'. This strategy, in turn, tended to place a greater emphasis on the more formal or 'basic' aspects of the curriculum than was generally thought to be the case. In mathematics, for example, which occupied about one-third of curriculum time, over half of this allocation was given to straightforward computation and work on number, a further 37 per cent had to do with using the four rules to solve abstract problems, leaving only 13 per cent of the time available for using these computation skills to solve practical mathematical problems. Nearly 38 per cent of the remaining curriculum time was given over to language work, and over half of this time was devoted to exercises concerned with grammatically correct writing. Planned activities on spoken language, in contrast, received only 3 per cent and creative writing just under 20 per cent of the language allocation. Of the remaining 29 per cent of the time, art and craft occupied just over 10 per cent, leaving just under 20 per cent for general studies including science and other forms of topic work involving the humanities.

This picture is in very sharp contrast to that portrayed at the time by the critics of primary practice, who argued that the 'basics' were being neglected as a result of these modern methods. Support for these figures came from various surveys, for example Bassey (1978) and Bennett *et al.* (1980), although in Bassey's case the figures were based upon teacher estimates rather than on observations.

ORACLE and classroom interaction

Turning to the kinds of conversations that were observed between teachers and pupils there was a heavy emphasis on what might be termed 'lower-order interactions' – to do with factual statements, telling pupils what to do, or giving guidance on routine. Twelve per cent of all exchanges had to do with questions: 30 per cent of these were questions of fact, 32 per cent of task supervision and a further 15 per cent concerned routine matters. Nearly 45 per cent of exchanges were teacher statements. Of these, 15 per cent had to do with facts, 28 per cent concerned telling a child what to do, while a further 15 per cent concerned routine information. This picture hardly matches the critics' view that in some modern primary classrooms children were never told anything but were left to find things out for themselves (Cox) and Dyson, 1969b). *Needs to be a balance - structured independent work*

Comparing ORACLE and PRISMS

The PRISMS study, carried out eight years after the ORACLE field-work, showed very similar patterns in relation to these interactions. The PRISMS study was mainly concerned with the curriculum provision in small primary schools. Unlike ORACLE, the emphasis in the observation was therefore placed on recording details of the various curriculum categories. For example, those concerning number work were broken down to provide details of the actual task (addition, take away, multiplication, division, fractions, etc.) and also to indicate whether the problem involved one, two or three digits. As a conse-quence, the ORACLE behaviour categories were reduced to make the observer's task a manageable one. Nevertheless, it is possible to make some comparisons with ORACLE data. What gives added interest to these results is the fact that in the PRISMS study, unlike ORACLE, both infant and junior classes were observed.

Table 3.1 shows the proportion of different curriculum activities at infant and junior levels in the 86 infant and 102 junior classes in the PRISMS sample compared to the 58 junior classes in the ORACLE study. The PRISMS data were adjusted to exclude play and music, which were not observed in the ORACLE study. Within possible sampling errors the proportions of curriculum time given to the different subject areas were remarkably similar across both the infant and junior classrooms in the PRISMS sample and also in ORACLE.

Table 3.1 *Curriculum activities PRISMS and ORACLE (% of all observ-ations)*

Activity	PRISMS		ORACLE
	Infant	*Junior*	
Maths	23.7	23.7	28.5
Language	39.1	37.1	36.2
Art and craft	16.1	14.6	10.9
General	21.1	24.6	24.4
	100.0	100.0	100.0

In ORACLE there appears to have been slightly more mathematics but less art and craft than in the PRISMS classrooms. If the various categories within the PRISMS curriculum areas are examined in more detail, there were similar patterns to those previously described for the ORACLE study. For example, at infant level, practical mathematics accounted for 4.2 per cent of the curriculum observation compared to 17.5 per cent for number computation and 4 per cent compared to 18.4 per cent at the junior level.

Looking at the overall patterns of interaction in the two studies the figures were again remarkably similar. These data are presented in Table 3.2. In PRISMS around 10 per cent of the observations concerned questioning, compared to 12 per cent in the ORACLE study. Teachers made more statements in ORACLE than in PRISMS, but the small school teachers tended to compensate for this by engaging in more non-conversational interactions, particularly demonstrating to pupils, and doing less marking, in the latter case because presumably there were fewer pupils in the class. In the small schools there were nearly two-thirds as many questions about task as about routine in both the infant and junior classrooms, compared to the ORACLE study where about 85 per cent of all questions were to do with task. The same pattern is evident when teacher statements are considered. In the infant small school, 30 per cent of all statements had to do with task, 30 per cent with feedback to pupils about their work, and the remaining 40 per cent concerned routine matters. The small school junior classes had slightly different proportions in that nearly 40 per cent of statements were about task, 34 per cent related to routine and just under 27 per cent concerned feedback. The corresponding figure for ORACLE task statements was just over 53 per cent, with the remaining proportion equally divided between routine and feedback.

Table 3.2 *Overall pattern of interaction – PRISMS compared to ORACLE (% of all observations)*

	PRISMS		ORACLE
	Infant	Junior	
1. Questioning	10.8	10.4	12.0
2. Statements	34.8	37.6	44.7
3. Non-conversation interaction	49.9	45.3	38.4
4. No interaction	4.4	6.5	4.4
5. Not coded	0.1	0.2	0.5
	100.0	100.0	100.0

The schools in both samples, therefore, show similar patterns, with the differences largely accounted for by different methods of sampling.

One interesting feature of the PRISMS study, which could not be replicated by ORACLE, concerned the type of individual interactions in which the teacher engaged. These are shown in Table 3.3. In the PRISMS study, the time interval between one observation and another was 5 seconds compared with the 25 second time-sampling unit used in the ORACLE study. Whereas in ORACLE the observer simply noted whether the interaction was with an individual pupil, the PRISMS observers also noted whether the individual interaction was with a different pupil from the previous observation, whether it involved one pupil in a group or one pupil in a class. For the infants, 69 per cent of total teacher–pupil interaction concerned individuals ($100 \times 57.8/84.0$) while for the juniors the overall proportion was 66 per cent ($100 \times 54.4/82.8$). Bearing in mind that different ground rules operated in the two studies – for example, an interaction was still coded as individual in PRISMS as long as one pupil remained the principal focus of the teacher's audience, even when the remainder of the class was expected to listen to what was being said – the figures here are very close to those in the ORACLE study.

Given these differences in interpretation, the most interesting finding concerns the categories which were recorded when a different pupil from the one in the previous observation was in focus. In infant schools, 41 per cent of all observed teacher interactions with individual pupils took place with a different pupil 5 seconds later ($100 \times 21.1/30.0 + 21.1$). The corresponding figure for juniors was 31 per cent ($100 \times 14.9/32.5 + 14.9$). Clearly, some of these exchanges may have marked

Table 3.3 *Type of individual interactions in infant and junior PRISMS classrooms*

Teacher interacts with:	% of total observations	
	Infant	Junior
Individual pupil	30.0	32.5
Different pupil from previous observation	21.1	14.9
One pupil in a group (whole group involved)	2.9	3.3
One pupil in the class (whole class involved)	3.5	3.5
Different pupil in group from previous observations	0.3	0.2
Total individual interaction	57.8	54.4
% of all teacher–pupil interactions involving individuals, class or group	84.0	82.8

the end of an extended conversation between one pupil and the start of another, but it is reasonable to infer that the majority of these conversations corresponded to very short interactions which hardly allowed sufficient time to engage in 'challenging discussion'. The data were therefore consistent with the descriptions of the ORACLE classroom earlier where many of the exchanges were very short – to do with information about tasks or to do with routine activities connected with behaviour.

The ORACLE teaching styles

The ORACLE study also investigated variations between groups of teachers in order to develop an understanding of a teacher's style that was somewhat different from that used by Bennett (1976). Initially, style was defined solely in terms of the teaching tactics, which consisted of all observations recorded during lessons. These styles were then related to the organisational strategies that teachers employed in the classroom. From the initial analysis, four teaching styles emerged, three of which were clearly linked to a particular organisational strategy.

The first group, consisting of 22.4 per cent of the sample, were called *individual monitors*. They interacted with children for around 80 per cent of the time and nearly 84 per cent of these interactions were with individual pupils. Contrary to the expressed opinion of critics of modern practice that such teachers 'left children to find out things for themselves', this group of teachers tended to emphasise facts (both questions and statements) and had some of the lowest levels of interactions concerning challenging questions and providing feedback on children's work, a category of behaviour that many American studies have shown to be important for pupil progress. These individual monitors were also high on marking, which was defined in the study as correcting work either without the child present or silently as, for example, when the teacher stood and corrected a worksheet while the child was waiting at the desk. Given the information from the previous discussion of the PRISMS results, it is possible to build up a picture of the individual monitor as a teacher who tended to organise the classroom so that children worked on individual tasks, often making use of worksheets or published schemes of work, and who then either moved rapidly around the class, checking and monitoring work, or had children come to the desk. With thirty children in a class organised in this way the managerial difficulties were considerable. Teachers directed much of their effort to reducing the size of the queue or to keeping the number of hands raised for help to a minimum. Interactions with individual pupils tended to be short and mainly concerned with enabling the children to continue with their work with as little interruption as possible; hence the emphasis on providing pupils with either information or task directions or routine help. Working in this way left little time for extended conversations with pupils about work (feedback) or any opportunities to challenge children by asking open-ended questions of the kinds advocated in the Ford Teaching Project as an aid to discovery learning.

The second group of teachers, accounting for 15.5 per cent of the sample, were called *class enquirers.* As the name suggested, they engaged in the highest level of whole-class interaction. Like the individual monitors, the class enquirers, overall, were interacting with children for around 80 per cent of the time, but nearly 39 per cent of these interactions involved the whole class. Again, the popular image of a class teacher as one mainly concerned with drill and practice did not emerge from the observation of this group of teachers. While class enquirers did engage in as high a level of factual recall interactions as did other teachers, they had the highest level of challenging questions and statements in the whole sample. They also appeared to cultivate a positive climate within their classrooms in that they used praise more often than any other group of teachers. In these classes pupils tended to learn by example, in that these teachers were often observed demonstrating and showing children. For instance, they would read information to the whole class from a book and illustrate points through reference to pictures or make use of objects brought in for display. The classroom organisation seemed somewhat reminiscent of the pre-Plowden pattern and, indeed, one characteristic of this group of teachers was that they were among the oldest in the sample. Most children were engaged in the same or similar work, topics would be carefully introduced to the whole class and the teacher would then move around helping individual pupils who had particular difficulties with the work.

In their comparison of formal and informal classrooms, Gray and Satterly (1981) used the results for the individual monitors and the class enquirers to represent ORACLE versions of progressive and traditional teachers. While there is some evidence of similarity between these ORACLE styles and those characterised by Bennett (1976), there are also many differences. Like Bennett's formal teachers, the ORACLE class enquirers were less likely to allow children to have choice of seats or to have free movement, and they made greater use of tests of arithmetic and spelling. However, unlike Bennett's informal and formal styles, individual monitors and class enquirers did not differ appreciably in their demands for quiet in the classroom or in the balance between single and integrated subject teaching – an important characteristic of the earlier definition of 'progressiveness'. Presumably class enquirers tended to engage in integrated teaching as part of topic work at those times when children were working in groups. Nor were the individual monitors like the informal style described by Barker-Lunn, who found that teachers favouring 'less traditional methods' were likely to be more permissive (Barker-Lunn, 1970). While a higher proportion of class enquirers had been observed to smack children (at the time that this was permitted), nearly three times as many individual monitors would send children from the room for disciplinary purposes. From these data, therefore, the evidence that these two groups of teachers can be readily identified with progressive and traditional methods of teaching is inconclusive. The ORACLE study suggests that, if 'progressiveness' is defined in terms of freedom, activity and a curriculum based upon the needs and interests of the child, then such practices were characteristic of some teachers in each of the different ORACLE styles.

Of the remaining teachers in the sample, 12 per cent made use of 'above-average' amounts of group interaction (approximately 23 per cent of all interactions with pupils). These teachers tended to emphasise factual statements compared with the presentation of ideas but, by working through groups rather than with individuals, they were able to provide higher levels of feedback. They also tended to demonstrate to the groups in the same way as the class enquirers. The observers' descriptions of these teachers emphasised their concern to structure the work of the group carefully before leaving them to carry on the tasks among themselves. Once all groups had begun to work then the teacher would rejoin an earlier group and respond to the pupils' ideas and solutions by providing feedback. Although there was some evidence of problem-solving, the main emphasis of these teachers' style was on the informational aspects of their teaching. Consequently they were described as *group instructors.*

These three styles between them accounted for 50 per cent of the sample of teachers observed during the first year of the study. In the initial analysis the remaining half of the sample were classified as *style changers* because they tended to adopt modified versions of the various patterns of interaction associated with the different degrees of emphasis placed upon individual, class and group organisational strategies. Further analysis allowed these style changers to be broken down into three distinct clusters. In retrospect, however, the association with a change in the organisational strategy tended to divert attention from important differences within the patterns of observed interactions between these teachers and their pupils during the lesson.

Thus one group was called the *rotating changers* because of the way in which groups of children would move from table to table according to the curriculum activity being carried out upon it. In many of these classrooms there would be an art and craft corner, a mathematics corner, a language corner and a topic (science and humanities) corner. When children moved, for example to the mathematics table, they would either engage individually on worksheets or work on a common topic. But, in emphasising the notion of rotation, this description tended to obscure the fact that for much of the time these teachers operated rather in the fashion of unsuccessful group instructors. Whereas group instructors kept firm control in the classroom, so that the time was usefully spent in teaching the children, in the classes of the rotating changers there appeared to be considerable disruption as a consequence of groups of pupils having to move physically from one table to another. After each interruption, the time taken for a class to settle down inevitably reduced the time available for teaching. Rotating changers therefore tended to have the lowest levels of interaction across all categories, except the disciplinary ones, in comparison with the other groups of teachers in the sample.

In contrast, another group of teachers was initially labelled *infrequent changers*, because they deliberately, on a few occasions, switched their main organisational strategy to take account of particular circumstances in the classroom. This label again obscured the fact that in their interaction with pupils these teachers were, in many ways, more successful versions of the individual monitors. In general, they made planned switches of organisation from individual to whole-class teaching but, when working with individual children, seemed able to overcome some of the disadvantages associated with the individual monitors. The most distinctive feature of these teachers was their ability to maintain high levels of questioning across all categories so that they elicited both factual information and challenging responses from the children. They were able to provide feedback to the pupils about their work and had far lower levels of 'silent' marking or pupils waiting in queues. They come nearest to the descriptions of the Plowden style of teaching, although constituting only 10 per cent of the sample.

One of these teachers explained why, in an effort to maintain the level of questioning, she changed her emphasis from individual to whole-class teaching. In the class there were several disruptive pupils. The teacher found that more and more of her time was taken up in having to deal with these troublesome children rather than engaging in the kinds of challenging questions that she believed promoted learning. She therefore made a deliberate switch in strategy and included more class teaching in her lessons so that she could keep tighter control over these pupils until they had 'settled down'. In general, this group of teachers appeared to give much more thought to the use of different strategies. Whereas in some of the other styles the observed interaction in the classroom (the tactics) seemed to be a consequence of earlier strategic decisions about how to organise the class, in the case of the infrequent changers it appeared that strategies were deliberately chosen in order to maintain a desired pattern of teaching tactics.

The final 25 per cent of the sample were difficult to describe in terms of their classroom interaction patterns. In almost every category of verbal interaction observed, they typically had the lowest frequencies of any group in the sample, the exception being general conversations of a social nature as against those to do with the task. In these class-rooms children spent more time waiting for the teacher. A lot of time was also spent demonstrating and showing to pupils. These teachers, the *habitual changers*, seemed to vary organisational strategies in an unplanned way and, as a result, they appeared to experience all the disadvantages and none of the advantages of the other styles.

ORACLE and pupil performance

The ORACLE study also measured pupil progress using the Richmond Tests of basic skills (France and Fraser, 1975). The results of this progress–product study were reported in *Progress and Performance in the Primary Classroom* (Galton and Simon, 1980). On tests of mathematics and language the *classroom enquirers* performed best of all, although not appreciably better than the *infrequent changers*. In reading, pupils in the classrooms of the *infrequent changers* out-performed all other groups, with *class enquirers* coming second.

When the various results were combined and points awarded according to the magnitude of the statistical differences between each style, then the results shown in Table 3.4 were produced. Here, by virtue of smaller levels of significance, the *infrequent changers* appear

Table 3.4 *Comparative performance of ORACLE teaching styles*

	No of tests	MS	NSD	S5	S1	Total points
Infrequent changers	3	1	2	0	0	7
Class enquirers	3	2	0	1	0	7
Group instructors	3	0	1	2	0	4
Individual monitors	3	0	0	1	2	1
Habitual changers	3	0	0	0	3	0
Rotating changers	3	0	0	0	3	0

Key: MS   Most successful style   3 points per test

        NSD   Not significantly different from most   2 points per test
                  successful style

        S5   Significantly different from most successful   1 point per test
                  style at the 5 per cent level

        S1   Significantly different from most successful   0 points
                  style at 1 per cent or beyond

Source: Galton and Simon (1980), p. 187)

at the top of the table, closely followed by *class enquirers* and then by *group instructors*. *Individual monitors* gained their points by the superior performance of their pupils in reading, again emphasising the link with the *infrequent changers*. The remaining two styles, the *habitual changers* and the *rotating changers*, did not appear very successful, in terms of standardised tests at least.

The ORACLE study also assessed pupils on a variety of other tasks normally associated with study skills and with other qualities deemed important by teachers, such as communication and listening skills. Here, however, the results were inconclusive, so that there was no support for the idea that, although some styles did not achieve much success on the tests of basic skills, they nevertheless compensated by superior performance in other areas of the curriculum. Both styles and their associated pattern of test results were replicated during the second year of the study, an important factor in observational research of this kind, where the sample of teachers and the actual sample of lessons is but a small part of the total (Croll, 1986). By replicating the study on a substantially different sample of teachers, it becomes possible to have more confidence in the results, even though the samples are not a random selection from the general population. If, for example, one argues that the results during the first year of the

ORACLE study were atypical of patterns of teaching in primary schools in general, then, by the same token, one must also draw similar conclusions in the case of the second-year sample. If, however, the patterns of interaction and the trends in the relationship between teaching style and pupil progress were similar in both years, as they were in ORACLE, the two samples, although atypical, must be atypical in similar ways. Such a proposition would statistically be very remote.

More Recent Research in the Primary Classroom

The above general portrayal of teaching in the primary classroom seems to match the descriptions from other recent studies where systematic observation has been used.

It has already been shown, for example, that the PRISMS research, which used similar instruments but operated across a much wider cross-section of local authorities, including some where Bennett's (1976) study was carried out, produced similar descriptions of teaching behaviour.

A study of reading in the infant classroom carried out by Southgate at about the same time as the ORACLE project (Southgate *et al.*, 1981) found that the total time devoted to reading and writing activities was considerably less than most teachers claimed. This time could often be reduced by a quarter or a third as a result of interruptions by children within the class or from other people coming into the classroom. Southgate found, for example, that during reading and language activities, on average, teachers spent 25 per cent of their time doing things unrelated to the actual purpose of the lesson. Apart from the problem of interruptions, the next most frequent reason for this reduction in the time available for teaching activity was given as marking work unrelated to the current lesson or arranging equipment and materials for subsequent activities. This behaviour was reminiscent of the *individual monitor* in the ORACLE study.

Southgate also commented on the low proportion of 'high-level' exchanges between teachers and children, including the review and discussion of books. She drew attention to the extremely short periods of time spent by teachers in listening to an individual child reading: the average time spent concentrating on a particular child was only 30 seconds. This provides yet another example of what has earlier been called the 'perception gap' in teaching, since the teachers' logs usually set this figure at a much higher level, making no allowance for the frequent interruptions that occurred as teachers broke off from listening to the child to help other pupils with spellings, comment on a piece of work, answer a question or issue a reprimand. This supports both the ORACLE and PRISMS findings that many interactions were of short duration so that teachers rarely engaged in any high-order questioning.

Further support for the main ORACLE findings can be found in a study by Croll and Moses (1985), who were concerned with the behaviour of junior pupils whom teachers identified as having special learning difficulties. A sample of such pupils was compared with a control group of children from the same classrooms. Although pupils with learning problems received nearly twice as much individual attention from the teacher as the control children, this still accounted for only 4 per cent of the time spent in the classroom. For both groups, however, work levels were high. The children with learning difficulties spent 69 per cent of their time either 'on task' or on some work-related activity. The corresponding figure for the control group was nearly 77 per cent. An important finding concerned what Croll and Moses described as the major feature of the 'slow learning behaviour pattern'. When these slow learners were working by themselves, nearly one-third of their time was spent in 'solitary distraction', double that for the control group.

More recent data can be found in two studies of London schools, one at junior level (Mortimore *et al.*, 1987) and one in the early years (Tizard *et al.*, 1988). The junior study provides direct comparisons with the ORACLE data in that the same observation instruments were used. Like the teachers in the ORACLE study, teachers in the ILEA junior study set limits on the amount of pupil mobility and on the level of noise they permitted in their classrooms. Very few children were allowed to leave the room in connection with their work. In subjects such as mathematics children were generally required to stay in their places, but they were allowed to move around and collaborate during project or topic activities. Approximately 10 per cent of all interactions were concerned with managerial details, although, unlike the ORACLE study, this proportion decreased slightly as the pupils moved up the junior school.

The overall pattern of interaction was very similar to that of ORACLE, although there were greater variations from year to year in Mortimore's sample of teachers. In the second year, for example, 23 per cent of all teachers' interactions were with the whole class, 9 per cent were with groups and the remaining 67 per cent were with individual children. In the third year, there was slightly more group work. As in the ORACLE study, teachers spent most of their time talking to individuals, and pupils mostly worked alone for 68 per cent of the observed time (Mortimore *et al*., 1988, p.82). Mortimore also comments that, although most teachers made use of groups when organising their classrooms and although many teachers grouped children of similar ability together (particularly in the basic subject areas), 'not a great deal of collaborative work was observed'.

The ILEA junior study also examined differences between higher-order contacts and interactions concerned with task supervision. Only 2 per cent of observed time appeared to be devoted to questions that might be regarded as offering challenge. Over two-thirds of the teachers were observed to make no use of open-ended questions where more than one answer might be acceptable. There were wide variations in the amount of time that different groups of teachers spent in talking to children about 'task' matters. At one extreme, one in ten teachers devoted less than 6 per cent of their time to this kind of interaction while, at the other extreme, one in ten spent over 17 per cent on task statements. On average, 11 per cent of the teachers' time was spent supervising pupils' tasks, mostly in the form of telling the child what to do. Positive feedback in the form of praise about work was observed very infrequently. Generally, feedback without any emotional tone occurred during $11\frac{1}{2}$ per cent of the interactions, but there was a wide range across the sample. Some teachers gave feedback in approximately 2 per cent of all observed interactions while others managed to raise the level to around 25 per cent.

The ILEA junior study did not use the notion of 'teaching style' and, indeed, argued that the variations within the different groupings were so great that there was little point in trying to describe teachers' practices collectively. Pupil progress was measured, however. In general, the amount of time teachers spent on class interaction was positively correlated with the amount of time teachers spent talking about work, which in turn correlated with improved performance. As in the ORACLE study, the proportion of time spent on communicating with the whole class was associated with the use of higher-order questions and statements, and this factor too was strongly correlated with performance.

Tizard *et al*. (1988) in an 'early years' study of ILEA schools, confirm these patterns. They also describe results that can be interpreted as similar to those provided by PRISMS, although the comparisons are more difficult because different observation instruments were used.

Tizard's sample of London schools contained a large proportion of children from ethnic minority groups, but few of the classroom observations differed in respect of race. As in the PRISMS study, most teachers made considerable use of workcards and published schemes for mathematics and language. However, 80 per cent of teachers did use several schemes for reading, as did 77 per cent for mathematics, although here there was a marked tendency (as in PRISMS) mainly to use only one scheme supplemented occasionally either by others or by home-made materials.

In the 'top infants', somewhat less than half the school day was devoted to work activity (which Borg, 1980, calls 'instructional time'), while 43 per cent of the day was given over either to routine activities (registration, toilet visits, and either lining or tidying up) or to meal and playtimes. In mathematics, 62 per cent of the time was devoted to number work, 14 per cent to time and 12 per cent to weight and length. Direct comparison with the PRISMS data is difficult since, if a pupil in the small schools study was adding two weights, both the number and weight categories would have been ticked by the observer. Overall, however, number activities in PRISMS featured in 64 per cent of all mathematics activities. In language, most work observed by Tizard consisted of completing worksheets or pages from workbooks. Prose writing consisted mainly of drawing a picture and then writing about it. These patterns were also similar to those observed during the PRISMS study.

The pattern of teacher–pupil contacts as described by Tizard also bears a remarkable similarity to those recorded in both the PRISMS and ORACLE studies. In only one in five contacts was the target pupil the focus of the teacher's attention. Group work was uncommon, and over half such contacts were concerned with non-work activity. Serious disruptive behaviour was rare – less than 1 per cent of all observations. In spite of this relative isolation, engagement rates were high. During the time pupils spent on their own, interacting with neither the teacher nor other children, 'on task' behaviour was recorded during 66 per cent of all observations. Tizard *et al.* concluded:

> We found that children were mostly busy and involved in their work . . . working individually on basic subjects of language and mathematics. However, although individual working was common, individual teaching was not. Most children's contact with the teacher was listening to her address the whole class about work . . . children's active

contribution to contact with their teachers declined over three years of infant school.

(Tizard *et al.*, 1988, p.69)

Some General Conclusions

In general, a clear pattern emerges from these results. Whatever the style of teaching adopted, it would appear that the greater the emphasis the teacher gives to organising and directing the curriculum the greater the progress pupils make in the areas of mathematics, language and reading when these are assessed in terms of traditional tests. In order to obtain this success teachers tend to make more use of whole-class or group instruction; this inevitably means that they restrict the proportion of time when children work on integrated tasks. In classrooms where there are high levels of individual attention, teachers tend to spend less time concerned with the task. This is particularly true of reading where, as Southgate *et al.*'s (1981) study shows, teachers engage more often in class supervision and routine interactions of a fairly low-level kind. In these circumstances, it becomes more difficult to engage pupils in open-ended extended discussions about their ideas. Nearly all teachers, whatever the prevalent organisational strategy adopted, managed to conduct such open-ended discussions more successfully when they were addressing the whole class. The conclusions drawn by Mortimore *et al.* (1987) from their research echo those of Bennett (1976, 1978). Both researchers argue for more closely directed curriculum activities with higher proportions of class teaching.

Such results, however, have been criticised, particularly by Scarth and Hammersley (1986, 1987) and by Edwards and Westgate (1986), on the grounds that the categories used to define teacher behaviour are highly problematical ones. Similar criticisms, in more contentious forms, have been made by Barrow (1984) and are discussed by Croll (1986). Both Hammersley and Edwards are concerned to query the use of the question categories to define teacher behaviour, particularly those to do with 'higher-order' interactions. They point out that there is a considerable problem with defining questions and in particular trying to infer a teacher's intention from a particular utterance.

In both the ORACLE and the ILEA junior study, however, such questions were categorised, not in terms of the teacher's intention but in terms of the reply that the question elicited from the pupil. This, at one level, seems preferable to trying to code the initial utterance by the teacher, since observation suggests that some experienced practitioners can elicit a whole range of responses from pupils by the simple expedient of joining a group and asking the children, 'How are you getting on?' Another person who approaches children with, 'What do you think is happening?' might merely receive a response, 'It's changed.' In practice, having spent some time in the classroom, an observer will begin to get a feel for the nature of the exchanges between the pupil and the teacher. Thus, observers rarely code utterances in isolation but take account of the interaction preceding and following the exchange occurring at the specified time interval when the coding is made. As McIntyre (1980) observes, unless the observer is party to the particular classroom culture, there can be no understanding and therefore no possibility of interpreting events that take place during the lesson. Certain judgements will always be difficult, as, for example, when the observer is trying to work out whether a pupil who is staring out of the window is thinking or simply distracted. Nevertheless, the claim by Scarth and Hammersley that, because of the problematic nature of these decisions, one should suspend judgement on the whole of the ORACLE findings does seem somewhat extreme (Croll and Galton, 1986).

The similarities in the interaction patterns observed in different classrooms in the various studies described in this chapter do at least point to certain common features in primary classroom practice that appear to have remained relatively stable over the ten-year period that these studies were being carried out. Furthermore, the studies have taken place in different locations involving local authorities with varying reputations for emphasising progressive practices. Over and above different interpretations of the concept of 'progressiveness', therefore, there seems to be something about characteristics of individual primary classrooms that is akin to those of living cells. Each class, like a human cell, has a life of its own and requires the application of considerable external pressure in order to disturb its equilibrium and bring about a shift in the internal organisation. Primary practice appears therefore to be very resistant to change.

A second important feature concerning primary practice, which has emerged through systematic study, is the finding that certain patterns of teaching are associated with pupil performance. When we look at the progress that pupils make in school we normally expect that, if pupil A does better than pupil B on the first occasion, they will generally do better on the second occasion also. The process–product studies of the type carried out in ORACLE, however, show clearly that the pattern of pupil progress was also strongly related to the particular style of teaching. Over the whole sample, if the position of two groups of pupils, the one taught by a more effective style and the other by a less effective style in year one, was reversed in year two, then so would the progress these pupils made between the two test administrations. The notion, therefore, that what teachers do affects the way that pupils behave, and that this in turn affects the way that pupils perform, does have important implications for the study of teacher effectiveness. So far, however, the discussion has concerned the variations in teaching behaviour. The way in which a teacher's style largely determines what pupils do and say in the classroom will be considered in the next chapter.

CHAPTER 4

Pupils in the Primary Classroom: Loneliness in a Crowded Room

One of the most dramatic features of the primary classroom, described in the previous chapter, concerned the 'asymmetry of the interaction process'. Both the ORACLE and PRISMS studies, and also those by Southgate *et al.* (1981), Mortimore *et al.* (1987) and Tizard *et al.* (1988), show that one consequence of the decision to implement the Plowden prescription of individualisation is that the time the teacher spends in one-to-one interaction with an individual child is in direct proportion to the time the remaining pupils will work on their own. Primary classrooms may be busy places but they are also places where a child can spend part of the day working in isolation from the teacher and from fellow pupils. This is because, in the period when pupils are not involved with the teacher, there is little likelihood of their interacting with their peers, even when some form of collaborative group work strategy is a desired aim of the teacher. Just why this is so will emerge in later discussion, but the first concern here is to examine the behaviour of pupils during those periods when the teacher is engaged elsewhere in the classroom.

Intermittent Working in the Primary Classroom

In many instances the activity of the pupils appeared to be characterised by avoidance. In the ORACLE classes of the *individual monitors*, for example, nearly 48 per cent of the pupils were described as *intermittent workers*. This type of pupil tended to work when they were the focus of the teacher's attention. At other times, when the teacher was involved elsewhere, the children sitting around the table engaged in conversations that rarely related to the work in hand. In the busy atmosphere of a typical primary classroom there are many opportunities for behaviour of this kind. Although most experienced practitioners develop what Kounin (1970) termed 'withitness' – the capacity to have 'eyes in the back of one's head' – the frequency with which the teacher glances up to monitor activity in other parts of the classroom can vary when they are preoccupied with learning problems of various pupils. Intermittent workers seemed to take advantage of these opportunities and were adept at appearing to work hard whenever the teacher glanced their way. The observation data suggested that, as far as the typical pupil was concerned, nearly one day each week was taken up by behaviour of this kind. However, the range of intermittent working varied considerably, with, in some cases, a pupil spending nearly half the week on 'off-task' activity. Similar findings emerge from American studies (Berliner, 1979).

Few teachers would argue that children should have to work continuously throughout the day, and in most classrooms there are plenty of opportunities to relax. The point about intermittent working is that, to a large extent, it reflects a classroom climate where this kind of behaviour occurs without the teacher's knowledge or approval. Studies that have examined the nature of pupil activity (although not in a systematic manner) have emphasised the extent of practice tasks in primary classrooms where there is a high degree of individualisation (Bennett *et al.*, 1984). It was shown in the last chapter, when the results of the PRISMS study were discussed, that in many of the classrooms there was a high degree of reliance on worksheets and published schemes of work. These classes would be typical of the individual monitors. It would seem that in many cases children who have completed a worksheet in, say, mathematics are required to do additional examples by way of practice, until the teacher is ready to introduce a new idea or to change to a different topic. In these circumstances the pupils seem to pace the work for themselves, slowing down the rate at which they complete the original worksheet, since the reward for speedier work is to get more practice examples of the same kind.

Solitary Working in the Primary Classroom

It would seem likely that this problem would disappear when the amount of individualised working is reduced and more class teaching takes place. It is now easier for the teacher to monitor the whole class and hence the opportunities for children to engage in intermittent working are fewer. In keeping with this hypothesis it was found in the

ORACLE analysis that only 9 per cent of pupils were intermittent workers in the classrooms of the *class enquirers*. Instead, nearly 65 per cent of children could be described as *solitary workers*. Such pupils tended to receive very little individual attention from the teacher, but were more usually part of the teacher's audience when they were addressing the whole class. During class discussion, they tended to listen and watch while another pupil was the focus of the teacher's attention. These pupils also showed great reluctance to engage in conversations with other children and, even when they did so, few of these conversations were sustained into the next 25 second interval. Of all pupils they achieved the highest levels of concentration on the task.

This group of children was named *solitary workers* because in some ways they could be identified with a similar group of older science students whom McClelland (1963) called 'undeflected workers' because, like human cannon balls, they remained undeflected by the vagaries of the teaching. Although, like these pupils, the solitary workers were not active participants in class discussions, they were a considerable asset in that they could be trusted to maintain high work-rates, irrespective of the presence or absence of the teacher in their vicinity. One puzzling effect concerning these pupils, however, was that, when allowance was made for different teaching styles, no differences were found in the progress made by solitary workers and intermittent workers in the ORACLE primary classrooms. This was in direct contrast to studies that identified 'time on task' as a major determinant of pupil progress (Good and Brophy, 1986). In Britain, Mortimore *et al*. (1987) have also obtained positive correlations between levels of pupil engagement and pupil progress. However, none of these studies controlled for the differences between teaching styles in their analysis of 'time on task' and pupil performance.

Easy Riding in the Primary Classroom

Part of the explanation for this discrepancy in research findings can be found in the further analysis of pupil behaviour carried out during the ORACLE transfer study, the results of which are presented in *Moving from the Primary Classroom* (Galton and Willcocks, 1983). There a group of pupils, not unlike solitary workers, was further divided into two sub-categories termed *hard grinders* and *easy riders*.

Hard grinders were, in every way, an extreme type of the solitary worker, seemingly being able to maintain concentration in whatever kind of classroom they found themselves. The second, and perhaps more interesting, sub-group adopted a strategy of working but doing so as slowly as possible without attracting the teacher's attention. In one classroom, for example, children were instructed to begin the lesson by getting out their books, rulers and pencils. They were then told to start a new page, with the date at the top right-hand corner, while making sure that a margin of $2\frac{1}{2}$ centimetres was constructed using a 'sharp' pencil. Some pupils made these activities last considerably longer than other children. They would, for example, take the various items from their tray or from their bag one by one. First, they would take time to find the required workbook, then they would rummage for a ruler, then a pencil. Having written their name they would accurately measure $2\frac{1}{2}$ centimetres at the top, at the middle and at the bottom of the left-hand side of the page. They would then re-measure the margin width, glancing up to see that the teacher was not showing a particular interest in what they were doing. After beginning to draw the margin if, for a moment, the teacher's attention was engaged elsewhere, they would contrive to break their pencil point and have to get up from their seat to go and sharpen it. They would remain out of their place busily sharpening the pencil until they felt that further absence might elicit an adverse comment from the teacher.

Such pupils seemed very adept at knowing just how long they could prolong each stage of an activity before the teacher questioned its legitimacy. The net result was that by the time the easy rider had begun the task proper – for example, completing a worksheet of mathematical problems – the hard grinder was already half way through the exercise. The observers noted that these differential rates of working presented considerable problems for teachers who, in some cases, attempted to slow down the quicker pupils and speed up the slower ones. Pupils who finished a piece of writing quickly would be allowed to draw a picture and colour it in or, if in an older age group, would be invited to start work that the slower pupils would have to finish off as homework. In mathematics, nearly 80 per cent of the pupils engaged in this type of easy riding (Galton and Willcocks, 1983).

When 'time on task' and its relationship to progress was analysed in the ORACLE classrooms, it would have been likely that most of the pupils classified as solitary workers in classes of *individual monitors* and *rotating changers* would have been *hard grinders*, whereas *class enquirers* may have had more pupils from the *easy riding* sub-group.

Katie?

Attention Getting in the Primary Classroom

A similar elaboration of the behaviour of a group of pupils originally called *attention seekers* also occurred as the result of further analysis during the transfer study. These pupils comprised 18–27 per cent of all classes apart from those of *group instructors*, where they accounted for only 5 per cent. From the observers' accounts it was clear that attention seeking in the primary classroom involved two different kinds of pupil.

The first type, later christened *fuss pots* in the transfer study, seemed over-anxious lest they did something that the teacher would not approve of. Thus they tended to be the centre of the teacher's attention more often than other pupils. They would often come out to enquire whether they were performing the task correctly or whether they had got the right answer. Typical of these pupils was the reported remark of one who asked her teacher, 'I've done No. 1 now Miss. Shall I go on to No. 2?' Such pupils were easily dealt with but obviously took up a proportion of a teacher's time throughout the day. This pattern of behaviour corresponds to that reported by Southgate *et al.* (1981) in their comments on the behaviour of other pupils when the teacher was hearing a particular child read. During this time a queue of pupils would form with various requests for information about the task they were doing. These requests, although distracting for the teacher, were dealt with quickly and rarely required a teacher to engage in any lengthy discussion with the pupil.

Perhaps more interesting was a group of pupils who might more aptly have been described as *attention getters*. These pupils did not so much seek the teacher's attention as were the objects of it, usually as a result of a misdemeanour. The observers described such pupils as being very adept at finding things to do in other parts of the classroom that allowed them to avoid getting on with their own tasks. For example, they would appear to be intensely interested in another pupil's work and if required to queue at the teacher's desk they would, on occasions, step backwards when another child joined the line, allowing them to step to the front, thereby delaying their own encounter with the teacher.

Quiet Collaboration in the Primary Classroom

Finally, there was a group of pupils who in some ways were similar to the solitary workers but were associated with group work. These pupils were termed *quiet collaborators* and were usually to be found in classes of *group instructors* (37.5) per cent) or of *habitual changers* (17.5 per cent) who, as we have seen, tended to use a mixture of the three organisational strategies at will. These pupils were given their name because, although they were clearly working in groups, they for the most part appeared reluctant to engage in conversation about their work. When such pupils did collaborate, it generally involved the use of materials. In the PRISMS study, where the behaviour associated with certain curriculum activities was examined in some detail, group collaboration of this kind, as might be expected, was more often associated with topic work of a practical nature than with aspects of language that required pupils to discuss ideas. When not involved in practical activities of these kinds, quiet collaborators tended to be identical, in many respects, to solitary workers, the main difference being that the behaviour of the former took place within a group instructional setting while the latter were more often a part of whole-class teaching.

The replication study provided support for these trends observed during the first year of the ORACLE research. In the second year the pupils who had previously been observed moved, for the most part, to a different teacher. Although the overall proportions of the various pupil types naturally differed over the two years (within allowable sampling variation), the trend for a particular teaching style to be associated with a particular pupil type was maintained. Thus *individual monitors* continued to have the largest proportion of *intermittent workers,* while *class enquirers'* classes were dominated by the presence of *solitary workers*. What had changed was the proportion of different teaching styles and it was this that resulted in differences in the overall proportions of pupil types.

It was, therefore, the teaching styles that determined the pupil behaviour, contrary to the often-quoted statement that teachers varied their styles to suit the needs of pupils. Pupils who in the first year had behaved as *intermittent workers* in the class of an *individual monitor* tended to become *solitary workers* if they moved to the class of a *class enquirer*. Unfortunately, the analysis was not able to break down the categories further because of the relatively small numbers that would have been involved. However, it is possible to speculate that the majority of these intermittent workers would become *easy riders* in this situation rather than *hard grinders*.

These patterns of pupil behaviour, dominated as they appear to be by the teacher's preferred method, are at variance with the proposition that progressive education is concerned to organise classroom activity in accordance with the 'needs and interests' of individual pupils. Over 75 per cent of the pupils who moved in the second year to a teacher with a different style from that which they experienced in the first year changed their behaviour. In contrast, none of the small proportion of teachers who over the three years of observation were seen on more than one occasion (12 per cent) changed to a different teaching style.

Pupil–Teacher Influences in the Primary Classroom

Although the overall control of what goes on in the primary classroom seems to be largely determined by the teacher, establishing this balance is the result of a complex process. Clearly, pupils behave in ways that influence teachers' actions in the same way that the teachers' actions obviously influence those of the pupils. The picture presented in the ORACLE research describes what might be termed the 'equilibrium' position, but this equilibrium is not a static one. The 'moment-by-moment' teaching events during a lesson all have a personal history of their own, each one evoking a response from the other participants, whether these be the teacher or the pupils. Moreover, as in a chemical reaction where the dynamic equilibrium usually favours the reactants on one side of the equation, so in the classroom the overall balance tends, on the evidence presented here, to favour teachers rather than pupils.

In this respect, the analysis of classroom behaviour in terms of teaching styles and related pupil types has an important use in that it allows teachers to assess the overall consequences of adopting a particular pattern of classroom and curriculum organisation. What systematic analysis of this kind cannot do, as pointed out by both Bennett (1987) and Mortimore et al. (1987), is to offer explanations concerning the reasons for these patterns or for the effectiveness of one style rather than another. Bennett (1987) argues that because styles, whether defined in terms of indirect teaching (or 'progressiveness') or in terms of patterns of interaction, as in the ORACLE study, inevitably consist of combinations of different variables, it is extremely difficult to isolate the key factors that are responsible for pupils' improved performance.

The second and perhaps more important reason why the analysis of teaching style has a limited value, beyond description, when developing a theory of practice is that teachers within any one style are likely to use a range of behaviour, and are therefore likely to achieve differential results on measures of pupil performance. In the ORACLE study, for example, some teachers in the less effective groups achieved excellent results and in Bennett's (1976) original study one of the most successful teachers in the whole of the sample was in the extreme informal cluster. Certain effects – such as providing feedback, raising questions and minimising routine instructions – seem important determinants of pupils' progress. Different styles achieve these effects in different ways. There is no 'one best buy' in teaching.

Explanations of Pupil Behaviour in the Primary Classroom

To look for explanations for these patterns of pupil and teacher behaviour in the primary classroom and to account for their success it is necessary to go beyond the quantitative data supplied by systematic analysis and to collect qualitative information by a variety of means, such as the observers' impressions backed up by interviews with pupils and teachers. The aim of this approach is to explain, from an outsider's point of view, what it is like to be part of the classroom process under investigation. Participant observation was used as part of the ORACLE transfer study (Delamont and Galton, 1986) and also in the follow-up study, *Effective Group Work in the Primary Classroom* (Galton, 1987).

As part of an investigation into why so few teachers were able to sustain collaborative activity between pupils, other than during the kinds of task involving practical activity, a series of cartoon pictures of different classroom settings was provided. Children were given a set of pictures, each picture showing five pupils seated round a table. The children were shown engaged in four different activities:

1. Doing art work on individual sheets of paper.
2. Writing individually on sheets of paper.
3. Discussing, with a tape recorder in the centre of the table.
4. Collaborating together in measuring and drawing on a large sheet of paper.

For each of these four different activities, three different teacher positions were shown. In the first, no teacher appeared in the picture at all, in the second the teacher was seated at the table with a group, and in the third the teacher was standing near the blackboard addressing the whole class. The combination of teacher position and activity produced twelve pictures in all. The gender of the teacher in the picture could be altered according to whether the class teacher was a man or a woman, and in every case the group of children consisted of three boys and two girls.

Pupils were asked to choose a picture that showed the lesson they would most like to be part of and to give the reasons why the particular lesson was preferred. They were also asked to describe what one of the pupils in the picture was saying and what another might be saying in reply. Pupils were then asked to repeat the procedure but this time to select the lesson that they would least like to be a part of.

The results tended to support the patterns of working that emerged from the studies based upon systematic observation. In terms of type of lesson, 50 per cent of all choices showed a strong preference for working individually with materials rather than with writing. Of these, 19 per cent preferred it when the teacher sat with a group, 17 per cent when the teacher was nowhere in the picture, and 14 per cent when the teacher stood at the blackboard. The remaining pictures – depicting children holding discussions and working collaboratively on a joint piece of work – received between 7 and 4 per cent of choices.

Two pictures were rejected more often than others. In both cases no teacher was present. The least popular picture, accounting for 17 per cent of rejections, was the one where the pupils were tape-recording a discussion, and the second least popular was when they were engaged in writing. Only 4 per cent of pupils rejected the most popular picture, in which the children were doing individual art work with the teacher present. The remaining nine pictures were rejected by 6–9 per cent of pupils.

The conversations that the children added to the pictures were generally of the kind that observers in the early ORACLE study had reported. For the most part, the children either checked with each other whether or not they had got the correct answer or listened to what the teacher was saying to another pupil who was doing the same piece of work in another part of the classroom. It seems clear from these responses that one of the means by which pupils overcome the 'asymmetry' of classroom interaction, whereby they spend much of the time on their own, is by listening to the teacher when he or she is engaged elsewhere. In this way children often pick up information about what to do next or gain clues when they have problems with the work. In most of the pupil conversations reported, the teacher was mentioned. The pupils were clearly anxious to please the teacher and do what the teacher wanted. The influence of the teacher was generally very strong, supporting the earlier analysis of the relationship between teacher styles and pupil types in which children adapted to the teacher's needs rather than, as progressive theory would demand, pupils' needs and interests being paramount.

To investigate the extent of the teacher's influence further and to probe the reasons for it, the cartoon picture exercise was repeated but this time with only six pictures in which:

5. A child was alone with the teacher with the curriculum unspecified.
6. A group of children was talking without the teacher present.
7. A teacher was engaged with the whole class with mathematical symbols on the board.
8. A group of children was sitting with the teacher and having a discussion that was being tape-recorded.
9. Children were sitting in a group but working individually on worksheets.
10. The children were working on a practical task with the teacher present.

The exercise was modified in that pupils had to say what the teacher was saying (if present) and what the pupils were saying or *thinking*. The extent of the exchange in conversation was also predetermined by giving two opportunities for the first pupil to speak and two opportunities for the second pupil to respond. Again the pupils were asked to choose their overall favourite and their least favourite picture.

In most of the schools studied within the second sample the patterns of choices were similar to those in the previous exercise. Children preferred working individually with the teacher or by themselves. The next favoured alternative was whole-class teaching. Any form of group work, particularly that involving discussion, was the least favoured. In only one school were there noticeable differences in attitudes to group work. In this 8–12 middle school there was a gradual increase in liking for group work as the children got older. The first-year children disliked the picture that showed them discussing without the teacher present because:

'There's no teacher. You're worried if you get things wrong.'
'My friends make me silly.'

whereas the older children were much more positive in their response:

'One can learn more from each other when there is no teacher to nag.'

'You can have a laugh when you discuss.'
'It's good to work things out without the teacher.'

Most exchanges between first-year pupils betrayed anxiety about getting things wrong or were exhortations to their companions to 'shut up' or 'get on' in order to please the teacher or to avoid attracting their attention. The pupils tended to see the teacher as someone who was continually 'getting at them' for lack of effort:

'Do your work good or you'll stay in at playtime.'
'Now listen to me.'
'Now pay attention.'
'Sit still.'

Only the children in the top class rejected this kind of pattern – arguing, for example, that class teaching was boring because. 'Nobody is learning anything, only the teacher. You have to copy everything the teacher says.'

Subsequent interviews with the pupils in this final year class revealed complex patterns of pupil behaviour. Pupils developed several strategies for coping with the demands that were made upon them by teachers. For example, if the teacher said that unless they wrote at least two sides during the lesson they would stay in during break, they revealed that. 'You just make your writing bigger'. Pupils' accounts of how they behaved during class discussion also helped flesh out the descriptions of *solitary workers* who, it may be remembered, tended to listen rather than participate in class discussion. When asked during the interview what it felt like when the teacher asked a question, one pupil replied:

'It's like walking on a tightrope.'

Pupils volunteered the information that, when the teacher questioned the class, a variety of strategies would be used. First, one had to put one's hand up because,

'If you don't the teacher will think you are not paying attention and pick on you.'

Next, pupils took their hands down if they believed that the teacher was about to pick on them to answer the question. The strategy behind this tactic was to persuade the teacher that one was just trying to do a little more thinking. This impression would be reinforced by writing something down or screwing up one's forehead. If all else failed then 'you guessed'; if your guess proved to be wrong and if the teacher did not pass on to someone else but gave you the answer, 'you pretend it was the same one that was on the tip of your tongue'. In another context, Measor and Woods (1984) refer to such behaviours as 'knife – edging strategies'. Similar behaviours are described by Woods (1980) and Pollard (1985) with respect to infant pupils.

What emerges from these pupil descriptions of classroom events are what, in an earlier study of American college freshman, Becker *et al.* (1988) refer to as 'exchange bargains'. These were exchanges whereby the college freshmen allowed their instructors to perform effectively and give the appearance of being in control but at the cost of setting work from which the students could achieve satisfactory grades. The world of the primary classroom seems to exhibit similar features. Pupils are quiet, obedient and complete reasonable amounts of work so that the teacher can appear effective in the eyes of his or her colleagues, the headteacher, parents and governors. In return, the pupils demand the kind of work that does not force them into positions where they have to expose their ignorance to the class or to their teacher.

Thus Mr Aspin, in the episode described at the beginning of the book, received excellent co-operation from all the children when the task was something that they could do easily (colouring the squares of the crossword). When, however, he began to press the children to solve the crossword clues, which consisted of mathematical problems, some pupils, who experienced difficulty with this task, began to disrupt the classroom while others came out to Mr Aspin's desk and tried to persuade him to give them sufficient 'guidance' so that they could achieve success.

Pollard (1985, 1987) extends the above analysis by describing how pupils attempt to cope with the teacher's demands while seeking to maintain harmonious relationships with different sets of children within their peer group. Pollard's pupils belonged to either the *goodies*, the *jokers* or the *gang*. According to Pollard, pupils bargain within the context of the 'working consensus' only in so far as it meets with their 'interests-at-hand'. The 'working consensus' consists of shared social understandings between the teacher and the pupils which 'structure and frame the classroom climate in terms of routines, conventions and expectations' (Pollard, 1987, p.177). Interests-at-hand represent 'various facets of self which are juggled in the ebb and flow of classroom processes to produce an overall level of satisfaction of self' (p.179). Interests-at-hand are primarily concerned therefore with the maintenance of self-image and the retention of personal dignity, which is closely linked to the way in which we are viewed by both the teacher and our peers.

Within this framework, *goodies* placed much importance on the way they were perceived by their teachers. They therefore conformed totally to the 'working consensus'. *Gangs*, on the other hand, often because they had learning problems, stressed the importance of peer group membership and were prepared to reject the 'working consensus' for the sake of this group solidarity. *Jokers* tried to have the best of both worlds by being prepared sometimes to 'have a laugh' during lessons at the teacher's expense although not to such an extent that it earned the teacher's disapproval. In constructing these images of themselves children were faced, at times, with stark choices between taking the side of the teacher or joining in with other pupils. As we have seen in the earlier descriptions of the ORACLE pupil types, one important tactic for reducing the stress caused by the need for such choices was to try not to be noticed, so that one was not called a 'swot' by the gang group or labelled disruptive by the teacher. Hence dependency and avoidance – taking one's cue from the teacher or leaving it to another pupil – are the two most significant features of pupil behaviour in many primary classrooms.

Whenever possible, strategies are adopted that encourage increased teacher involvement until sufficient clues emerge for the pupil to produce the answer required. Hence group discussion (presumably of abstract ideas) without a teacher present was the least liked situation depicted in the cartoon pictures because it was the most difficult to manipulate. Faced with these pupil strategies and tactics, teachers come to adjust their overall aims, arguing, as some did in the ORACLE study, 'that pupils of junior age just aren't capable of discussing things sensibly in groups'. Teachers then revert to what are, for pupils, the safer forms of class and individual organisation where the children can more readily use various strategies to reduce the level of cognitive demands made by the task the teachers set.

Plowden and Today's Primary Teacher

In *Inside the Primary Classroom*, Simon provides a 'a general sketch of the ideal Plowden type teacher and her class', drawn from the various recommendations outlined in the 1967 Report.

> The children are active, engaged in exploration or discovery, interacting both with the teacher and with each other. Each child operates as an individual where groups

are formed and reformed related to those activities which are not normally subject differentiated. The teacher moves around the classroom, consulting, guiding, stimulating individual children, or, occasionally, for convenience, the groups of children which are brought together for some specific activity or are 'at the same stage'. She knows each child individually, and how best to stimulate or intervene with each. In this activity she bears in mind the child's intellectual, social and physical levels of development and monitors these. On occasions, the whole class is brought together, for instance for a story or music, or to spark off or finalise a class project: otherwise class teaching is seldom used, the pupils' work and the teacher's attention being individualised or grouped.

(Galton *et al.*, 1980, p.49)

It is clear from the evidence presented in this and in the preceding chapter that today's typical classroom practice departs considerably from this ideal. Whether any but a few teachers ever manage to reach these high goals must remain debatable. Twenty years on from Plowden we are now in a position to see that this disjunction between the Plowden prescription and actual practice is the result not of any lack of effort on the part of teachers but rather of a lack of understanding, at the time the Report was written, of what a complex, demanding activity such a teaching approach entails.

Both the ORACLE study and the ILEA study of junior schools contain descriptions of classrooms that demonstrate, beyond doubt, that many things have improved over the last twenty years. Classrooms are more relaxed places to be. There is less drill and practice, much more tolerance and still little disruption and violence. Yet beyond these gains there remains an over-emphasis on intellectual transactions that are largely of a low cognitive level. Much of the work still consists of routine rather than challenging tasks, so that children with above-average ability tend to work below their capacity. There is also a lack of collaborative activity between pupils when the teacher is not present. If the Plowden Report was in fact 'the progressives' charter', then it would appear that, for the most part, progressivism did not fail but was not really fully tried. In the next chapter, a number of explanations for this failure to translate principles into practice will be considered. This then leads to the notion that we perhaps need to reinterpret the definition of 'progressiveness' as part of the development of a more practical theory of primary pedagogy.

CHAPTER 5

Plowden Revisited: What Went Wrong?

Twenty years after the publication of the Plowden Report (1967), described at the time by one commentator as the 'progressives' charter' it is perhaps natural to seek explanations for what the previous research overview suggests was moderate progress in the attempts to change certain aspects of classroom practice. In making this reappraisal, it is important to recognise that, even before the setting up of the Committee under Lady Plowden, considerable changes were taking place in primary education in Britain. Before the Second World War, according to Whitbread (1972), the separation of infant pupils into schools in which most of the 5–7 year olds were grouped vertically tended to promote a progressive ethos. This ethos arose because of the need to cope with a mixed age range by the use of individualised learning and group work. According to one Leicestershire adviser, as reported by Jones (1987), Stewart Mason's period as Director of Education marked considerable changes in ways of involving children in the learning process. Teachers were driven to look for a means of motivating children other than by using the carrot of the 11 + examination. Jones reports one adviser as remembering that when he visited classrooms he would find children making up their own novels – 'Anything between five and one hundred pages in length, editing each other's work and illustrating and binding them ready to be placed on a book shelf'. Similarly in art and craft, when weaving was being done, 'the whole process from raw wool to dyed cloth was followed'. Further evidence of these new approaches is provided by Jones from an unpublished paper by an American enthusiast of progressive teaching who describes seeing a class making a collage of a street scene. Although there were over thirty children, 'there was little confusion', the American remarked. 'Teachers had a special interest in the kind of work and were proud of the fact that every child had a chance to make a contribution'. The visitor saw handwriting patterns in the style of Marion Richardson, listened to music played on the recorder and observed a science experiment carried out according to the instructions on work cards devised by the teacher. He also noted the mathematics work cards that a teacher had developed during the summer vacation (Jones, 1987, p.43). Later the same American visitor published a further account entitled 'Leicestershire Revisited' (Hull, 1971). Coupled with the publication of three articles by Joseph Featherstone (1971) entitled 'The School Revolution in Britain', this created, according to Jones, something of an explosion in American interest in England, leading to the setting up of summer vacation workshops in the United States on which Leicestershire teachers and colleagues from the West Riding and Oxfordshire worked.

Jones also describes how, at the end of his career, Stewart Mason, looking back on this period, argued that there was little doubt that much progress had been achieved. In a talk to teachers entitled 'The Changing Face of the Primary School', Mason describes the scene twenty-five years previously when, as an HMI in Cambridge, he had gazed at the serried ranks of children,

'seated at iron framed desks, built for two, four and sometimes eight children, more often than not screwed to the floor... The teacher was the chief, perhaps the only centre of interest, and the whole class at any moment was doing the same thing. Now, the teacher's role had changed to that of facilitator and adviser. By far the most significant change was the place occupied by the library in the primary school. Children today move freely in and out of the classroom, bring reference books from the library... the whole trend being to get children to discover for themselves with more attention being given to the differing pace and interests of each child. The individual was supreme.'

(Jones, 1987, p.47)

Summing up twenty years on however, Lady Plowden (1987, p. 122) lists as the main areas of progress not these aspects of classroom practice but 'the increasing emphasis and understanding of the importance of there being an active relationship between schools and parents... the increasing recognition of pre-school provision for all children... and the development of educational priority areas which eventually developed into the Warnock Report (1978) on Special Educational Needs'. On this analysis, therefore, by the time of the Plowden Report the brief summer flowering of progressive education was already on the wane.

How Typical was the Progressive Classroom?

Even if we grant that the reports of experiments in Oxfordshire, the West Riding and Leicestershire were an accurate reflection of what was taking place in the schools that were visited, the question remains how far such descriptions typified general practice throughout the rest of Britain's primary classrooms. Simon (writing in *Research and Practice in the Primary Classroom* – Simon and Willcocks, 1981 – about the primary school revolution as myth or reality) attempts a reconstruction of what was happening, generally, in primary schools of the 1960s based upon the Plowden Report itself. For the report, Her Majesty's Inspectors undertook to categorise over 20,000 primary schools in England under nine mutually exclusive headings. Although from the scant information available it would seem that the HMI based these judgements upon impressions rather than specific criteria, they reported that

> 'about ten per cent of schools were good and even outstanding, about one third of the schools were good in general, although twenty-three per cent of these were good "in most respects without any special distinction". Of the remaining schools, sixteen per cent were classified in category 4 where "there was hope they might improve, six per cent were good on personal relations but were poverty stricken or swamped by immigrants!", twenty-eight per cent, in category 6, were defined as decent run-of-the-mill schools, while nine per cent were defined as "curate's egg schools".'
>
> (Simon and Willcocks, 1981, p. 18)

Simon goes on to argue that, even if the twenty-three schools defined as good in most respects without any special distinction were added to the 10 per cent that were good and even outstanding, it would seem that only a minority of primary schools had been transformed along 'modern lines'.

The report also gives descriptions of three schools that were 'run successfully on modern lines' but, as Simon remarks, it is the feel and the tone of the classroom as a whole that they describe and seem most interested in, 'rather than the teaching–learning process going on within them'. Further evidence is deduced by Simon on the basis of the surveys carried out for the Plowden Committee and reported in volume two. HMIs, for example, were asked to rate schools, using a five-point scale, on the extent to which they 'were in line with modern educational trends' (Simon and Willcocks, 1981, pp. 19–20). They rated 3 per cent of the sample as very good and 18 per cent as good. Again, if these two categories are combined, it suggests that only one-fifth of all schools were operating these 'modern educational trends' with a degree of success. In their ratings, HMIs were asked to note such matters as permissive discipline, provision for individual rates of progress, readiness to reconsider the content of education and awareness of the unity of knowledge. As Simon remarks, these perceptions seem to have very little to do with the nature of the teaching and learning process taking place within these structures and nowhere is any indication given of how such detailed judgements about the educational process were arrived at. What is known from these surveys, however, is that 55 per cent of the schools in the sample still classified children by 'age and achievement' and that 'junior schools in this sample were much more likely than others to be streamed so that, for example, sixty per cent of JMI schools were streamed and seventy per cent of schools with five hundred or more pupils were streamed' (Simon and Willcocks 1981, p.19). Yet, as Simon observes, by 1971 research evidence was available that indicated that the vast majority of primary schools were by then unstreamed (Bealing, 1972; Bennett, 1976; HMI, 1978).

The possibility exists, therefore, that many observers, including the many American visitors, tended to look more closely at these organisational characteristics of classrooms and to infer from them that there had been a radical change of teaching methods at the tactical level. The increase in the local authority reorganisation of secondary schools along comprehensive lines, and the move to non-streaming as a result of the abolition of the 11 + , forced teachers to move away from whole-class teaching as the main method of instruction. We have already seen how Simon, as a *Forum* observer (1966), saw three teachers attempting to come to terms with the problem of teaching a mixed-ability class. It is all too easy to imagine how hard-pressed teachers, faced with questions from anxious parents about whether their sons or daughters would be held back by the presence of slow learners in the class, would have had recourse to the Plowden Report to justify their methods.

Particularly useful would have been key paragraphs that claimed that able children would gain from working in such mixed-ability groups, since they would 'make their meaning clear to themselves by having to explain it to others and gain some opportunities to teach as well as learn' (Plowden, 1967, para 758). In this way Plowden and progressive theory legitimated what at the time was seen to be the only practical solution to the problem of mixed-ability classes. Teachers needed to believe in the Report's rhetoric.

A further factor in this legitimation process concerned the abolition of the 11+, at a time when there was a strong tide of educational opinion against formal testing of any kind for children in the primary age range. This placed increasing emphasis on teachers as 'professionals' with expertise in devising their own record-keeping systems. Again, anxious parents needed reassurance that, although their children might be working within an integrated timetable, the teacher was still able to determine whether they had done their share of computation and number work. Plowden specifically endorsed such approaches to monitoring, arguing that 'although tests are useful there is some danger of spending too much time on testing at the expense of teaching' (para 422). It may be, therefore, that the revolution was never as revolutionary as claimed by these American visitors. Even in those local authorities (such as Leicestershire and the West Riding) with a reputation for progressivism there were probably favoured schools that received more than their fair share of visitors and thus came to represent practice in general rather than being seen as exceptional cases. We still need to explain, however, why more schools did not follow in the footsteps of these 'outstanding' examples and adopt the new approaches to primary teaching.

Explaining Failure

Pressure theory

The first of the explanations why the initial blossoming of enthusiasm for new approaches did not extend beyond a small proportion of the schools – with the result that in the majority the changes were more cosmetic than real – can be classified as the *pressure* theory.

This states that many teachers have been forced to limit the extent to which they make use of progressive methods of teaching because of the pressures exerted by parents on the school and by the public generally on local education authorities. These anxieties are the result of a vociferous campaign by certain sections of the media, taking their lead from central government. Typical of such media treatment, for example, would be that of the *Daily Mirror* newspaper, which, under the headline 'Stop Being Kind in the Classroom', informed its readers:

> American education researchers have discovered that too much praise is bad for children. The way to get results in the classroom they say, is to tell the children what to do and keep them hard at work . . . And they found the worst results were in classrooms where teachers praised the children, encouraged them to ask questions – and answered them – and gave them a say in the decision making.

The authors of the article concluded:

> Parents who are disturbed by modern classroom methods will be reassured by the findings of the American researchers.

(*Daily Mirror*, 10 March 1981)

This campaign has extended beyond the popular press and includes the serious papers and TV reportage. According to some critics, the campaign is orchestrated by the government and Department of Education officials who wish to exercise greater control over the primary curriculum.

Indeed, some writers argue that the whole period since the creation of the Schools Council in 1964 has seen repeated attempts by the central authorities to wrest control of the planning process away from teachers. Kelly (1982, 1986), for example, measures the extent of the success of this challenge by contrasting the 1969 speech of the then Minister of Education, Sir David Eccles, who referred to the curriculum as a 'secret garden' where people, other than teachers, 'who attempted to trespass there were very firmly warned off', with the present-day situation where considerable inroads have been made into the garden, culminating now in the 1988 Education Bill with a statutory core curriculum. Kelly (1982) sees as landmarks in this gradual erosion of teacher autonomy the abolition of the Schools Council in the wake of its own evidence of the negligible impact and poor take-up of its projects (Schools Council, 1978, 1980) and the articulation of parental anxieties about 'modern or informal methods in primary schools'. The same period saw the publication of the *Black Papers* (Cox and Dyson, 1969a,b), the report of events at the William Tyndale School (Auld, 1976) and the establishment of the Assessment of Performance Unit (APU) with a remit to monitor standards of attainment in six major areas of the curriculum (Dennison, 1978). In the wake of these events came Prime Minister James Callaghan's (1976) Ruskin College, Oxford, speech, which heralded 'The Great Debate', the basis for which was a green paper, *Education in Schools* (DES, 1977). There followed a number of major surveys by HMI dealing first with primary education (HMI, 1978) and then middle schools (HMI, 1983). Central government subsequently demanded that local authorities should provide clear statements of their curriculum aims and policies, demands that in turn were passed on to schools.

According to Kelly (1983), 'these demands for greater teacher accountability, for the monitoring of standards and for greater public control of the curriculum' were the main reason for the shift of emphasis 'towards the teaching of subject content as justifiable in itself rather than in relation to its contribution to the growth and development of pupils and the teaching of basic skills in isolation from the wider educational context'. 'In short,' Kelly concludes, 'the needs of society are being held to take precedence over the needs of pupils so that a totally different philosophy is being foisted upon the primary school' (Kelly, 1983, p.18).

For Kelly and for others this developmental tradition in the primary curriculum (Blyth, 1984) was 'the fruits of those seeds sown much earlier by theorists such as Rousseau, Froebel, Montessori and Dewey' and was 'given the official sanction not only by the Hadow Report (1931) but also by Plowden' (Kelly, 1983, p.10). Throughout its existence this view of primary education has had to struggle against the deep-rooted elementary school tradition, which, according to Cohen and Cohen (1986, p.ix), 'with nineteenth century administrative thoroughness and efficiency, produced a pedagogical system of class teaching allied to a curriculum geared largely to utilitarian preoccupation with skills of literacy and numeracy'. Accounts of curriculum development in the United States (Kliebard, 1986, p. 123) describe a similar struggle between 'subject realignment and vocationalism and a curriculum based upon development and experience'. According to Kliebard, during this struggle a period of *hybridisation* took place in which the two traditions merged and became confused. It could be argued that in the United Kingdom, particularly in the twenty years following the Second World War, a similar process took place but that the degree of hybridisation varied from local authority to local authority and from school to school, giving rise to a range of different

interpretations of primary practice equivalent to a system based upon
laissez-faire.

Support for the pressure theory comes from the sociological
research of Andrew Hargreaves (1978, 1979), who seeks to explain the
gap between the rhetoric and the reality of progressive education in
terms of the competing external pressures put on teachers by the
demands for accountability and the demands from parents. According
to Hargreaves, the teacher is 'a crucial lynch pin in the wheel of
causality that connects structural features of the society to inter-
actional patterns in the classroom and back again, thereby
reproducing the structural arrangements' (Hargreaves, 1978, p.75). In
order to do this the teacher devises 'a set of coping teaching strategies
which will make life bearable, possible and even rewarding as an
educational practitioner'. Teaching styles are developed 'only insofar
as they enable successful coping with experienced constraint'
(Hargreaves, 1978, p.75), the major constraints being the pressures
exerted by society through central and local government interference,
parental aspirations, and institutional constraints such as buildings
and class sizes. Hargreaves sees the teacher as one who tries, as far as
possible, to 'educate and relate to children in the spirit of liberal indivi-
dualism' while at the same time preparing children for 'the reality of
the society in which they will one day live and work' (Hargreaves,
1978, p.78).

Hargreaves argues that teachers, such as those who took part in the
Ford Teaching Project, tended heavily to guide the pupils in the introductory question and answer sessions leading to a discovery lesson in
an attempt to cope with a situation where they wished to implement the
progressive ideology (that children learn best when they actively
pursue their own interests), while at the same time ensuring that pupils
did not attempt a particular task that was beyond them. This avoided
any possibility that, by the end of the topic, pupils would have
achieved little and gained a poor assessment, producing criticism by
parents of the school and the teacher.

Quality control theories and inadequate teachers

The second set of explanations for the failure to implement Plowden's
theory of progressivism might be called the *quality control* theory, the
idea that too many of the profession lack the intelligence and skills to
practise progressive teaching effectively. This particular theory was
given official backing by the Labour government during Prime

Minister Callaghan's (1976) Ruskin speech when he voiced the unease allegedly felt by parents and others 'about the new informal methods', arguing that these appeared to work well only in 'well qualified hands'. This seemingly was a reference to Bennett's (1976) Lancaster study where the class of one informal teacher obtained among the highest scores on the standardised tests and was subsequently the subject of a study by Wragg (1978).

Writing twenty years after the publication of her report, Lady Plowden (1987) appears to endorse Callaghan's view:

> Looking back, it seems that our report could not have come out at a worse time. For the rapid increase in birth rate meant a vast increase in the numbers of teachers needed... The staff in the colleges, mostly secondary orientated for they were all graduates, coped as well as they could to convey to their students the best that we had described. But the difficulties of the new, young teachers, with the high turnover which there was, entering possibly overcrowded infant and junior schools – some with still fairly formal approach, militated against an understanding against what was and what was not possible. No wonder there were shortcomings and misinterpretations, and methods were tried which were entirely impracticable. There was sufficient fodder for the Black Paper enthusiasts to make quite a convincing case and the affair at William Tyndale school made its special contribution to this misunderstanding. No wonder that teachers who were trying to see what could be done became depressed by all the criticism – some must have given up in despair.
>
> (Plowden, 1987, p.120)

This view was also endorsed by Colin Richards, later to become an HMI with responsibility for fashioning some of the recent government curriculum initiatives. In a review of primary education from 1974 to 1980, Richards (1982) does not disagree with Kelly's (1982) interpretation of the important events that caused the public shift away from the more rosy view of education as a social panacea. Richards, like Kelly, highlights the Great Debate and the growth of the accountability movement as important factors in the gradual loss of teacher autonomy in the matters of what and how they teach in their own classrooms. Richards, however, profoundly disagrees with Kelly's external pressures analysis. He argues instead that the *laissez-faire* approach to progressive practice arose largely because leaving 'all curriculum decisions (or non-decisions) in the hands of individual practitioners, operating in comparative isolation', assumes 'a degree of individual self-sufficiency which could only be sustained if the task in question was simple, uncontentious, fully understood and self-contained' (Richards, 1982, p. 25).

During this period much evidence was collected, both in Britain and in the United States, on the quality of entrants into the teaching profession. Applicants for BEd courses at universities and polytechnics, for example, have some of the lowest 'A' level admission grades. Like Lady Plowden, Richards seems to imply that many of these teachers were not intellectually capable of the rigorous analysis required to come to grips with such complex issues as discovery learning, subject integration and, more recently, continuity and progression in the curriculum. If philosophers such as Dearden (1976) have considerable conceptual difficulty with these terms, it is unreasonable to expect any consistency of practice amongst those charged with translating these theories into action within the classroom.

Many of the changes in primary education have, therefore, been the result of an enthusiastic response to various bandwagons or the result of expediency. In neither case have the implications of such changes been fully worked out or understood. As a result, far from leading to all-round improvements in practice, the period of experimentation has produced, at best, teaching that is 'occasionally exciting, usually competent in the so-called basics at least, but not infrequently mediocre or inadequate' (Alexander, 1984a, p. 11).

Alexander's verdict may seem, to so me, unduly harsh, but one has only to observe the attempts of some experienced and generally recognised 'effective' teachers to design an activity based upon freedom of choice according to the child's interests to appreciate the magnitude of the problem. For example, in collecting examples of effective group work as part of the ORACLE project, two teachers in an inner city infant school offered a lesson that they had recorded on video tape. These children, top infants, had previously been on an outing to the seaside and, in the enthusiasm generated by the trip, asked to go on another excursion. Conscious of the limitations of family finance, it was decided by these two teachers that the children should be allowed to plan a local outing at a cost of no more than 50p per head. This money had to include the costs of the journey and the picnic lunch.

Quite the largest part of the video tape was given over to the introductory sessions where the children were told about the trip and asked to decide where they wanted to go and what form of transport they would use. The children made various suggestions ranging from hiring coaches to going by train. In fact, given the financial situation, bussing or walking were the only valid alternatives and, in terms of safety and suitability, the local park the only location for the picnic.

Once this decision had eventually been arrived at, with much guidance from the teachers, the learning activity became truly autonomous with pupils ringing up the bus company (having first learned to use the telephone directory), plotting journeys (using the bus timetables), and planning elaborate menus consisting of ham sandwiches, fruit and chocolate 'cup' cakes. Subsequently, after carrying out a pricing exercise at the local supermarket, the groups eventually settled on a picnic lunch of paste sandwiches and thin slices of jam swiss roll. The class drew maps of the park, plotted their routes and organised their own activities and games.

The point of this description is not to argue about the rightness of the teachers' decisions but to suggest a possible dilemma on their part when seeking to interpret 'freedom of choice' either in terms of '*what* to do' or in terms of '*how* to do it'. Emphasising the *what* rather than the *how* appears to diminish the importance placed by writers such as Taba (1966) and Bruner (1966) on teaching the processes of discovery when developing children's thinking. According to Kliebard (1986), it would also arguably run counter to Dewey's view: by emphasising the choice of activity rather than the more important choice of how to carry out the activity, these teachers were in danger of placing too much stress on 'the more negative aspects of progressivism'. Both the school and the teachers were regarded as outstanding by colleagues and the local authority. If such issues as 'freedom of choice' remain problematic for such skilled practitioners, then those of us with less 'craft knowledge' may experience more difficulty in putting progressive theory into practice.

Impossibility theory: It's all too difficult

The third type of explanation for failure to put progressive ideas into practice might be termed the *impossibility theory*. The view that such practice is physically too demanding of teachers is strongly argued by Simon (1981), writing as part of the ORACLE project. Bennett *et al.* (1984) also conclude from their study of teachers attempting to match the tasks in the classroom to the individual pupil's needs and ability that,

The philosophy of individualised instruction has informed the education of young children for many years. We do not doubt the validity of this, but like all ideals, it is easier to theorise about than practise. Nevertheless, teachers of this age group have made significant steps towards its successful implementation. Learning environments have been created which are characterised by good social relationships, expert utilisation of resources, happy and industrious pupils. What this study has revealed is that a number of cognitive aspects of this environment appear to have been hidden from the teachers.

(Bennett *et al.*, 1984, p.221)

Simon argues in a similar vein concerning the Plowden prescription that, as an alternative to whole-class teaching, the class should be split into four, five or more groups and each group engaged on co-operative tasks involving discussion and the use of materials and apparatus so that 'all are effectively and meaningfully occupied'. Simon comments:

To think out, provide materials for and set up a series of group tasks having the characteristics just described in the different subject areas which comprise a modern curriculum would in itself clearly be a major undertaking, even if use is made of relevant curriculum development projects. To monitor activities; to be ready and able to intervene in the work of each group when this is educationally necessary or desirable; this also would clearly be a major undertaking for the teacher.

(Galton and Simon, 1980, p.160)

By implication, therefore, Simon reinforces the admission in the Plowden Report that the demands now máde on teachers were 'frighteningly high' (Plowden, 1967, para 875). On the ORACLE evidence Simon concludes:

The fact is that the teacher does not have time to devote her mind to, or engage in, the kind of interactions with individual pupils which Plowden prescribed. This kind of probing, questioning relationship with individual pupils is characteristic of University teaching, a point specifically made in Plowden (para 669). It is particularly characteristic of the one-to-one University tutorial, when twenty-nine other students are not also present, requiring the same simultaneous relationship. Even at the University level teaching of this kind is generally recognised as an art requiring a high degree of skill. A teacher with a classroom populated by young children is in a different situation altogether and cannot easily afford either the time or the mental energy to engage in such discussions with individual children. On the contrary she must always be conscious of the other twenty-nine pupils who, in this case, are present and who, given the same system of individualisation, are also, if in varying degrees, demanding her attention. Our conclusion, then is that given contemporary class sizes, the Plowden 'progressive' ideology based essentially on individualisation is impractical.

(Galton *et al.*, 1980, p.158)

Studies of class size (Glass, 1982) agree with the ORACLE estimate that to raise the level of interactions to the rate achieved by the more successful 'infrequent changers' (whom it may be remembered had above-average rates of one-to-one exchanges with pupils) would require class sizes to be reduced to fifteen. Within existing financial constraints this would be totally impractical unless a solution adopted in Iceland was followed where classes of thirty are divided into two, and each half attends for only the morning or the afternoon session. This would not necessarily result in a decrease in instructional time, since on the evidence of Tizard *et al.* (1988) the current situation with between twenty-five and thirty children to a class results in pupils spending half the day in non-work activity. Findings from both the ORACLE (Galton and Simon, 1980) and the ILEA junior study (Mortimore *et al.*, 1987) suggest that some teachers are well aware of the limitations of individualisation and make use of class teaching whenever possible, in order to maximise the amount and the quality of their interactions with the children.

The lack of theory theory

The fourth and perhaps more interesting explanation for the failure to implement Plowden practice to any considerable extent derives also from Simon. This theory might be termed the *lack of theory* in that Simon argues, convincingly, that the very philosophy of the Plowden Report, with its emphasis on individualisation of the teaching and learning process, has 'created a situation from which it is impossible to derive an effective pedagogy' (which he defines as 'the science of teaching'). This is because,

> To develop effective pedagogic means involves starting from the opposite stand point, from what the children have in common as members of the human species: to establish the general principles of teaching and, in the light of these, to determine what modifications of practice are needed to meet specific individual needs.
>
> (Simon, 1981, p.141)

Others have echoed this view. Writing towards the end of the 1960s, William Taylor, former Director of the London Institute, argued that the world of teacher training was one of 'social and literary romanticism' (Taylor, 1969, p.12). Simon implicitly endorses Taylor's view when he argues:

> the most striking aspect of current thinking and discussion about education (in England) is its eclectic character, reflecting deep confusion of thought and aims and purposes, relating to learning and teaching: to pedagogy.
>
> (Simon, 1981, p.124)

Simon considers that the omission of any serious consideration of 'the science of teaching' has arisen largely because of the elitist system of education in Britain, which has for so long 'dominated the thinking concerning educational policy and provision, as represented by the dominant influence of public schools and the Universities of Oxford and Cambridge' (Simon, 1981, p. 126), particularly the influence of their examination boards. He points out that one of the crucial events in the demise of an interest in pedagogy was the ending of the elementary school system as the vehicle for mass education. Once secondary education developed in parallel but quite separate from the elementary school, then a shift of emphasis took place. Prior to the growth of the secondary system the training manuals written for students who intended to teach in the elementary school tended to stress the need for self-evaluation. Only rarely was school failure attributed to disabilities in the child such as lack of intelligence. Instead, the emphasis was placed on the examination of teaching behaviour when seeking a cause for an individual child's learning difficulties. The need to separate children at the end of the elementary stage and to select those who continued into the secondary school changed this situation.

> The old belief in a positive pedagogy based upon scientific
> procedures and understanding and relevant for all was no
> longer seen as appropriate or required . . . The social discip-
> linary 'containment' function of elementary education was
> now especially emphasised.
>
> (Simon, 1981, p.132)

These new requirements of the secondary system were well served by the development of psychometric theories in which inherited ability, rather than the quality of the teaching, was seen as the major determinant of attainment. Such developments eventually put an end to the search for an effective pedagogy. At primary level, even prominent exponents of 'progressivism' such as Susan Isaacs accepted as axiomatic the concepts of intelligence and supported streaming. At the time, Piaget's ideas were used, mistakenly, to place undue stress on the effective teacher's ability to detect when a child 'was ready' to engage in a particular activity and to create the necessary environment that could then 'spark off' the child in a spontaneous way. Progressive educationalists such as Susan Isaacs argued that, just as different plants needed different conditions for this kind of spontaneous growth, so children of different abilities required different environments and it therefore made sense to group those individuals with similar needs together. Teachers needed to develop a sense of each child's needs through the use of creative imagination rather than by reference to a set of generalised procedures. Progressive teaching was therefore much more of an art than a science.

In bringing his criticisms up to date, Simon cites the work of the Schools Council from its establishment in 1964 to its demise at the beginning of the 1980s. He defines as the key feature of the Council's attempt to reform the curriculum 'The atheoretical pragmatic approach adopted'.

> . . . the overall approach has not been informed by any
> generally accepted (by publicly formulated) ideas or
> theories about the nature of the child or the learning–tea-
> ching process – by any science of teaching or pedagogy. In
> particular there has been an almost total failure to provide
> psychological underpinning for the new programmes
> proposed. In general, the Schools Council approach has
> reflected a pluralism run wild – a mass of disparate
> projects.
>
> (Simon, 1981, p.124)

These sentiments echo those earlier reported by both Taylor and Alexander. However, Simon goes on to absolve the Schools Council from blame because,

> The concept of pedagogy – of a science of teaching embodying both curriculum and methodology – is alien to our experience and way of thinking. There are, no doubt, many reasons why this is so; among them wide acceptance of the unresolved dichotomies between 'progressive' and 'traditional' approaches, between 'child-centred' and 'subject-centred' approaches, or, more generally, between the 'informal' and 'formal'. Such crude, generalised categories are basically meaningless but expressed in this form deflect attention from the real problems of teaching and learning. Indeed so disparate are the views expressed that to resuscitate the concept of a science of teaching which underlines that of 'pedagogy' may seem to be crying for the moon.
>
> (Simon, 1981, p.125)

Nowhere is Simon's argument more clearly demonstrated than in one of the final publications of the Schools Council, the 1983 Working Paper entitled *Primary Practice: A Sequel to 'The Practical Curriculum'*. In this paper the authors make the point that today's schoolchildren will be young adults in AD 2000. While accepting that educating the young is now a more daunting responsibility than ever before, they nevertheless argue that

> fortunately, we are better equipped to tackle this task, professionally, than ever before. We understand more about how children develop, how they learn, and how they are sometimes prevented from learning, we are beginning to see how to match teaching and learning to their stages of development. We have marvellous insights into the working of the brain's two hemispheres. The left hemisphere handles words and numbers while the right remembers shapes and tunes . . . Most significant, creative activities depend on the collaborative work of the left and the right cerebral hemispheres. Both have to be nurtured.
>
> (Schools Council, 1983, p.11)

The introduction, however, contains no reference to any characteristics that might define effective teaching in terms of teachers' behaviours, other than in a most general and unproblematic manner. To be a successful teacher means working to more detailed objectives, since 'agreeing the terms to be used in defining part of the curriculum leads to statements about the kind of progress children are expected to make and how their progress is to be assessed' (Schools Council, 1983, p.35). This is followed by statements of objectives for various subject areas including science, mathematics and language. At the end of each chapter various points are offered as an aid to further discussion. For example, under language and literacy, teachers are asked:

(i)   Do your reading guidelines provide adequately for the reading of several different kinds?
(ii) Are satisfactory guidelines for talking, listening and writing in regular use at your school?
(iii) Can you prepare a list of listening skills appropriate as objectives for your own pupils?

Nowhere in the document is there any reference to the difficulties, such as those described by teachers in the Ford Teaching Project, involved in facilitating pupil talk in the classroom, or to the likely problems associated with children's responses to teacher's questions, although most teachers would agree that getting children involved in class discussion is highly problematic.

The document specifically rejects the kind of argument advanced by Simon concerning the need for a generalised theory of pedagogy that gives less priority to children's individual differences. The Schools Council Working Paper, in fact, maintains the opposite view, specifically when referring to the processes of assessment and record keeping. Here it argues:

> We know that children differ greatly by the time they arrive at reception class. They differ in physique, general ability, achievement and personality. To some extent their differences are clearly hereditary: pigmentation and sex are genetically determined and physique largely so. To some extent their differences are environmental: differences in interests and verbal abilities are probably attributable to family influence.
>
> Teachers need to be aware of these differences, and the reasons for them because they are of such importance in shaping strategies for teaching. Teachers may sometimes find it helpful to draw on research findings to enrich their

understanding. But they should do so with caution. Some research studies are based on quite small samples and their conclusions are necessarily tentative. Above all, *they tend to generalise about whole groups of people, whereas teachers need strategies for helping the twenty, thirty or forty individuals in their class*.

(Schools Council, 1983, p.116)

There is then, in this and other documents – such as those emanating from government sources (DES, 1985; HMI, 1985) – very little evidence of any perceived need for a theory of effective teaching, let alone any attempt to define its major components.

Towards a Redefinition of Effective Teaching

Summarising these various explanations for the failure to implement progressive practice in the aftermath of the Plowden Report, it is probable that all these theories have some validity. Certainly, some of them are complementary.

The external pressures that teachers face day in and day out, as part of their professional life, are enormous, as Lady Plowden (1987) argues when writing in the wake of the teacher unrest:

What of the teachers themselves, those whose predecessors made progress which we described? The past months of bitterness in the teaching world have produced a situation which in the days of 'Plowden' we could not have imagined.

(Plowden, 1987, p.124)

The pressures created by the 1988 Education Act allowing schools to opt out and by the introduction of regular testing programmes at both 7 years and 11 years will contribute further to this pressure. However, the existence of attribution theory is not always recognised by those researchers who collect their data about the constraints on innovation in classroom practice primarily through extended interviews with practitioners. As we have seen, one of the key features of attribution theory is that it suggests why a person will explain their actions by factors that lie outside their immediate control. Such a person will therefore see themselves as powerless to effect change.

The argument for a reduction in class size is illuminating in this respect. Research studies of class size are ambivalent (Burstall, 1979). Many have tended to show a positive correlation between increasing size and pupil progress. More recently, however, studies such as PRISMS and the ILEA junior school study (Mortimore *et al.*, 1987) have shown the opposite trend. In the case of PRISMS, the correlations, although positive, were small and in the ILEA study they were in the negative direction. More interestingly, the PRISMS study showed that in many respects the observed patterns of interaction in large and small classes were similar. In the PRISMS classes there were more opportunities for children to receive extended periods of individual attention as class size decreased. The corollary of this, however, was that, although pupils spent more time with the teacher, they also spent more time waiting for the teacher. Overall, therefore, the total amount of attention that a pupil received was of the same order in small classes as in large ones. While it is obviously less stressful and more pleasurable to work with a small class of children, this result suggests that there are other factors involved in teachers' explanations for low levels of individual attention other than the pressures of class size. These other factors, to do with classroom organisation, are in the control of the teacher, as is the nature of a classroom relationship that requires pupils to spend extensive time waiting for the teacher rather than taking greater responsibility for their own learning. Low levels of interaction in large classes cannot therefore be explained solely in terms of 'pressure' theory.

The quality control argument also merits some consideration. Recent government initiatives, such as the setting up of the Council for Teacher Accreditation (CATE), have attempted to raise standards of entry to teacher training by insisting on 'O' levels in mathematics and English, together with appropriate knowledge in a 'core' subject area of the primary curriculum. These regulations have caused considerable criticism, particularly in relation to teacher training for the early years. That particular discussion lies beyond the scope of this chapter, but it should be recognised that these changes in the pattern of teacher training in England are part of a much wider debate about the standards of entry to teaching that is going on throughout Europe and the United States (Neave, 1987). If the quality argument is accepted, it follows that, since many of the concepts used to describe 'modern practice' are badly defined, 'What teachers do not understand they will not value and what they do not value they will not teach well', to paraphrase Alexander (1984a).

One unfortunate consequence of the quality theory is that it implies a critical view of teachers and undermines their confidence in their ability to bring about change. Indeed, both Richards (1982) and

Alexander (1984b) are at pains to stress that the greater responsibility for the present situation lies with those who have developed the educational theories and particularly those who have had responsibility for inducting new entrants into the profession (Galton, in press). It is only too easy for critics of modern primary practice to draw over-simplistic conclusions from the data on entry qualifications and to conclude that there is a need to standardise and control what teachers do in order to reduce diversity and to produce more consistency of practice. There is, in any case, little evidence that quality of teaching at primary level is highly correlated with academic grades. In one unpublished study at Nottingham University, during a transition period when the regulations for the BEd were being changed so that no entrant could be admitted without two 'A' levels, comparisons were made between a group gaining entry with only 'O' level qualifications and those who had completed 'A' level study. 'O' level grades rather than 'A' level were found to be better predictors of the final teaching practice grade. Clearly such questions are complex, in that the factors to do with different experiences during training must be taken into account as a predictor of future success, as well as the limitations of teaching practice grades. However, the general point is that no strong evidence exists that suggests that students with better academic qualifications are more likely to implement progressive practice successfully as defined by Plowden.

One reason for rejecting both pressure theories and quality control theories has already been discussed in earlier chapters. Both these notions begin with an assumption that teaching is, in large part, an *intentional activity*. Hargreaves' coping theory, described earlier with respect to discovery learning, assumes that teachers are consciously weighing up the balance between their need to give guidance in order to ensure that the pupil produces a satisfactory product and their desire to maintain, as far as possible, independent pupil enquiry. In a different context, the same assumption lies behind the initiatives to provide a framework for the primary curriculum (HMI, 1985), which Richards (1982) earlier saw as 'the much needed corrective' that would restore the 'professionalism' of the individual practitioner by allowing teachers to respond to varying circumstances in the classrooms within clearly defined curriculum structures. While there is a place for clearly defined objectives that can be assessed, the use of the national curriculum planning model has regularly failed to deliver the corresponding 'national desired' practice contingent upon these objectives.

While, therefore, intention is a necessary part of developing a teaching strategy, it is not sufficient to account for its implementation. Intention, as argued earlier, concerns what Allport termed coping behaviour, which is, largely, consciously determined. However, practice in the classroom also derives much of its impetus from Allport's second category of behaviour, which he terms 'expressive' and which is largely motivated by our unconscious needs.

In our classroom practice, whenever difficulties arise, we generally define the problems in terms of solutions that we find acceptable to us. How, for example, do we get the class to be quiet? How do we stop children wandering around the room? But a central idea of John Dewey's view of progressiveness was that problems were to be defined not solely 'in terms of acceptable solutions' but also 'in terms of competing needs' (Gordon, 1974). To begin an analysis of this kind requires answers to such questions as, 'Why do I need these children to be quiet and sit still?' which immediately demands explanations in terms of our expressive actions as well as our coping ones. Such analyses can be extremely stressful, forcing us 'to face what we do not wish to face' (Hoggart, 1980 p.41), and are therefore difficult to contemplate. Thus we revert to 'safer', more familiar practices and take comfort in the notion of an impossibility theory that suggests that progressive teaching is only for others, the few outstanding members of the profession.

This 'conservative' view is explored by Gage (1985). He notes 'the persistence of teacher-centered classroom teaching', and refers to the work of Cuban (1984), who documents 'a seemingly stubborn continuity in the character of instruction'. Cuban found that classroom practices tended to be stable and to resemble the approaches used by previous teachers. Given this remarkable stability and using his definition of pedagogy as 'the science of the art of teaching', Gage goes on to argue that to attempt to introduce new paradigms is in effect like trying to change the basic art form that constitutes classroom teaching. This would be 'tantamount to trying to persuade poets to stop writing sonnets and start writing sonatas'. Gage continues:

> My analogy with art forms seems to apply to the approach to research and development in teaching and teacher education that I see as most promising. If we cannot replace the art form, we can perhaps change the quality of what is done in that form. Within the sonnet form there are poor sonnets and good sonnets. The same is true of concertos, watercolors and mobiles. Within the art form called classroom teaching there is also great variation in

quality. What I see as promising is research that accepts the basic parameters of classroom teaching: teacher-centeredness, whole-class organization, subject matter orientation, and much recitation interspersed with short lectures, discussions, tutoring and seat work. Such research will study the infinite variations possible within this stable art form, the variations that make the difference between superb, average and atrocious classroom teaching.

(Gage, 1985, p.49)

There remain many teachers, however, who would wish to reject this view as unduly pessimistic. They would maintain, as Simon (1981) does, that it is the lack of an adequate pedagogic theory of progressiveness that undermines their attempts to change their practice. Research into teaching that seeks to move from the merely descriptive to developing explanatory theories of action is relatively recent, judging by advances in other disciplines. The developments of new paradigms in science have often depended not so much on a 'leap in the dark' as on the improved technology through which the processes studied can be observed. The progression from Galileo's telescope to the latest radio instruments illustrates the point well in relation to the development of theories about the origin of the universe. What has been lacking in teaching until relatively recently are research techniques that enable investigators to focus on the needs of both teachers and pupils in ways that deal with their unconscious motivations so that explanations of practice do not reflect simply aspects of attribution theory. The works of Nias (1984, 1985) and Pollard (1985) are but two examples of these more detailed penetrating analyses.

The theory of progressive education, if it is to be redefined or perhaps restated, must take such research into account so as to identify and then resolve problems that arise because of potential conflict between the teachers' and pupils' needs in the classroom. Gage's model of classroom teaching continues the traditional view of teacher–pupil relationships – defined in the way that teachers who favour this approach often talk about '*my* classroom' or '*my* children'. This contrasts sharply with those who favour the 'Plowden' approach, where 'freedom of choice' and 'giving responsibility to the pupils' are interpreted as surrendering this authority so that the children are now told that 'it's *your* classroom'.

The 'new' progressivism, or perhaps the rediscovered original version, has to begin with an understanding of 'our classroom', where teachers and children both have rights and responsibilities that need to be jointly agreed, without at the same time undermining the authority of the teacher. For too long, perhaps, we have talked in general terms about 'the importance of relationships' in teaching without defining their nature. There is now an adequate research methodology to enable the working out of these relationships to be studied in more detail and for the results of these investigations to be used as a basis in the reformulation of progressive theory.

If this view is the correct one then it suggests that the pedagogy that Simon (1981) calls for will make full use of social learning theories, which emphasise that learning is not only a cognitive but also a social activity. Within this kind of framework, it becomes possible to understand why, in the opening chapter of this book, Mr Aspin's class of twenty-eight 9-year-old children responded so differently to the two kinds of task he set and why 'intermittent workers', 'easy riders' and 'attention getters', such as Darren in Chapter 1, make use of strategies for task avoidance.

Such an approach has the added advantage that it enables teachers to use their own experiences as learners in adult settings to reflect on their own classroom practice and so contribute to this theorising. By concentrating on cognitive approaches to learning, as we often do during teacher training, new entrants to the profession receive very strong messages that children are different from adults in the way in which they assimilate new knowledge and new skills. By emphasising the social aspects of the learning process – the manner in which we behave in groups, the way we try to avoid being the first to answer the question – we stress the communalities of learning between adults and children. This allows us to 'put ourselves in the child's place' and more readily look for the reasons for the child's failure in terms of our own performance rather than the pupils' inadequacies. At the same time, a progressive theory based upon the idea of 'our classroom' requires children to 'put themselves in the place of their teachers', so that teaching and learning become, truly, a collaborative effort.

Before exploring this theme further, however, we return to Gage's (1985) argument that it is possible, using recent research, to improve the quality of 'classroom teaching'. Unlike Coe's account (1966) of a teacher who claimed she 'never taught the class but only children', most practitioners now find themselves making use of this strategy on many occasions. In the next chapter, therefore, I consider those factors that appear to be important characteristics of Gage's 'superb' classroom teacher.

CHAPTER 6

Direct Instruction and Factory Models of Teaching

In the last chapter we saw that one response to the problems that have arisen when teachers have attempted to implement the 'Plowden' model of progressive teaching is to conclude that it is more sensible to abandon the attempt and to concentrate on improving what teachers have done throughout the ages: namely to organise the classroom so that most of the initiatives stem from the teacher, with the emphasis on teacher talk and teacher-initiated questioning. The pupils spend a large proportion of their time either listening to the teacher, practising what the teacher has taught, or taking turns to answer the teacher's questions.

We shall call the various models based upon this approach 'factory models of teaching', because they exhibit striking similarities to a non-automated factory production line. Although the models do bear a resemblance to the old 'traditional' notion of instruction, they are much more sophisticated and detailed in their descriptions of what teachers should do and say. For our purposes the factory in question makes biscuits and the task that has been set for the packers (the pupils) is to place a variety of biscuit assortments (the curriculum) into tins (the end product) under the supervision of a foreman (the teacher). The packers are placed on either side of a conveyor belt down which the tins move at a regular pace. The atmosphere is friendly and as they work the packers chat to one another against a background of pop music which is piped around the factory.

The key to the success of the enterprise lies in the rate at which the conveyor belts move. This is controlled by the foreman. If the conveyor belt moves too quickly then too many tins emerge from the line with certain varieties of biscuits missing from the assortment. If the conveyor belt moves too slowly then the tins emerge correctly packed but the number produced falls to such a level that it is uneconomic. The foreman therefore sets the rate so that only a small proportion of tins need to be returned for repacking. In this factory the speed of the conveyor belt is set, initially, so that the success rate for packing the tins is around 80 per cent.

Sometimes the conversation between packers rises to such a level that they become distracted and begin to make mistakes when packing the tins. At this point the foreman switches off the pop music until the noise level subsides and the tins begin to emerge correctly packed. Thus the working relationship between the foreman and the packers is friendly but firm. The whole exercise is carefully planned and under the control of the foreman, who decides which biscuits will be packed and by whom. Sometimes the conveyor belt has only one kind of biscuit (single-subject curriculum) while at other times different groups pack different biscuits into the same tins (integrated-subject curriculum). One refinement is to observe very carefully the different rates at which different packers operate and then group these together (setting within the classroom). In this way it is possible to run different conveyor belts at different speeds and so increase the number of tins that are packed correctly.

Under the general heading of 'direct instruction' a variety of teaching programmes have been devised in recent years, mostly in the United States, which bear remarkable similarities to the factory situation described. According to Rosenshine (1987, p. 258), 'direct instruction and similar terms can be summarised in the phrase: "If you want students to learn something, teach it to them – directly." ' Something of the style of direct instruction approaches can be seen from the example provided in a report of research by Anderson, Evertson and Brophy (1979). They offer the following advice to teachers for organising instruction in reading.

1. Once in the [reading] group, the children should be seated with their backs to the rest of the class while the teacher is facing the class.
2. The introduction to the lesson should contain an overview of what is to come, in order to prepare the students mentally for the presentation.
3. The teacher should work with one individual at a time, having the children practise the new skill and apply the new concept, making sure that everyone is checked and receives feedback during the lesson.

4.   The teacher should use a pattern (such as going from one end of the group to the other) for selecting children to take their turns reading in the group or answering questions (rather than calling on them randomly and unpredictably).

5.   When call-outs occur, the teacher should remind the child that everyone gets a turn and he must wait his turn to answer.

6.   After asking a question the teacher should wait for the child to respond and also see that other children wait and do not call out answers. If the child does not respond within a reasonable time, the teacher should indicate that some response is expected by probing.

7.   Praise should be used in moderation. The teacher should praise thinking and effort more than just getting the answer and should make praise as specific to an individual as possible.

8.   Criticism should also be as specific as possible, and should include specification of desirable or correct alternatives.

(Anderson *et al.*, 1979, pp. 196–8)

It is noticeable that such prescriptions go well beyond the rather imprecise notions of traditional teaching discussed in Chapter 2, which tended to be associated with whole-class teaching, didactic exposition and regular testing. These recent definitions of direct instruction employ a variety of sophisticated models based upon various interpretations of 'information-processing theory' (Gage and Berliner, 1988; Sternberg, 1982).

The Origins of Direct Instruction

In the early chapters we saw how the developments taking place during the 1960s in local authorities such as the West Riding, Leicestershire and Oxfordshire led to a great number of visits by Americans who wished to introduce similar practice to schools in the United States. Partly for propaganda purposes, some of these writers (such as Silberman, 1970, 1973; and Featherstone, 1971) appear to have exaggerated the extent of the so-called primary revolution. However, central features of what was described as 'British practice' were given theoretical support in the writings of Cazden (1969) and Bussis and Chittenden (1970). The programmes that these and other American educationalists proposed came to be known under the general heading of 'open' education. As in the Plowden classroom, American children experiencing 'open' education could choose to work alone or with a group and would not have a particular place in the class but would move from one activity area to another. Each child would be responsible for planning their personal timetable, although they were expected to do some reading, writing and arithmetic each day. As with the progressive methods described by Anthony (1979), it was argued that classroom activity should be mainly based on the interests of the pupils.

As in Britain, there was no shortage of studies in which 'open' education programmes were compared with more 'traditional' approaches. Such comparisons proved difficult to make, however, because not all programmes included the same features as part of the 'open' education package. Nevertheless, when global comparisons were made between 'open' education and more traditional practices, the same trends that operated in the British studies were discovered. There was a tendency for pupils in more traditional classrooms to show slightly superior performance in language, mathematics and reading (Giaconia and Hedges, 1982). In the United States, there has always been a greater emphasis on testing in the elementary school, so it is not surprising that the differences between open and traditional forms of education were as small as found in these studies. It would be as if the comparisons had been made in Britain using the 11 + results as the main criterion for effectiveness.

Nevertheless, the widespread use of test results, as part of the new accountability movement, led to increased questioning about the value for money that the education system was providing – in ways that were very similar to those described earlier for the United Kingdom. Researchers increasingly began to look for clues in developing teaching programmes that were more specific and enabled 'beginning teachers' to be provided with a package of skills to ensure not only their survival but some initial success (Denham and Lieberman, 1980).

The starting point for some of these early investigators was to return to the work of Flanders (1964), whose results had tended to support the use of 'indirect' teaching (low levels of lecturing and direct teacher questioning within a strong affective climate of accepting pupils' feelings, praise, etc.). It was pointed out by researchers such as Rosenshine (1979) that Flanders' distinction between direct and indirect instruction was flawed in that it incorporated two clusters of variables that were not necessarily mutually incompatible. To be a 'direct' teacher under the Flanders model, at least at the extreme of the continuum, it was necessary not to praise but to criticise, and not to accept pupils' feelings while emphasising teacher talk. Why, these critics asked, was it not possible for the teacher to exercise strong control of lesson content and procedures while at the same time creating a classroom atmosphere that was warm, friendly and generally supportive of the student? Direct instruction, so called to distinguish it from Flanders' notion of direct teaching, therefore emphasises time-honoured characteristics such as a focus on the academic content of the lesson, teacher talk in various forms of lectures and demonstrations, and pupil engagement in the activities of recitation, drill and practice. Teachers aim for around 80 per cent success rate initially (as in the biscuit factory analogy). The teacher operates a management system designed to maintain the pace of the lesson (the speed of the conveyor belt) so that the students are engaged on their task for most of the time. The pupils remain in their seats, while the teacher moves around monitoring their performance and providing individual feedback.

Research into Direct Instruction

The underlying principle governing the idea of 'direct instruction' is that of mastery (Carroll, 1963; Bloom, 1971; Block, 1971). In its simplest terms this model predicts that the amount learnt is a function of the ratio between the time that is allowed for learning (the *allocated* time) and the acdtual amount of time that the student spends upon the task (the *engaged* time). Direct instruction attempts to maximise these times. Superficially at least, these variables are appealing because they are easy to measure. Numerous studies have shown that they vary considerably from classroom to classroom (Rosenshine, 1980; Bennett, 1978). This has led Harnischfeger and Wiley (1978) to postulate that 'time on task is the major determinant of pupil learning'. As the mastery model developed it incorporated other variables, such as the pupil's motivation, the quality of the instruction and the capability of a pupil to understand the instruction provided.

Time allocation itself can vary considerably, as reported by Bennett (1978). In the PRISMS study, for example, the schools in one local authority showed a difference of five hours a week between the extremes in the range of time spent on classroom activities. Within the classroom, the individual pupil's time on task will also vary considerably, with some pupils working for only 30 per cent of allocated time. Research into direct instruction, therefore, usually measures the relationship between various teaching behaviours and the time that pupils are observed to be engaged upon their tasks. This engaged time is then correlated with pupil performance over a range of standardised tests. There are now a number of reviews of the effects of direct instruction (Rosenshine, 1987; Good and Brophy, 1986). These reviews stress the importance of structuring the learning experience – by proceeding in small steps at a rapid pace, and using frequent questioning – and of providing opportunities for overt, active practice, with plenty of feedback and corrections during the initial stages of learning new information. Frequent monitoring is necessary to achieve success rates of 80 per cent during initial learning. This makes it possible to extend mastery to the point of 'over learning', with pupils eventually achieving success rates of around 90–100 per cent and gaining confidence in their ability to make use of their newly acquired knowledge and skills.

A typical cycle of direct instruction begins with a review and demonstration by the teacher. Good and Grouws (1979), in a study of fourth-grade (10+) mathematics instruction, recommend a daily review for the first 8 minutes (except Mondays when it should last 20 minutes) in which the concepts and skills previously learnt are revised, homework assignments are collected and rapid checks are made on various mental computation exercises. This is followed by a developmental period, in which the teacher briefly focuses on the prerequisite skills and concepts to be taught and then develops these ideas by using good-humoured, interesting demonstrations, illustrations and explanations. The next step involves a check on the students' comprehension by means of rapid questions and by getting students to do one or two examples. If the initial success rate is below 70 per cent then this 'controlled' practice period is repeated.

Although these procedures seem obvious, there is strong evidence that they can be improved with training. In an experimental study of first-grade reading, Anderson, Evertson and Brophy (1979) found, as did Good and Grouws (1979), that, with training, the experimental group of teachers used more direct instruction skills in their classroom and their pupils obtained higher achievement scores and spent more time on task. Thus it appears that when teachers consciously attempt to put these processes into practice they actually increase their effectiveness. This supports Gage's (1985) argument that it is possible to help teachers to become better at what they do already.

A key feature of the guided practice procedure is the use of two types of question – those that ask for a specific piece of information and those that ask students to explain how they arrived at the answer. Teachers are trained to go through a cycle of asking factual questions, obtaining a student response and then giving immediate feedback, all the time maintaining a lively pace. Support for these procedures also emerges from the work of Stallings (1980), Soar (1977) and Coker *et al.* (1980). In the experimental studies, teachers who had been trained in direct instruction questioning methods had more of these kinds of interactions per minute than the control teachers, whose pupils did less well on the standardised tests (Anderson *et al.*, 1979).

Once the teacher is satisfied that the class or group have reached a reasonable level of understanding through this guided practice, they then set around 15 minutes independent practice (often described in American literature as 'seat work'). During this practice period the students go through two stages. At first they are quite slow while they gain confidence and gradually fit the new ideas or information into their existing knowledge structures. Gradually the pupils no longer have to think through each step and are then able to answer further questions 'automatically'. It is important for the teacher to manage this process so that pupils maintain high levels of time on task during this 'transition' stage. Thus Fisher *et al.* (1980) found that the higher the rate of interaction between the teacher and pupils during this period the greater student engagement and the level of achievement. Furthermore, teachers who had the highest numbers of interactions during the guided practice period needed fewer long contacts with pupils during independent practice, which suggests that their explanations had been better. Good, Grouws and Beckerman (1978), for example, found that high-achieving teachers who circulated continuously during the monitoring process averaged twenty-three student-initiated work contacts per hour, compared to twelve per hour for the 'low-achieving' teachers. These successful teachers tended to concentrate their help on those who needed it and were more likely to provide explanation by way of feedback rather than just telling the pupil the answer or giving a brief directive as to what to do next.

Maintaining a workmanlike atmosphere during seat work so that pupils remain 'on task' requires the use of the techniques suggested by Kounin (1970). Successful teachers exhibit 'withitness'. By moving round the classroom during seat work time, they more often diagnose correctly the source of any trouble and seem to intervene at exactly the right moment. Such teachers tend to warn rather than threaten their pupils and do not resort to personal criticism. They appear able to anticipate potential disruptive situations, demand and obtain compliance with their request for improved behaviour and are consistent in following up further breaches with reminders of what they expect of pupils (Evertson and Emmer, 1982). Most of these explanations, however, are concerned not to force the pupils to comply with authority but to maintain their engagement in academic activity. Thus the focus is on work rather than on behaviour. Good and Brophy (1986), summarising the lessons of nearly two decades of research, conclude:

> In general, the major finding was that students who spent most of their time being instructed by the teachers or working independently under teacher supervision made greater gains than students who spent a lot of time in non-academic activities or who were expected to learn largely on their own... These main effects were elaborated by interactions with student ability: frequent instruction by the teacher was especially important for the lowest ability students.
>
> (Good and Brophy, 1986, p.338)

Classroom Organisation and Direct Instruction

In their summary of the research, Good and Brophy argue that although the data do not say much about teaching the whole class as against small groups, there are obvious conclusions to be drawn. Whole-class instruction is simpler in that the teacher needs to plan only one set of lessons and can then concentrate on moving around the class during seat work times. The small-group approach will involve preparing several different lessons and assignments. The teacher is likely to be busy instructing different groups for most of the lesson and thus has less time to monitor and assist the majority of students who are working on their assignments. Small-group approaches therefore require the kind of assignments that motivate children to engage in high levels of on-task behaviour and also rules and procedures that allow the pupils to help each other when they cannot understand something or when they need new directions when they have finished their assignment. These conversations must be carried out without disrupting the flow of the instruction to other groups in the class.

Good and Brophy conclude that 'even teachers who are able to make the small group approach work may find that it takes too much effort to be worth the trouble' (Good and Brophy, 1986, p. 361). However, they do acknowledge that small-group instruction may be necessary for beginning reading where it is important for each individual to read aloud. It is also necessary in mixed-ability classes where, in their view, it is essential that the different groups be composed of children with similar abilities. While acknowledging that such an approach introduces 'the potential for undesirable expectations for labelling effects', Good and Brophy argue that 'there may be no alternative in many classes' (Good and Brophy, 198s6, p. 361)

Direct Instruction and Homework

According to Good and Grouws (1979), a further important element in direct instruction is the setting of homework. This should be assigned on a regular basis (giving Friday evening off!) and should involve, on average, 15 minutes work. As well as dealing with the topic of the day, this homework should include one or two questions that revise previous work.

In Britain, there has been a long-standing debate about the value of homework at primary school level. One of the largest investigations of the relationship between the time spent on homework and school achievement was carried out in the 1960s as part of an international evaluation of educational achievement (IEA). Although the effect of homework time may have been confounded by possible interrelationships with a large number of the other variables studied, these studies nevertheless showed a positive association between homework time and school achievement, particularly in mathematics and science. More importantly, in one group of countries (including England and Scotland), the relationship was stronger for pupils of junior and middle school age but tended to tail off at the top end of the secondary school (Husen, 1967). One possible interpretation of these findings is that homework is more suited for routine, less demanding tasks of the kind normally assessed in research on direct instruction.

Recent studies have suggested that it is important to match the homework to the particular child's needs. It has been found in most research that the content of the homework assignments in fact tends to be the same for all pupils within the class. For example, Cole and Lunzer (1978) monitored nearly 1,000 students in Nottinghamshire schools and found huge variations in the time that they spent doing the same homework: pupils took between 10 and 30 minutes drawing a simple diagram in science, and others spent between 15 and 90 minutes writing a short composition. There also seems to be a wide variation in the way in which teachers both set and respond to homework. Very few teachers appear to question pupils about the time it takes for them to do the homework, whether by asking the pupils to keep a record or by checking with parents. One Australian study that examined this and other issues found that, when secondary school teachers integrated the homework carefully into the structure of the lessons so that the results were used diagnostically as a basis for structuring subsequent lessons, student participation rates improved (Coulter, 1981).

In the ORACLE transfer study, observers' impressionistic accounts tended to confirm that homework was rarely used in this way. More often it was used as a device to cope with the problem of 'easy riding'. Pupils who were slow to finish their tasks would often be told to complete them for homework. 'Hard grinders' would be allowed to start new work in class, leaving the slower pupils to catch up later at home.

The main findings to emerge from these studies are that homework should be tailored to individual pupils and it should be structured in such a way that it helps to diagnose pupils' difficulties so that the results can be used to inform the preparation of the next series of lessons. The message about homework, therefore, is that it should be viewed as part of the 'feedback' cycle rather than as a means of providing a series of intermittent assessments.

Recent Developments in Direct Instruction

In the more recent development of research into direct instruction, less emphasis is given to the 'time on task' element in the model. Instead, 'opportunity to learn', or the pupils' 'engaged time', is regarded as a necessary but not sufficient determinant of pupil achievement. More emphasis is given to the appropriateness of the tasks that teachers set for pupils.

In Britain, the issue of the mismatch between the tasks set and pupils' capabilities was first raised by HMI (1978) in their primary survey, where it was suggested that high-attaining children were not being stretched. Bennett *et al.* (1984) have examined this issue in some detail. In their approach they reject the more familiar use of the term 'match' as applied by developmental psychologists such as Piaget, whereby tasks are set by the teacher according to the perceived readiness of the child to engage in a particular level (or stage) of reasoning. Critics have argued that to apply this model to a class of twenty-five junior pupils would involve the teacher in continually testing what pupils had already learnt rather than teaching new knowledge and ideas (Duckworth, 1979). Instead, Bennett and colleagues make use of the ideas of Donald Norman (1978), whose analysis is based upon the way in which the human mind processes information. In this context, the term 'information processing' has a wide range of meanings and refers to the way that people handle stimuli from the environment, organise data, sense problems and generate concepts to help to solve problems. It should not be thought of solely in terms of factual recall.

Many information-processing theories use the digital computer as an analogy for the human mind. Computers have a central processing unit with a short-term working memory and a longer-term storage facility. In order to solve a problem, an initial command or stimulus is necessary to activate the processing unit. In the classroom it will often be the teacher's voice or expression of body language that gains the children's attention. Research has shown that our short-term working memory is very limited in the number of chunks of information it can hold onto at any one time. Our success in transferring information from the short-term to the long-term memory store within the brain, and in retrieving it from time to time when it is needed, depends on our ability to use appropriate strategies to encode information and the repeated rehearsal of these procedures. It has been shown, for example, that only about 40 per cent of the material in a lecture is remembered immediately afterwards and that this drops to around 17 per cent after a week unless we take steps to slow down the rate of loss. For this purpose it is helpful to use routines to organise the information, in the same way that computers have sub-routine programmes that can simplify various complex operations. In computers, labelling parts of the programme to indicate the beginning, middle and end of a procedure is also helpful. In the same way, 'advanced organisers', where teachers provide pupils with a brief introduction to the main components of the lesson, help learners to fit together various pieces of information in an organised pattern which facilitates future recall (Ausubel, 1978).

While this computer analogy is helpful in telling teachers how to present new tasks to pupils, it still does not solve the problem of matching the task to the needs and ability of the child. Norman's approach extends the simple computer model of information processing to involve accretion, restructuring and tuning. *Accretion* is the direct acquisition of new information (facts, examples, skills), while *restructuring* involves possible reorganisation of existing knowledge in the light of this new information. Once the new pattern or new principle has been recognised, the newly created structure will guide the collection of further information until the model breaks down once more and has to be revised. The restructuring process is therefore mainly concerned with reconstruction, invention and discovery. The third stage, *tuning*, generalises the process so that the learner becomes so familiar with the new structure that they can apply it automatically to any new problem or situation of a similar type.

Bennett *et al*. (1984) use Norman's ideas to define different kinds of tasks that pupils perform in the classroom. *Incremental* tasks concern the process of accretion where the main aim is to introduce new material or ideas. Quite often in the primary school situation this involves using previously learned procedures but building on new features – for example the principle of multiplication to deal with hundreds, the child previously having mastered multiplication involving tens. *Restructuring* tasks require the pupils to look at familiar things in a different way and to discover or construct new ways of looking at problems. Discovering a spelling rule or inventing a method of calculating that does away with repeated addition are examples quoted by Bennett *et al*.

Enrichment tasks relate to a further period of accretion after the process of restructuring is complete. The process is very similar to that defined by Taba (1966) as 'productive thinking' during which the pupil demonstrates an ability to use existing knowledge in unfamiliar situations. Problem-solving in mathematics and comprehension exercises in language afford many examples. A pupil who has mastered the ability to multiply may be set an enrichment task in which he must recognise the need to use this procedure in order to answer the question 'If 1 metre of rope costs 20p what do 5 metres cost?'

Finally, *practice* tasks relate to the process of tuning. This mainly involves doing examples so that pupils become familiar with the use of the skill and can gradually speed up the process until it becomes fairly automatic. Practice tasks also include revision exercises in which the teacher sets out to check that the new information has now been internalised so that it can be moved back and forth from the short-term to the long-term memory store.

Bennet *et al*. (1984) observed children carrying out various tasks in classrooms. They followed this up with a clinical interview during which the observer either took pupils back a step if they failed to complete the task or took them forward if they had completed the work successfully. A simple example, in the infant classroom, might consist of children working through a series of cards in which they wrote down the number of objects displayed (three trains, four balls, five houses, etc.) and then coloured in the pictures of these objects. The observer might, during the subsequent interview, move ahead and ask the children to recognise groups of six, seven and eight until the child could no longer complete the task correctly. Other guides to assessing the match were to note the error rate, particularly with incremental tasks, where too many errors would suggest that the task was too difficult. Observers looked for improvements in the 'fluency of performance' during practice tasks which indicated that tuning was taking place. If performance appeared to have reached a plateau, it suggested that the child's achievement was being underestimated. Each task was assessed on a three-point scale: level 1 indicated that the child's ability had been overestimated, so that the task was too difficult; level 2 indicated that the task was approximately matched to the child's ability; level 3 indicated that the pupil's ability had been underestimated, so that the task was too easy.

In language activities, by far the largest number of tasks involved practice (156 out of 205 recorded). Only 5 per cent of tasks concerned enrichment and about 15 per cent were incremental. In number work, there were many more incremental tasks (72 out of 212), but still a considerable amount of practice (43 per cent). Given the small number of restructuring and enrichment tasks observed it was possible to look at the 'match' only in terms of incremental and practice tasks. Bennett estimated that, on average, around 40 per cent of all such tasks were approximately matched to the child's ability. In language, 31 per cent and 29 per cent of incremental and practice tasks, respectively, were overestimated, while 22 per cent and 28 per cent, respectively, were underestimated. The corresponding figures for number were 35 per cent of incremental tasks and 23 per cent of practice tasks overestimated, and 14 per cent and 34 per cent, respectively, underestimated. Teachers, on the other hand, rarely considered that a task they had set was too easy for a child.

Bennett et al. argue that considerable improvement in these figures could be attained if teachers would adopt a strategy for diagnosis similar to that employed by the researchers during the clinical interview. In general, they observed that teachers tended to decide the nature of the pupil's problem by drawing inferences from the child's answer rather than by asking the child to describe the process they used to arrive at the incorrect solution. As one example, they quote a child who had no difficulty in successfully completing a worksheet on 'take aways' provided there was no need to borrow from the 'tens' column. On several occasions the teacher showed the pupil how to carry out the procedure for 'borrowing'. Eventually, exasperated by the pupil's inability to do the task successfully, the teacher exclaimed, 'Show me what you are doing then', whereupon the child demonstrated that she had understood the 'borrowing' principle but was subtracting the tens before the units!

The inefficiency of the teacher's approach was easily demonstrated, since the teacher spent more time showing the pupil what to do and the pupil spent more time waiting her turn to see the teacher than was used up when the pupil was invited to show the teacher her working method. However, it must be doubted whether teachers faced with a queue of pupils would not always be tempted to risk a guess at the pupil's difficulty rather than allowing the child to take up precious time showing the working method. Bennett *et al.* are not very helpful in suggesting ways in which teachers can organise their time to make use of these 'matching' procedures. Indeed, anyone who has experienced the demands made by pupils in a typical primary classroom might be amazed at the 40 per cent success rate regularly achieved by the teacher under such conditions.

Nevertheless, Bennett's classification of tasks, and the various other recommended procedures emanating from the empirical studies of 'direct instruction' in the classroom, make an important contribution to Simon's (1981) plea for the development of an adequate pedagogy or science of teaching based upon sound, psychological principles. In particular, these ideas help move the debate away from the restrictive notion of 'traditional' teaching towards a 'theory of instruction' where teachers need to acquire a 'repertoire of teaching strategies' and employ these different strategies according to the demands of various tasks. The model supports the idea that higher-order skills of thinking need to be taught. Thus at primary level it may be more important for children to learn the appropriate strategies for solving certain kinds of problem rather than to solve the problem itself. The importance of teaching children to master the processes of discovery is convincingly argued by Joyce and Weil (1980) when, for example, they deal with the acquisition of concepts.

In Britain, however, teachers appear to receive very little help during training in how to promote the use of such strategies. As a result, they find it difficult to talk about and reflect upon the various ways that children learn new ideas. The Science Teaching Action Research project (STAR) at the universities of Leicester and Liverpool, for example, has found that teachers experience great difficulty in describing their strategies for teaching new ideas in science, other than that of telling pupils and then illustrating their definition with examples. This may, in part, explain an earlier finding from the PRISMS study. As a result of various initiatives on the part of the advisory service, teachers in one local authority had raised the proportion of science in the primary curriculum to over 10 per cent. However, 60 per cent of this curriculum allocation was taken up with teachers talking and demonstrating to the pupils.

Joyce and Weil make use of Bruner *et al.*'s (1977) distinction between the act of concept formation and concept attainment, and assert that the two processes require different teaching methods. Concept formation is a process, akin to Taba's (1966) inductive thinking approach, in which the pupil has to identify items, identify common properties and determine some kind of hierarchical network so that the items can be ordered into various groups. Essentially, therefore, this activity requires pupils to collect, organise and manipulate data. Concept attainment, on the other hand, requires the pupil to identify and understand a category of objects that already exists. Concept attainment strategies begin with the teacher grouping the objects for the children but not indicating the reasons for the classification. A teacher might, for example, begin by saying, 'Today we are going to study mammals.' She then produces a series of pictures of animals and says to the class, 'When I look at this animal I think of a mammal but when I look at this animal I don't.' Eventually, all the pictures are placed in two piles, only one of which the teacher classifies as mammals. The pupils' task is then to collect information about these animals and from this information to work out the basis on which the teacher has made a judgement of what is and what is not a mammal.

The purpose of this exercise, taken from the MACOS (Man a Course of Study) programme, is to teach children the process of acquiring concepts by learning principles of classification. These introduce pupils to a strategy that allows them to identify the various properties connected with a particular idea by contrasting certain objects that have these properties with others that don't. In the process they may learn that there are several possible classifications. For example, in a vignette provided by Joyce and Weil (1980), a teacher asks the pupils to use the information provided in the social studies textbook in order to determine a way of grouping various major cities in the United States.

Teaching concepts in this way would be a legitimate activity in a direct instructional approach (as opposed to the more familiar procedure associated with 'traditional' teaching in which the teacher simply states the concept and then gives pupils a number of illustrative examples). The main feature of the direct instruction model is that control over what is taught and which strategy to use remains with the teacher. The teacher directs the pace of the learning and is responsible for the diagnosis and the evaluation of the pupils' performance. Used in these enlightened ways the direct instruction approach is as demanding and perhaps therefore as difficult to master as the Plowden prescriptions of progressive practice described earlier.

Possible Limitations of Direct Instruction

There are a number of reservations concerning the view expressed by Good and Brophy (1986) that direct instruction should become the main teaching strategy in the primary classroom. In particular, there are dangers in seeking to translate the experiences of the United States to the English context with its different tradition. The logic of the model, whatever the intentions of its proponents, suggests that it is most effective when children can be taught as a class rather than as groups or as individuals. Inevitably, as the factory model analogy demonstrates, maximum output is obtained when the range of tasks available to pupils at any one time is limited. It is also easier to 'match' tasks correctly if the class contains a limited range of ability. Denham and Lieberman (1980) are clearly aware of this danger when they conclude their review of the Beginning Teacher Evaluation Study (BTES) with the following entreaty:

> At a time when 'back-to-basics' is popular, there is a danger that the BTES may be misunderstood. When the casual reader of the report thinks of ALT (Active Learning Time) he or she might think of straight rows of desks and long periods spent in academic drills. But the BTES researchers argue that BTES ideas can be used in class-rooms with different educational philosophies and goals. It would be unfortunate if policy makers moved too quickly towards mandates based upon BTES. The potential benefits of the BTES lie not in mandates by policy makers but in the extent to which it leads to increased under-standing by those involved in education.
> (Denham and Lieberman, 1980, p.238)

Already some writers on classroom management for beginning teachers have attempted to offer a simplified version of the rather sophisticated ideas embodied in the full direct instruction model. For example, in the Simple Cycle of Teaching (adapted by Laslett and Smith, 1984), the student teacher should

Start with seat work, recapping work previously taught.

Introduce new work through teacher talk or demonstration.

Make sure pupils grasp the new ideas by question and answer session.

Practice examples by working as a group and then individually.

Look back by reviewing the new learning and linking it to previous skills and knowledge, and

End with some short relaxing activity, a game, a quiz, some conversation on a topic of interest to pupils, etc.

(Laslett and Smith, 1984, p.18)

Many English classrooms have not, however, been built to operate a 'whole-class' approach of this kind. Some open plan schools, for example, have been built on an 'architectural two-thirds rule' – it was assumed that only two-thirds of pupils would be present in the classroom at any one time, while others were engaged on individual work in various quiet areas throughout the school. Teachers find it very difficult to operate whole-class sessions for any length of time under conditions where there is inadequate table space for all the children or where room to sit on the mat and listen to the teacher is not sufficient to prevent children from knocking into one another, thus creating conditions for disruptive behaviour. In these classrooms, although teachers can operate the direct instruction model with groups of children, it is still necessary, as Good and Brophy (1986) concede, to have some children working independently of the teacher. But direct instruction is, by implication, designed to increase the dependency of pupils upon the teacher because it is claimed that without an 'imposed' structure pupils became anxious and lose motivation. This presents the teacher with a formidable problem of monitoring, as was shown in the case of the 'group instructors' in the ORACLE study, who in many ways operated a modified form of the direct instruction approach. In their classes, levels of pupil involvement fell considerably within the groups that were not receiving attention, owing in part to this dependency.

The need for some alternative strategy that encourages autonomous learning in some pupils so that the teacher can engage in direct instruction with others is well illustrated in Bennett *et al.* (1984). Early on in their book they record a teacher's account of her attempt to focus her attention on one child in order to diagnose a learning problem.

'The class contains children aged 4–7 years. Twentyeight children were present. Robert sits at the table with seven other children. Each of his group was working on a different number task and the four other tables were working on number games (e.g. attribute dice, number dominoes, threading beads). The children doing number were constantly asking for help or wanting work marked. The other children interrupted frequently to ask for disputes to be settled, for permission to go to the toilet, to complain of toothache, to talk about things that happened last night or were going to happen later. There was no chance to concentrate attention on Robert. There were constant interruptions from within the class and from children coming into the class with lost property, taking the numbers for school lunch, junior children to borrow infant books and so on. I started to record the number of interruptions but I soon lost count . . . I felt very tense and found myself getting impatient and getting sharp with the children.'

(Bennett *et al.*, 1984, p.58)

Even if the teacher had assigned the same task to each group of pupils, it is doubtful whether many of the interruptions described in this extract would have been prevented. Attempts to diagnose pupils' learning problems using the suggested 'clinical interview' technique would be extremely difficult under such circumstances. Without the use of some independent learning strategies in combination with 'direct instruction', the model must – like that of 'Plowden progressiveness' – remain an impossible theory.

A further reservation about the adoption of the direct instruction model to the exclusion of alternative approaches (as suggested by Good and Brophy) concerns the contribution that children can make towards the creation of the classroom environment. In addition to the various explanations for the failure of teachers to implement the 'Plowden prescription', which were considered in the previous chapter, one can add what might be termed the 'sabotage theory', whereby pupils seek to undermine the teacher's intentions. One alternative explanation for the hypothesis that the children prefer direct instruction might be that its highly organised structure provides opportunities for pupils to exploit the system to their own advantage rather than that it reduces their anxiety.

Thus Bennett *et al.* (1984) reported the ineffective match of practice tasks on the basis of evidence that the pupils' fluency when tackling a worksheet of similar questions did not improve. Under certain conditions, however (as described in Chapter 4), children develop a variety of strategies to slow down the completion rate of this kind of work. Faced with the possibility that completing one worksheet ensures another containing more difficult examples, pupils not unnaturally prefer to make the first exercise last as long as possible in order to avoid having to do a second one. It is not difficult to see, given the large body of research concerning teacher expectations, that a concerted effort of this kind by a class, particularly during the first few weeks of a school year, soon creates a situation where the new teacher expects these children to manage only a certain amount of work during a session on the assumption that 'they lack concentration'. In these circumstances, therefore, it is the pupils rather than the teacher who determine the mismatch. A complete theory of pedagogy needs to take such pupil behaviour into account and offer a means of reducing such expectancy effects.

The final reservation against an exclusive use of the direct instruction approach concerns its application to the full range of learning experiences offered in the typical primary classroom. This reservation is borne out by the research conducted in the United States into the effectiveness of direct instruction. In summarising these results Rosenshine (1987) concludes:

> The findings on direct instruction are most relevant when the objective is to teach explicit procedures, explicit concepts, or a body of knowledge. Specifically these results are most applicable when teaching mathematics concepts and procedures, English grammar, sight vocabulary, historical knowledge, reading maps and charts and science knowledge and procedures.
>
> These findings are less relevant when teaching in implicit

areas, that is, where the skills to be taught cannot be broken down into explicit steps. Such areas include mathematics problem solving, analysis of literature, writing papers, or discussion of social issues.

(Rosenshine, 1987, p.258)

Put in more general terms it would appear that, the more challenging and complex the cognitive skills to be taught, the less effective will be direct instruction approaches. But the ORACLE research shows that it was precisely these kinds of challenging tasks that gave rise to the pupils' avoidance tactics (described in Chapter 4) that are characteristic of many primary classrooms. These tactics, in general, describe pupils' attempts to give responsibility for the control of the learning back to the teacher, a situation that the direct instruction model actively encourages.

If children are to engage in these more demanding cognitive activities, they need to have the confidence to think for themselves. One regular feature of the research into the effectiveness of open education in the United States was that children in these classrooms developed higher levels of self-esteem and better self-concepts (Giaconia and Hedges, 1982). Such qualities seem essential if the 'learned helplessness' (Dweck, 1975; Brown and Inouye, 1978) characteristic of Mr Aspin's class in the first chapter, when faced with the challenge of mathematical problem-solving, is to be avoided. Effective teaching in the primary classroom, while it may incorporate direct instruction strategies as part of a teacher's total repertoire, nevertheless needs to find ways of modifying current notions of progressive or 'open' education so that it becomes a practical realisation for a majority of teachers. At the end of the previous chapter it was suggested that the starting point for this restatement of progressivism was the development of the idea of 'our' rather than 'my' or 'your' classroom. The next chapter will attempt to outline a method by which teachers can develop such an approach. The conclusion from the present chapter is that, when teachers say that 'they use mixed methods', they are expressing a viewpoint in accord with the research evidence. What is needed, however, is the translation of this idea of a mixed repertoire of teaching strategies into a set of pedagogic principles. Some of these principles are embodied in the direct instruction approach. Those required for more challenging learning activities will now be considered.

CHAPTER 7

Progressive Theory and Negotiated Learning

Chapter 5 offered a number of theories why the pedagogic prescriptions presented in the 1967 Plowden Report – which was seen as a highpoint in the development of progressive theory – were not generally implemented at classroom level. One explanation for this failure had to do with the pressures placed upon teachers by the more 'conservative' elements among the general public, fuelled by criticisms in the media. Another explanation had to do with the inability of teachers to understand, and therefore implement, these very complex ideas. Perhaps more convincing an explanation, however, was Brian Simon's (1981) argument that the failure to develop a coherent set of principles governing modern primary practice should be blamed upon the lack of an appropriate pedagogic theory. Such a theory should, above all, be informed by psychological principles of learning backed by empirical research. In Chapter 6 it was suggested that parts of this theory have begun to emerge. These are based upon notions of 'direct instruction', which in its best and widest interpretation could encompass many of the aims of modern primary practice, providing the temptation is resisted to regress to more traditional methods associated with a high degree of teacher control and rote learning.

Sabotage Theory and the Primary Classroom

At the end of the chapter a further explanation for the failure to implement the Plowden prescriptions was considered briefly. This suggested that the intentions of Plowden were foiled, not so much because of the teachers' inadequacies or because of external pressures but because the pupils decided to sabotage the teachers' attempts to give them responsibility for their own learning. Instead, children preferred a relatively highly structured curriculum in which it was possible, because of their pre-knowledge of the sequence of events, to manipulate events to their own advantage. In this respect, the similarities with the factory model analogy are striking. In the biscuit factory described in Chapter 6, the foreman's aim was to try to improve productivity by getting the conveyor belts to move at the fastest possible rate commensurate with the maximum number of correctly packed biscuit tins. The workers, however, had other ideas. Their aim was to persuade the foreman to run the conveyor belt as slowly as possible, in the belief that this represented a reasonable level of performance to be expected from the average worker. The workers aimed to give the appearance of 'busyness', while at the same time performing their tasks as slowly as possible, without making the strategy so obvious that the foreman discovered what they were doing. There was, therefore, a constant battle of wits between foreman and workers.

In Chapter 4, similar kinds of exchanges were described in which pupils attempted to reduce the proportion of 'time on task' by means of either *intermittent working* or *easy riding*. Children found all sorts of legitimate things to do that prevented them from getting on with their task – such as pretending to consult a reference book or sharpen a pencil, which they had deliberately broken. Pupils became very adept at estimating just how long they could remain out of their places without attracting the teacher's attention and being told to get on with their work. Even when this happened, a number of avoidance strategies were still open to the pupil. For example, if a pupil was discovered time-wasting by the teacher, they might be told, 'You will not go out to play until you have done a page of your writing'. In these circumstances many children did as the pupil described in Chapter 4 who reported he 'wrote bigger'.

Exchange Bargaining in the Primary Classroom

The above process constitutes one of the main items on the agenda of the 'hidden curriculum'. It has been termed 'exchange bargaining' and was also discussed briefly in Chapter 4. It was first reported by Howard Becker and his colleagues in a study of college freshmen attending liberal arts colleges in the United States (Becker *et al.*, 1968). Becker and his colleagues described the 'covert' bargaining that went on between the instructors and the freshmen as 'exchanging performance for grades'. In these colleges freshmen's classes were more likely to be taken by newly appointed instructors on temporary contracts. These new recruits needed to establish reputations as effective lecturers if they were to stand a chance of becoming permanent members of the college staff. One obvious way of demonstrating their effectiveness was to obtain the approval of the students. Ineffective instructors were those whose students did not turn up to the lectures, handed in assignments late and complained to senior staff about the quality of the teaching.

The students, on the other hand, also had to do well during their first year in order to remain in college. Throughout the year they needed to maintain a certain average grade in their various assessments. This, in part, depended on the difficulty of the assignments, since the more challenging these were the more difficult it was to get a good grade. Becker and his colleagues described the subtle, unconscious negotiation that went on between the students and the instructors, particularly during the early part of the course. If the students felt that the work was too difficult so that it would be hard to obtain a good grade, then they would exhibit a degree of restlessness during the lecture or tutorial and complain about the poor teaching to other members of staff. The instructor, faced with the evidence that the students were not responding to his teaching, would then consult a more experienced colleague who, on the basis of his conversation with the students, might suggest that perhaps the work was pitched at too high a level. The instructor would, therefore, prepare less complicated lectures and set easier assignments. The students' behaviour would improve and they would express greater satisfaction about the course and about the instructor's performance. In this way a bargain would be struck so that at the end of the year the freshmen obtained 'above-average' grades and the instructor obtained a sufficiently good rating to be offered a permanent position on the staff.

The process of 'exchange bargaining' can be discerned in the opening extract of Chapter 1. Mr Aspin begins with a relatively undemanding task that all pupils can easily perform but then moves to a more difficult and challenging activity, whereupon the pupils no longer collaborate in providing Mr Aspin with the kind of classroom that would be approved of by his headteacher and his colleagues. Faced with the difficulties of class control that Mr Aspin experienced during the problem-solving part of the crossword exercise, it is easy to see how he might have concluded that the task was too difficult since the children continually had to come out for help and support. In the same way, a teacher faced with examples of *intermittent working* or *easy riding* as described in Chapter 4 could readily conclude that the amount of work produced by such children was probably the most that might be expected, given their 'inability to concentrate'.

The ORACLE transfer studies, in particular, provided many examples of this bargaining process at work because during the first few weeks in a new school (or in a new class) it is important for pupils to set these teacher expectations at a reasonably undemanding level. Measor and Woods (1984) observed similar incidents in their study of transfer. They described the pupils' behaviour in terms of 'knife-edging' strategies: pupils did enough work to ensure that the teacher did not think that they were 'silly' or 'stupid' but not so much as to get a reputation as a 'swot' (what Americans call an 'apple-polisher'), thereby earning the dislike of the badly behaved pupils in the class who would regard them as 'teacher's pets'. As we have seen in Chapter 4, Pollard (1987) described how infant-aged children coped with the daily life in classrooms by adopting one of three different patterns of behaviour. 'Goodies' conformed to the demands of the teachers and the official school system during lessons, whilst 'gangs' tended to reference their actions to their peer group. The success of the 'jokers' lay in their skill and flexibility in bridging both types of 'social system' so that they were able 'to square their reference groups in both systems in ways which "goodies" do not attempt and which "gangs" would not attempt' (Pollard, 1987, p. 179).

In the ORACLE study, parallels to Pollard's categories of pupil behaviour can be seen in the various pupil types. 'Hard grinders' were the conforming pupils, the 'goodies'. Pupils such as Wayne, Dean and Darren, who were the 'attention getters' on account of their misbehaviour, might be expected to develop into the 'gangs'. The majority of pupils – in Pollard's description, the 'jokers' – would be those who adopted various avoidance strategies such as *intermittent working*, *quiet collaboration* and *easy riding*. Such pupils are also described by John Holt in his book, *How Children Fail*, as 'fence-straddlers'. They are

afraid ever to commit themselves – and at the age of ten. Playing games like twenty questions which one might have expected them to play for fun, many of them were concerned only to put up a good front, to look as if they knew what they were doing, whether they did or not. These self-limiting and self-defeating strategies are dictated above all else by fear. For many years I have been asking myself why intelligent children act unintelligently at school.

(Holt, 1984, p. 91)

Holt, like Becker, is essentially describing a bargaining process, where 'one is continually amazed to see the children hedging their bets, covering their losses in advance, trying to fix things so that whatever happened they could feel that they had been right, or if wrong, no more wrong than anyone else' (Holt, 1984, p. 91). Both writers attribute these behaviours to a 'fear of failure' resulting from the highly competitive American system of education with its emphasis on regular testing. In Britain, however, until recent years, there has been less emphasis on formal testing procedures. It would seem, therefore, that testing is just one manifestation of a much stronger determinant of this kind of pupil behaviour, which is based, as Pollard argues, 'upon the need to preserve, as far as possible within the ebb and flow of classroom events, an overall level of satisfaction for self' (Pollard, 1987, p. 179).

The importance of a child's self-concept in learning has generally been recognised (Burns, 1982) but, as Kutnick (1988, p. 166) points out in his review of the literature, there is a tendency to equate the construct largely in terms of academic self-concept. An equally important component concerns the child's self-image in regard to interpersonal relationships with both the teacher and his peers. As Pollard's results testify, pupils can develop a high self-concept through strong identification with either pro-school or anti-school groups; the degree of self-esteem that they derive from these relationships may then determine their academic performance. Teachers in primary schools have always attempted to build up good personal relationships between themselves and their pupils in the hope of improving the children's academic self-concept. Paradoxically, the strength of this relationship may be in itself problematic – the more that a pupil's self-concept is dependent upon a strong relationship with the teacher, the greater the risk involved should the pupil fail to satisfy the teacher's demands publicly in front of the other pupils. Hence the widespread strategy used by pupils during class discussion and questioning of trying to avoid answering the question until they are certain of the answer that the teacher requires.

Answering Questions to Please the Teacher

The pupils' need to please the teacher by attempting to offer the answer that they think the teacher wants is illustrated by the experiments reported by Donaldson with respect to 6-year-old children who were being tested to discover whether they were able to conserve number. In one experiment carried out by McGarrigle, children were shown two rows of equal length each containing five buttons. Having confirmed that the children knew that there were the same number of buttons in each of the rows, the researcher then rearranged one row so that the spaces between the buttons were no longer the same, thereby making one row longer than the other. When pupils were then asked if there were the same number of buttons in both rows, 84 per cent of the children appeared not to understand number conservation, confusing the number of buttons on each of the rows with the length of the row. This finding confirmed the earlier work of Piaget concerning the age levels at which children might be expected to reach this developmental stage. However, when the researcher no longer asked the question directly but instead introduced a small mischievous teddy bear who 'messed things up' by moving the buttons, the children's responses changed. McGarrigle told the children that 'naughty teddy often got things wrong' and 'needed help'. Naughty teddy wanted to know whether the two rows of buttons were still the same. When the question was put in this way 63 per cent of the children were able to conserve number (McGarrigle and Donaldson, 1975).

Although, as Meadows (1986) points out, the reasons for failing to make satisfactory comparisons between the two sets of buttons are complex, one factor clearly concerns the effect of the perceived relationship between the adult researcher who was asking the questions and the child. In much the same way as in the earlier discussion of 'guided discovery' lessons, the children in this experiment appeared to offer the adult the answer that they thought was wanted, whereas with the 'naughty teddy' they felt able to be more open in their response. There is evidence that the response of the child is not simply a function of an adult presence but relates to the perceived role of the adult in the learning situation, since the teddy bear can be replaced by a friendly clumsy adult who comes into the room and accidentally upsets the buttons (Hargreaves *et al.*, 1982). Thus it is the social context that largely determines the pupils' response. A teacher may be warm and friendly, as prescribed by the direct instruction model, but this classroom climate may induce in the children a dependency upon the teacher and an unwillingness to take risks when answering the teacher's questions or working independently on a challenging problem.

Fear of Failure and Pupils' Self-concept

One striking example of this kind of pupil behaviour occurs in John Holt's book, *How Children Fail*. From descriptions of his lessons,

Holt is obviously a very charismatic teacher with a warm relationship with his pupils. They often engage in friendly banter and talk, particularly towards the end of a teaching session when things are relaxed and the work has been satisfactorily completed. On one of these occasions Holt describes how he jokingly asked the students in a matter-of-fact way what it felt like when he asked them a question. He recounts how he saw suspicion in every child's eyes and how the relaxed atmosphere in the class suddenly evaporated. Eventually one child responded, 'We gulp'. Holt goes on to comment:

> He [the child] spoke for everyone. They all began to clamour and all said the same thing, that when the teacher asked them a question and they didn't know the answer they were scared half to death. I was flabbergasted... I asked them why they felt gulpish. They said they were afraid of failing, afraid of being kept back, afraid of being called stupid, afraid of feeling themselves stupid.
>
> What is most surprising of all is how much fear there is in school... Most children in school are very scared. Like good soldiers they control their fears, live with them and adjust to them. But the trouble is, and here is a vital difference between school and war, the adjustments children make to their fears are almost wholly bad, destructive of their intelligence and capacity.
>
> (Holt, 1984, pp. 70–1)

The exchanges with 9 year olds who were part of the follow-up project of the first ORACLE study, 'Effective Group Work in the Primary Classroom', describe similar feelings. In response to the same question that Holt asked his students – 'What do you feel like when the teacher asks you a question?' – these pupils replied:

First Pupil: It's like walking on a tightrope.
Second Pupil: We guess.
First Pupil: And then we get found out and you don't know the answer.
Third Pupil: Then you wait until the teacher tells you and says 'Oh yes, that's it.'

Here the third pupil goes to extraordinary lengths to save face in front of the teacher and the other children, thus preserving his self-image as a competent student.

Kutnick (1988), however, argues that the global concept of self, with its components of 'self-identity, self-worth, self-esteem' may not be solely academic or socially related as the above exchange would suggest. It may also be influenced by the pupils' 'sense of control over the environment and the quality of the relationships' (Kutnick, 1988, p. 167). There is support for this view from the open education studies in the United States. Giaconia and Hedges (1982) found a consistent effect of enhancing the student's self-concept when comparisons were made between the more successful open education systems and those where there were only small differences between the classrooms practising the open education and the controls. In the successful classes, not only were teachers able to provide a warm co-operative atmosphere but pupils also made good progress and the pupils' self-concepts were enhanced. In English classrooms it may also be that the pupils' feeling of control over their immediate environment exerts as important an effect on the way in which the children perceive themselves as does avoiding getting things wrong.

Ownership and Control of the Learning Process

Certainly, this view is supported by researchers such as Michael Armstrong (1980, 1981) and Stephen Rowland (1984, 1987). Rowland, the teacher in whose class Armstrong carried out his observations, rejects the main assumption of the direct instruction model 'that the teacher should be in control' of the learning environment. Instead he wishes to reconceptualise teaching as being principally 'a task of active observation and interpretation, rather than one of informing and instilling' (Rowlands, 1987, p. 121). Rowland characterises the traditional debate between formal and informal teaching in terms of a didactic and an exploratory model of learning. Within each model is a set of strategies that constitute what might be termed a 'two stage theory of teaching'. In the didactic model the teacher defines the student's needs and provides the appropriate stimulus and instruction at stage 1. Stage 2 marks a sequence in which the student responds to this stimulus and then the teacher marks and provides feedback and further instructions if necessary. Rowland comments:

> Even in the most favourable circumstances of teaching a single child to play the piano, under no pressure of time or space, it is very difficult not to teach in a didactic manner. Afterall, I have the knowledge and skill. Isn't my task to transfer this knowledge and skill to the child? Am I not the

one who knows best which activities will promote these abilities?

(Rowland, 1987, p. 129)

In the exploratory approach to learning, the teacher initially guides the task (stage 1) to a point where the children can be left to find their own solutions to the problem as jointly defined (stage 2). According to Rowland, the teacher's role is to be 'a provider of a stimulating environment' rather than 'an instructor', so that the learners have more control over their language and the ideas that develop as a result of these activities. Rowland goes on to observe that:

> The idea that learning takes place when individuals are put in a position of finding their own solutions fails to recognise the essentially social nature of learning. Left on their own during activity with only their own resources to call upon, children may rely only upon that knowledge and those strategies with which they are familiar. Anyone trying to learn on their own easily becomes stuck into their own ways of thinking . . . without teachers or peers with whom to interact during the process of learning, children are liable to become more entrenched in their present position. This problem arises whether the subject matter is a mathematical investigation which may require new insights, or a social enquiry which demands a new perspective on the issues of racism. The danger is that an exploratory model of learning, while intending to be a radical alternative which empowers the learner with greater autonomy, may actually have the opposite effect by protecting the learner from the challenge of social interaction. Confidence may be gained but the opportunity for growth lost.

(Rowland, 1987, p. 131)

Rowland also questions the advice that teachers should use mixed methods incorporating both these didactic and exploratory models of teaching, since this could well 'ensure that the children receive the worst of both models'. In place he offers what he calls the interpretive model of learning: 'at its heart lies the idea of the interaction between teachers and learners as essentially an attempt by each party to interpret the expressions of the other' (Rowland, 1987, p. 131). Unlike earlier forms of progressivism which emphasise freedom of choice, either child or teacher may provide the initial stimulus for the activity, although the child must be free to interpret the stimulus in a way that excites their interest. In this way the pupil is not trying to guess what is in the teacher's mind as in the earlier examples of questioning. Once the child has embarked on the task, the teacher's role is to

> act as a reflective agent, aiming to help the child identify concerns and needs and also to provide positive yet critical feedback to the student. The child, in turn, critically responds to the teacher's contributions. Neither is 'right' or 'wrong'.
>
> (Rowland, 1987, p. 131)

Rowland illustrates this notion that children should take control of their learning by relating a story about Dean, a 10-year-old boy who was engaged in examining and making homes for a collection of caterpillars. Dean offers a strategy for developing a classification system that is totally different from that proposed by Joyce and Weil (1980) during the process of concept attainment described in the previous chapter. Rowland describes how, initially, Dean decided to call his caterpillars by special names rather than the real names of the different varieties. Some were called 'Mr Diet' while some were called 'Arthur' or 'Cyril' and others 'Stannage'. While watching another pupil draw the caterpillars, Dean noticed that one of his 'Cyril' varieties had six legs and ten suckers, whereas most of the other 'Cyrils' had only four suckers. Rowland, thinking to use this difference in order to suggest a criterion for classification, proposed that together he and Dean list the various varieties and make up a table on which they record the number of legs, the number of suckers and other characteristics.

However, after the conversation, Dean went away and recorded in his table a totally different set of categories based upon colour, fatness, degree of hairiness, the location in which they were found and a further category called 'sameness'. Rowland was puzzled by the need for the column 'sameness', having assumed that 'the purpose of such a table was to list the attributes of different classes of caterpillar' whereas 'Dean, apparently, saw it as a way of recording the attributes of his different individual creatures'. Dean decided to put the caterpillars in pairs and then say whether they were identical, at which point Rowland questioned the need for the column headed 'sameness'.

On the following day the reasoning behind Dean's classification became clear. It appeared that sameness was defined solely in terms of the entries into the column and did not relate 'directly to the appearance of the insects or whether, on some evidence, he thought they were of the same type'. Having selected a pair with the same attributes of colour, fatness, hairiness and location, Dean then decided he needed a name, not like those that he had invented but 'their real names'. At this point, according to Rowland

> Dean seemed to have discovered the need for a taxonomy. Having selected (what he considered to be) criterion attributes by which to describe the caterpillars, he saw that a class could be made of those creatures with identical attributes, and that such a class should be given a name. It was this identity of selected attributes rather than direct appearances which characterised Dean's conception of class and is indeed central to any such system of classification.
>
> (Rowland, 1987, p. 125)

From this account, Rowland argues that, although Dean's approach may seem somewhat eccentric (and therefore unpredictable) to us, Dean 'would never have confronted problems of classification and taxonomy in such depth' if he had followed the teacher's suggestions of tabulating his inventive names for the caterpillars against the teacher's selection of attributes. More importantly, when Rowland looked back on the episode he was able to say that Dean's search for understanding 'actually sharpened my own understanding of what a taxonomy is about' so that 'these three ideas of inventing, discovering a need and the teacher acting as a reflective agent are crucial elements in the learning process' (Rowland, 1987, p. 126).

During this 'reflecting' process the roles of the teacher and pupil are often exchanged, so that sometimes the teacher reverts to the position of an instructor. Following on from the early observations, Dean decided to weigh the caterpillars and devised a method for doing so. This involved the use of fractions, which Dean had not yet reached in his graded primary mathematics scheme, so Rowland carried out a small lesson on the blackboard. After this Dean was able to add various fractions in order to record the weight of each caterpillar. Rowland then suggested that Dean did some more work on fractions and Dean made use of books that were two to three years ahead of his age group. Dean had 'no difficulty in tackling the tasks set so long as such tasks bear a direct and understood relationship to the activity over which he has recently exercised control' (Rowland, 1987, p. 128).

This description of a lesson by Rowland is given prominence because it illustrates several features of the redefined version of progressivism discussed briefly at the end of Chapter 5. This redefined version is based upon the concept of 'our classroom' and differs from our commonly accepted understanding of progressive or informal practice based upon 'freedom', 'activity' and 'discovery' in a number of important details.

First, 'freedom' is not equated with letting children choose what to do according to their interests. It is equally permissible for the teacher or the pupil to suggest the topic for investigation. It is, however, important that the child is free to negotiate with the teacher how the original idea is to be translated into an activity. Once the activity has begun, the pupil should make the major decisions on how the investigation proceeds. Put simply, it is not necessary for the pupil to 'own' the task but it is essential that the pupil should 'own' the process by which the task is carried out.

Second, this ownership does not preclude the use of direct instruction where it is appropriate for developing the necessary skills required to carry out such investigations. While this instruction will often be part of the general curriculum – in Rowlands's class, for example, graded mathematics schemes were in use – there will also be times when it will be specifically introduced into an investigation. However, this will only be done if the pupil is persuaded of the need for this help.

Third, unlike the more common form of progressive practice where the teacher 'heavily' guides the pupil during the period when ideas are at the 'incubation' stage, in the 'negotiated' model the teacher's interventions become more frequent and more direct as the activity progresses. In the 'guided discovery' approach, an assumption is made that this guidance helps to build up the pupils' confidence to a level where they can then work independently of the teacher. In the negotiated approach, the teacher's interventions are kept to a minimum until pupils are sufficiently confident in the value of their ideas to admit publicly to their 'ownership'. Once this stage has been reached, the pupils will no longer try to hand back control of the learning to the teacher by feigning dependency, as frequently happens during guided discovery. Once pupils have accepted 'public ownership' of their ideas, the teacher can act as critic rather than judge in ways that many teachers often find difficult because, as we have seen, children interpret the teacher's evaluations as personal rejection and so lose self-confidence. In the 'negotiated learning' model, however, pupils become sufficiently confident in what they have achieved to welcome the teacher's comments because it shows that their work has been taken seriously.

The results of interviews carried out with pupils during the second stage of the ORACLE project, 'Effective Group Work in the Primary Classroom', confirm the importance of this idea of 'ownership'. In the classroom where pupils rated working in groups in the absence of the teacher as the 'most liked' activity – unlike the remainder of the sample – the children said this was because:

PUPIL 1: When you are in groups you can discuss it, can't you, instead of working on your own. It's better working on your own than working with the class.

PUPIL 2: I think it is best when the teacher comes because they don't want you to mess about. Because when you are on your own you are always talking about other things but when you are with the teacher you start working harder.

PUPIL 3: Yes, the teacher helps you. She gives you different ideas.

PUPIL 1: I think the teacher wants to put her view into what you are thinking which might make you change your mind about something. You know, instead of keeping to your own idea.

PUPIL 4: Teachers stop you if you are right. Say you get, say your answer's right and they think it is wrong, well they will stop you and put what they think they want you to do. They don't like you to do your own work but sometimes they do.

PUPIL 2: When you have to do something, like we have had that before and you have got to do a certain number of things, when the teacher comes up telling you you've got a right good idea you go away and do it and they will come back and alter it all and they will make you do something else and [tell you] it's got to be like this.

INTERVIEWER: Now, why do you think that is?

PUPIL 1: Because they think it is best.

INTERVIEWER: Because they think it's best?

PUPIL 1: Because they think it could be improved.

INTERVIEWER:	Does that stop you putting your ideas as well?
CHORUS OF PUPILS:	No.
INTERVIEWER:	You can still put your ideas forward then?
CHORUS OF PUPILS:	Yes.
INTERVIEWER:	O.K. So what do you feel like if you think your idea is a good idea and then it happens like you say and the teacher comes and changes it?
PUPIL 2:	You feel a bit upset. You have put all that work into it and then the teacher suddenly changes it.
PUPIL 3:	You get a bit mad with her?
PUPIL 1:	You don't feel it is your piece of work. You feel as if it is the teacher's. When you have done everything to it and you think, that's my piece of work and no-one else has done owt to it. But when the teacher has done something to it it don't feel as good.

In keeping with the views expressed by these pupils, there is evidence that many teachers trained during the early 1970s are now seeking to modify progressive practice as it was presented to them in college by developing a style of teaching based upon the idea that, for learning to be 'purposeful', it must allow pupils actively to engage in constructing their *own* learning and solving their *own* problems. Jennifer Nias (1988), for example, provides a fascinating account of six teachers' attempts to define what, for them, constitutes informal practice in their classrooms. According to Nias, 'purposeful' learning has three possible meanings:

It describes an activity which contributes to the fulfilment of an end desired by individual pupils (for example finding the answer to their own questions; making something they want or need) or which contributes to the fulfilment of a goal set by the teacher (or other children or adults) but accepted by the learners as interesting... Frequently it also refers to situations in which pupils have initially accepted their teacher's aims or suggestions out of habit or

goodwill but have developed or converted them into activities which they themselves wish to pursue.

(Nias, 1988, p. 126)

With this third kind of 'purposeful' learning, where teachers had 'a
broad idea of what they would like to do', the children would be
encouraged 'to add to or modify this so that the final outcome was
jointly negotiated, agreed and pursued'. Significantly too, as Nias
comments, in writing about their teaching, the six teachers in her study
regularly referred to themselves and their classes as a unit, as 'we', thus
confirming the idea of a shared responsibility for learning.

Nias is careful to emphasise the speculative nature of these
accounts: 'in the past decade studies of teaching have revealed all too
clearly the gap which often exists between the rhetoric of the practitioner and the reality of his/her classroom practice'; 'ideally,
therefore, these descriptions should have been triangulated with
observers' accounts or have been subjected to analysis by the teachers
themselves' (Nias, 1988, p. 125). Surprisingly, Nias does not include the
possibility of providing the pupils' views of the same events as a way of
corroborating these teachers' accounts. For example, the descriptions
of their practice given by the six teachers in Nias's account of informal
teaching are not dissimilar to the views of the teachers in the school
where the pupils talked about ownership of their ideas to the interviewer in the ORACLE project. In that school, many of the teachers
were considered outstanding and there were frequent visits by other
teachers from the local authority to see the staff at work. They shared
the same determination, as did Nias's teachers, to provide children
with opportunities for ownership of their ideas. They saw the learning
experience as something to be shared with children and also, as with
Nias's teachers and Rowland, saw the importance of their taking the
role of 'critic rather than assessor'. Yet even in this school there still
remained some of the uncertainties in the teacher–pupil relationship
described by John Holt. This reflects the way in which the child in the
conservation of number experiment responded to McGarrigle's
question about whether there were more or fewer buttons in the
rearranged row.

This uncertainty emerged later on in the interview described earlier,
when the pupils began to argue that working in groups helped to
prevent the teacher from imposing their ideas:

PUPIL 1:   When the teacher comes over and they
                 disagree with something that you are

doing, if all the group agrees with it then the teacher has got no point of view really because if all the children don't agree with the teacher then there is just one person and they end up just not doing it. When there is just one teacher and one child working together, if the teacher says something and the child goes opposite, it's the teacher that gets their own way because the child's a bit frightened of the teacher.

OTHER PUPILS: Yes.

INTERVIEWER: Do you all think that is true?

CHORUS OF
PUPILS: Yes.

INTERVIEWER: But the teachers here are very friendly so why would you be frightened?

CHORUS OF
PUPILS (All shouting out and interrupting each other.)

PUPIL 2: You get nervous when someone is around. You feel uncomfortable . . . If you do anything wrong you think 'Oh No'.

INTERVIEWER: So it is fear of doing things wrong, is that what it is?

CHORUS OF
PUPILS: Yes.

PUPIL 1: You get a book and start reading because you know the teachers are watching you.

INTERVIEWER: O.K. So why can't we have a system, which is what I think the teachers would like, where, when they come to the group and sit down they just listen to what you are saying. They just listen and therefore learn what you are thinking about. They say, let me tell you what they say, that if they try to do that you all shut up and wait for them to take over the discussion group and tell them things. They find that's a problem. Is it true?

PUPIL 3: Some teachers try to do that but we won't let them listen because they [the

> pupils] think they [the teacher] will
> change your ideas about something.

One weakness of both Rowland's and Nias's accounts of teaching by negotiation is that the presentation of this key concept of ownership is relatively unproblematic. The teacher is seen as someone who helps to facilitate ownership by supporting and promoting pupils' ideas. Yet although the teacher's intention is to provide the appropriate amount of guidance and help so that the pupils produce outcomes of quality that increase their 'self-confidence and self-esteem', thereby 'motivating them to undertake further tasks' (Nias, 1988, p. 130) it seems from the above extract that the pupils found it difficult to distinguish between the different roles of the teacher as helper and guide on some occasions and as arbiter of behaviour on others. All Nias's six teachers, for example, argued that when they were engaged in purposeful learning based upon negotiation their relationship with the children had to be 'authentic' and 'reciprocal . . . a two way thing' (Nias, 1988, p. 135). They had to feel secure, that is, 'in control' and 'free from the constant need to shout'. In contrast, whenever they felt they were in a state of latent, potential or actual conflict with their pupils they were aware of the need to 'act a role, to be a policeman, a boss figure, the teacher'. Only 'when they felt relaxed, easy, not frightened any more – that is, when they could be themselves in the classroom – were they ready to pass more and more responsibility for learning to their pupils' (Nias, 1988, p. 133). But for the pupils in the ORACLE studies taking part in the interview about group work, there was still a problem:

> PUPIL 1: You never know when they are going to shout at
> you. Sometimes you can be saying something
> and they like agree with you but like next minute
> they can just turn against you and shout at you
> for something like that.

Ambiguity Theory and Progressive Practice

Thus the final explanation for the failure fully to implement progressive or informal practice can be termed the 'ambiguity' theory. A crucial stage of this concerns the setting or negotiating of new tasks and activities. As Doyle (1979, 1986) points out, when setting tasks in the classroom teachers have in mind a variety of purposes, based partly on their perception of the needs of individual children. The more complex the task, the greater the possible range of purposes and therefore the greater the ambiguity, with the risk that the child will misinterpret the teacher's intention. For example, in a recent observation of creative writing, a teacher encouraged the children to draft and redraft stories using the approach recommended by Graves (1983). When the stories were finally completed the children were allowed to use the word processor to produce a final version for inclusion in a book of stories. Seen from the pupils' eyes, the teacher displayed a remarkable degree of inconsistency. Some children, having produced pages of writing, were made to redraft it further, while others who produced six lines were allowed to use the computer. The teacher was able in each case to justify these decisions in terms of the pupils' special needs. One child who had written several pages was at a stage where the teacher felt 'she needed to develop her ideas further, they were becoming stereotyped', while the child who wrote six lines 'had concentrated well, which was unusual for him and had also worked well with the other children in his group'. The children, however, were not party to these deliberations. When asked by the observer how they knew when their work was ready to be published, they replied 'we take it to the teacher and he tells us'.

There is considerable evidence that tasks, such as story writing, do indeed appear to be carried out more successfully if the children can feel that they have ownership over their ideas (Cowie, 1989). However, in taking on this ownership, children have to accept the risk of having their ideas evaluated critically. This risk can be reduced if the child has some idea of the criteria being used for this evaluation. During the 'Effective Group Work in the Primary Classroom' project it was very noticeable how repeatedly children complained about not understanding why teachers made certain decisions. As one pupil put it,

> If I could see what it was learning me I could do it but I don't see what it's learning me. I am not really bothered because I want to know what it's learning me. One teacher, Miss Preston, did say that if you don't like what we are giving you come and tell us about it but I think lots of people are frightened to do that.

Teachers would emphasise the importance of the processes rather than the product of the learning, but rarely tried to explain to children why they were being asked to do certain activities at times when there was a need to direct the learning or to introduce a new topic. Indeed some teachers made a point of saying that they thought that 'children of this age don't need to understand why they do things'. In one example children were investigating various ways of measuring time, using an assortment of materials such as sand, water and plastic bottles. Both teachers under observation began by emphasising the importance of time and gave very precise instructions about *how* the children were to proceed with the task and *how* they were to not worry too much about results because what mattered was their ideas. As the children began to assemble the apparatus, it was noticeable that almost every pupil had on their wrist a cheap digital watch; to some of them, at least, it must have seemed strange that they should need to engage in an attempt to measure time in a variety of crude ways when a more accurate method was immediately to hand. With hindsight it would have been relatively easy for the teacher to explain that the main purpose of the exercise was not to measure time but to provide a problem-solving exercise where certain science skills could be developed. However, in the earlier example of developing children's writing skills through publishing, it would have been less easy for the teacher to explain the reasons for what appeared to be unfair treatment of some children as compared to others, without embarrassing the child who was allowed to publish only six lines. None the less, the pupils have eventually to face up to their limitations. The pupil who was allowed to publish six lines told the observer:

> When we have finished we have to read each other's stories. I watch what the others are reading but no-one reads mine.

Do as You Think and Do as You're Told

An even greater ambiguity in setting classroom tasks stems from the fact, as Doyle (1983) points out, that tasks have not only an academic content but also a behavioural purpose. The teacher's main purpose during a question and answer session may be to tease out the children's ideas so that the lesson may be shaped in terms of the pupils' concerns rather than the teacher's. At any one time a question may also be used to see if a child is paying attention. The pupil therefore has to work out what kind of question they are being asked. Is it the kind where a speculative answer will be praised or where a wrong answer will be seized upon as evidence of inattention? This sort of dilemma offers another excuse for pupils to adopt a strategy of avoidance – they leave someone else to make the initial responses until the purpose behind the teacher's questions becomes clear. Similarly, when writing it may not always be clear to the pupil what the difference is between redrafting and being made to do corrections.

Rowland (1987) argues that in negotiating ownership with children one removes the need to exercise authoritarian control over behaviour. Nias is more cautious and admits uncertainty about the causality of this process. It may be, therefore, that the form of the control exercised over the pupils' behaviour by the teacher largely determines whether pupils perceive the teacher's interventions as collaboration or as a 'take-over'. Thus when children regard control of the classroom organisation and of their behaviour as primarily the teacher's responsibility, then, because they are unable to distinguish easily between the teacher's role as 'policeman' and as 'negotiator', they play safe and seek to hand back responsibility for the learning to the teacher. Only in circumstances where the teacher is seen in a similar light to 'the mischievous friendly teddy bear' do the children appear able to resolve this basic ambiguity between a desire for 'ownership' and 'fear of getting things wrong' – which was so strikingly revealed in the interview transcripts earlier in the chapter. The strength of this 'fear of wrong-doing' is confirmed by other studies, notably that by Barrett (1986), who interviewed 5-year-old children during their first few weeks in the reception class. She reported the children's impressions when shown a series of photographs:

> A boy doesn't know what to do. He is sucking his pencil. He cannot do his work. He must tell the teacher.

> I don't know how to do it. I didn't know how to paint or mixed colours properly.

> I didn't like to write when I came to school. I couldn't make a snail. I couldn't draw a picture. It was too hard. I was too little. I feel miserable when I can't do it. I am frightened I might get it wrong.

> (Barrett, 1986, p. 82)

One difficulty with the work of Rowland and Armstrong is that it tends, by its very nature, to concentrate on those teaching moments where the relationship between the child and the teacher is at its most intimate and secure so that the potential of negotiated learning is seen at its best. Their approach does lead, as one reviewer put it, to a kind of 'reverential' description of what the child says and does, which is more akin to the hushed conversation within a cathedral than the sometimes boisterous and noisy environment of the classroom. Both

Armstrong and Rowland strongly emphasise 'that learning is a process of construction or reconstruction by the learner and that therefore teaching, which is a deliberate intervention in the learning process, must be founded upon an attempt to understand the learner's present state of knowledge' (Rowland, 1988, p. 122). It therefore seems strange that they do not extend beyond the cognitive domain into a discussion of the social context in which this learning takes place.

Social learning theorists, such as Bandura (1986), point out that all learning is influenced by the way in which the learner views what he is being asked to learn. If learners are to reconstruct knowledge, they require suitable explanations not only of *what* they are being asked to do but also of *why* they are being asked to do it. As Gage and Berliner (1988) argue, when commenting on Bandura's work:

> We exert personal control through reflective self-consciousness. Change in behaviour of any lasting kind always means a change in cognition has taken place. It is important not to lose sight of the fact that students think about what they do and what we want them to do and those thoughts affect what students do.
>
> Learning is, above all, an inter-active process where 'thoughts are always influencing actions, and actions are always influencing thoughts'.
>
> (Gage and Berliner, 1988, p. 271

Progressivism Restated

In summary, therefore, it appears that many teachers have, intuitively, modified the original prescriptions for progressivism as described by writers such as Bennett and Anthony and as contained in the Plowden Committee's Report (1967), with its emphasis on a curriculum based upon choice and the interests of the children, an organisation largely devoted to individual work, and a teaching method providing individual attention and emphasising discovery learning. In the 'revised form of progressivism', choice is no longer about *what* task to do but more importantly about *how* to do it. Whether the teacher or the pupil initiates the activity, it is important that the pupil feels they retain a degree of control over the way in which the task should be carried out. During this process the teacher tries to build upon the child's partial understandings so that the pupil can reconstruct their knowledge and ideas in ways that make them more generally applicable to a wider range of problems. The teacher also has a role as an instructor in this process but it is likely, on the evidence of the research findings on direct instruction, that this help will generally relate to lower-order cognitive tasks to do with areas such as reading, computation and study skills. During complex challenging tasks the introduction of these periods of instruction must be carried out skilfully so that children see them as useful additions to their own activities rather than as something imposed unilaterally by the teacher.

For children to feel in control of their learning, teachers need to explain not only what children are required to do but why a particular instruction is relevant to the activity. As part of this better understanding by children of the 'why' as well as the 'what', the teacher's role in relation to the outcomes of the activity changes. Rather than simply assessing the child's work, there is a need for a critical dialogue in which the teacher's and other pupils' views are offered as part of an ongoing debate about the quality of the final product. This is a most difficult area because the teacher needs to be simultaneously supportive of what the child has achieved but also critical so that clear standards are set and agreed between all participants in the learning process.

A crucial factor in ensuring that such evaluation is seen by pupils as a positive contribution to the development of their ideas, rather than as an indication of the teacher's displeasure, is the way in which the relationship between the teacher and the children extends beyond the learning activity to the management of behaviour and control in the classroom. It would appear that when setting out to implement the Plowden ideology, many teachers did so within a traditional framework of control. This created much ambiguity as children attempted to assimilate the teacher's hidden message – when it's learning 'do as you think', but when it's behaviour 'do as I say'. Children are particularly vulnerable at an early stage of an activity when they are uncertain about the status of the response that they can expect from the teacher. In these circumstances the pupils will return to well-tried strategies of avoidance in which responsibility for control of the learning is returned to the teacher. The evidence suggests that teachers who can successfully implement a 'negotiated' learning model also seem able to use similar strategies to control the children's behaviour. Yet this is not the usual model of classroom control presented to teachers during their training. Instead, student teachers are more usually offered 'softer' versions of the 'don't smile until Christmas' model (see the next chapter). There is, therefore, a need to try to sketch out a possible alternative to this somewhat authoritarian approach that can match more closely the model of 'negotiated' learning without, at the same time, creating the impression (given in earlier versions of progressive theory) that anarchy is about to reign in the classroom.

CHAPTER 8

It's All about Relationships: Turning Teachers into Teddy Bears

In any discussion with a group of primary teachers about children's learning, the exchanges will not have advanced too far before one of their number will exclaim, 'Well, it's all about relationships.' While others will nod sagely at this intervention, it is rare for the discussion to go on to consider the exact nature of the relationship that is necessary to achieve the desired learning processes and outcomes. The direct instruction models of teaching call for a classroom atmosphere that is 'warm' but 'firm and businesslike' (Rosenshine, 1987). Writers such as Helen Cowie see narrative writing as a means of allowing pupils to become 'more socially aware, to develop greater sensitivity to the needs of others, to experiment with social roles and to explore events in the world of imagination'. Cowie argues that such objectives require 'a collaborative environment in the classroom', which 'is most helpful for developing in children a sense of audience and enabling them to have control over their own writing processes' (Cowie and Hanrott, 1984, p. 217). On the other hand, sociologists such as Pollard see the classroom as a place of potential conflict. For Pollard it is the participants' needs that shape the classroom environment, which is one of a 'working consensus' representing 'a set of shared social understandings which structure and frame the classroom context in terms of the routines and expectations, and takes its dynamic from the power of children to threaten the teacher because of their numbers and from the power of the teachers to threaten the children because of their role and authority' (Pollard, 1987, p. 177).

Don't Smile until Christmas

Certainly, the idea that going into a new class for the first time is rather like going into battle has a long history. It is claimed that children respect a good teacher who is 'firm but fair'. Teachers who have argued against this approach have had to face criticisms from the media, particularly in the late 1970s and early 1980s, when it was generally alleged that the indiscipline shown by modern youth was largely attributable to the 'anarchic' atmosphere in many primary schools.

Something of the flavour of the 'firm but fair' approach can be seen in a teacher checklist devised by a local authority entitled *A Guide to Teaching*. The purpose of this document was to help probationary teachers, but it is claimed that the sections on the management of pupil behaviour might also help the more experienced teacher. One section, headed 'Relationships', with the sub-heading 'Good Working Relationships with the Children', advises the new teacher that:

> The formal encourages discipline, the informal indiscipline.
>
> See yourself from their viewpoint. Any teacher is expected to fulfil a role of authority.
>
> A tough new teacher deserves respect.
>
> A friendly new teacher is weak.
>
> A teacher craving to be popular never is.

Teachers are then offered the following rules, which they must operate consistently so that they provide a stable classroom behaviour pattern:

> Teach from a position where you can see them all.
>
> Keep them seated, you stand up and control the room from time to time.
>
> Don't over-shout a class, stand and wait, looking at your watch until they are silent.
>
> Speak quietly, save your outburst for the right moment – the more shouting and loss of cool from a teacher the more they believe *they are winning*.
>
> Never go to an offender, make him come to you.
>
> Never threaten what you can't carry out.
>
> Name the offender. (You must learn their names.)
>
> Practise using your eyes and hands until you bring about silence or quell a disruptive pupil.

The premise: Until you have got them where you want them no real teaching can be done. Discipline is primary, subject matter is secondary UNTIL YOU HAVE WON.

The writer, offers a number of hints to help teachers spot potentially disruptive pupils. The clues to look for are:

The way they enter, ignoring teacher, turning round to talk,
    sitting on desk with their back to teacher.
Late arrivals.
Chewing.
Condition of uniform, badge wearers, etc.
Wandering around room.
Slouching in their seats as they listen or write.
Aggressive – shouters-out, cheek, answering back, etc.

Shouters-out, according to the writer, must be seen as 'the first sign of a takeover bid'. If a shouter-out persists, then he or she should be 'made the reason for a test or a piece of written work so that the others will soon sort him out'.

The cheeky pupil should be viewed as one 'craving for attention'. They can usually be dealt with by 'showing them up' in front of the class:

'All of us want to be noticed. Those who have grown up show off through their work and doing well in school. Those not quite grown up show off through cheek, shouting out and silly behaviour. It just shows up those in the class who have not yet grown up. They need our help. Those of you who have grown up, try to help them.'

The writer also identifies a group of children called 'the last word pupil'. The problem is not so much what they say but 'how they say it'. The writer provides an example:

TEACHER: Are you chewing?
PUPIL: No.
TEACHER: You are chewing.
PUPIL: I'm not.
TEACHER: Empty your mouth.
PUPIL: Why should I, I'm not chewing.

Such confrontations are not recommended. Instead the teacher should say:

> 'I hope you are not chewing. (Stare them out.) If you are, put it in a basket. I'll make a note you are a chewer and check with other teachers.'

If the class will not stop talking then the teacher should walk round the room putting a piece of paper on each desk. They should then say:

> 'Write your name on the paper. It appears you don't want to be taught so I'll give you a test. Those doing badly on the test will be kept in to teach them to listen and not to talk in future.'

If this doesn't work, then the pupils should be kept back at 3.30 p.m. and given the lesson they have missed, remembering to take a register before the lesson.

The writer recognises that, for the probationary teacher, most problems are caused by 'the serious disruptive' who 'loves to have his admirers in close proximity'. Here the proper solution is to isolate.

> 'Sit there for the next month. You can return if you behave yourself.'

Or, if the time is around 3.30 p.m.:

> 'You are preventing work being done. You are preventing others doing as well in their work as they might do. Others in the class think you are rather silly. You are going to become very unpopular. One or two have asked if you can be taken out of the class. They are getting fed up with you.
>
> The Headteacher has asked me for names of anyone preventing work being done. I have written down your name. You can have one more chance then I shall hand over your name and your parents will probably be informed.'

Finally, the new teacher is provided with several 'helpful points':

> Don't smile for the first month. Develop your style while strict. Don't try to be popular.

> Children have crushes. Behave naturally and avoid a one to one situation.

Don't have favourites. Initial friendly contacts will turn sour. To a child, friendly contact pre-supposes special liberties.

Punish the same offence the same way each time. Be consistent.

Although from the tone of this document it appears that the writer is primarily addressing new secondary teachers, this 'two-stage' approach to classroom management – involving no undue familiarity until the class is firmly under control – is one that also operates in the primary classroom. Here, for example, is a teacher addressing a 9-year-old class for the first time:

'There's a song called "My Way". I am not going to sing it to you because there is a lady present [the observer] but this is my way.

I never have liked noise in my class and never will. If you all remember that then we will get along fine.'

The principle of isolation, of breaking down troublemakers into smaller groups, is also widely practised. Children enter the classroom one group at a time and each table is dismissed in turn. Sarcasm is also frequently used:

'You are being silly today. You are behaving like a class of infants, not like juniors. I shall have to treat you as infants then.'

Even when relationships are friendly the very warmth of the children's regard for the teacher can be used to blackmail pupils into doing what the teacher wants:

'Oh children. You have upset me by the way you have been behaving. I was really looking forward to what we were going to do this afternoon but now *you* have made me feel that I don't want to do it so you had better get out your maths books instead.'

Teachers appear to find it difficult to describe ways in which they provide positive reinforcement for the kinds of behaviour that they wish to encourage in the classroom. Ashton (1981), for example, attempted to discover commonly used strategies for dealing with pupils whose behaviour had caused the teacher serious concern (stealing, classroom disruption, etc.). The main strategy consisted of calling on a senior colleague. In a case concerning the loss of dinner money, the strategy favoured by some teachers was to reprimand the child who had lost the money, 'for being careless'. Similar findings emerged from a small-scale study carried out on behalf of the magazine *Child Education* (1986). Teachers were asked to respond to six vignettes dealing with problems such as bullying, racist abuse and challenges to the teacher about not doing work ('I'm on strike, like you'). By far the most commonly used strategy was 'putting the children in their place'. Children who made racist remarks of the kind 'Your God stinks. My God is better than your God' were told, 'Don't be silly'. The second most frequently used approach was to ignore the incident initially and then introduce a new topic in the hope that, by some process of 'osmosis', the new experience would improve the pupils' behaviour. For example, when children made racist remarks about other children's religious beliefs some teachers made no imme-diate comment but arranged a visit to a Sikh temple.

In some cases the teachers' response could be described as emotional blackmail. In one vignette a 7-year-old pupil told the teacher that he wished Mrs Thatcher had died in the Brighton bombing because 'she put my dad out of work'. The teachers' most favoured response was to ask the child, 'How would you have liked it if it was your mother who had been killed?' From interviews with children during the Effective Group Work Project this seemed a very common type of response, although it appeared to have little positive effect. According to one pupil,

> 'If you are messing around at dinner the teacher will say
> "You don't eat like that at home, do you?" and you say
> "No" because it shuts them up ... But you do.'

Uses and Abuses of Teachers' Power

All the above examples illustrate the use of teachers' power or authority to control pupils. In the primary school, however, the ap-proach is more subtle than at secondary level, where at the start of the year initial encounters between the teacher and the class can resemble those of the sergeant major with a new group of army recruits.

A number of arguments are often advanced by teachers to justify the necessity of using power to control pupils. First it is said that pupils themselves want teachers to put strict limits on their behaviour so that 'they know where they are'. Undoubtedly, there are strong psychological grounds for saying that children need a secure framework of rules and routines within which they can exercise independence. The assumption that the teacher must provide this structure, however, is open to question.

A second reason for justifying an authoritarian approach is that teachers are required by society to transmit important values, particularly those associated with the Protestant ethic of virtue and industry. Teachers, of course, find it very difficult to fulfil this role, particularly in a pluralist society where there are wide-ranging variations in attitudes towards race, religion, and morality in general. In small-scale study for *Child Education* (1986) one of the most frequently mentioned concerns of teachers involved parental attitudes to bullying. Teachers described how some parents stood outside the school railings at playtimes and urged their son to 'hit him first before he hits you'. However, it is questionable whether using power to prevent anti-social behaviour of this kind will bring about a genuine commitment to change. When the pupils are placed in a situation where their power is matched by the teacher's, they may either decide to defy the teacher or withdraw from the confrontation until the pressure is reduced. Teachers who use their authority to moralise and lecture pupils on good behaviour may, therefore, lessen their influence as 'transmitters of the culture'.

Third, it is often said about particularly difficult children that 'power is necessary with certain pupils who don't understand anything else'. Such descriptions usually apply to those children who are the most difficult to control and who are often violent in their behaviour towards both other pupils and teachers. These pupils, however, rarely seem to change as a result of this treatment. They often find more subtle ways of causing disruption or, worse still, take it out on another teacher whom they perceive to be weaker. In dealing with these pupils, teachers frequently find that they have to escalate the severity of the sanctions over time. Many studies of deviance show that these pupils can assume an heroic role in the eyes of their peers because of the way that they stand up to the teacher in these confrontations (Wood, 1977).

Finally, the use of the teacher's power to control pupils is often rationalised in terms of numerous research findings demonstrating that children want consistency in their treatment – the good teacher is one who is 'firm but fair'. Fairness is one of the main criteria that pupils use when describing a 'good teacher'. However, it is perfectly possible, as in Chapter 4, to see the pupils' needs for consistency of teacher behaviour not as something that is desirable in itself but as a means of enabling them to devise their own strategies of avoidance. Given the premise that a teacher is determined to impose their rules on the pupils, then it is naturally to the pupils' advantage for these rules to be applied consistently. For example, we saw in Chapter 4 that when the children knew that if they did not write a page of story they would be kept in and miss play, then they practised 'making their writing bigger'. Using a 'firm' approach, particularly at the beginning of a relationship with a new class, while it achieves its main objective of providing well-mannered, well-behaved, industrious pupils, may also create an environment in which the safest strategy for children to adopt is to submerge themselves within the mass. They then do not attract the teacher's attention and, at the same time, avoid being seen by the more deviant pupils as being on the side of the teacher. The use of what Measor and Woods (1986) term knife-edging strategies is a direct result of this kind of power game.

To summarise, the present approach to classroom control presents pupils with contradictory messages about learning and behaviour. Put simply, children are expected to understand that in the primary classroom 'you do as you think when learning' but 'you do as the teacher says when behaving'. Unfortunately, as we saw in the previous chapter, the tasks teachers set in the classroom have implications for both learning and behaviour. Children faced with this ambiguity play safe, and adopt a strategy of 'learned helplessness' until the teacher resolves the pupils' dilemma. It would seem that the more challenging the task set by the teacher, the greater this ambiguity. Redrafting, for example, can be seen as something positive, an indication to the pupil that the ideas in the story are worth developing. The process can also be viewed negatively as 'doing corrections'. In the same way, a pupil's answer can be seen as an inspired guess, a 'silly response' or an indication that they were not paying attention. It is no coincidence that activities that require pupils to exercise their own judgement and tasks such as narrative writing, problem-solving and creative art are the very areas where direct instruction does not appear to be effective (Rosenshine, 1987).

Wanted: An Alternative Approach to Dog-Training

The 'softer' uses of teacher power, commonly employed in the primary classroom, are well illustrated by the behaviour of Miss Lavine in the opening chapter. The techniques she used for controlling the class bore a remarkable similarity to those applied in dog-training. Miss Lavine controlled the children, it may be remembered, with familiar gestures and commands. She put her finger to her lips to indicate her wish for silence. If pupils still continued to talk she would tell them to 'listen' and then more firmly to 'listen carefully'. The children, when asked by Miss Lavine, 'What do I mean when I say listen?', responded, 'Fold our arms and look at you, Miss', again illustrating the ambiguity between learning and behaviour in the classroom. Other examples, particularly in the reception class, consist of games such as 'Simon Says', where Simon says, 'Put your hands above your head', then 'Fold your arms', and, 'Listen to me.'

In the same way, dogs are told to 'sit', 'stay' or 'heel' in a very special voice, and each owner will employ non-verbal cues to support these commands until the conditioned response becomes automatic. Although, initially, these instructions need to be reinforced, 'being cruel to be kind' does not appear – outwardly, at least – to affect the dog's attachment to the owner. However, a close study of the animal in any unfamiliar situation shows that, as with the description of pupils in Chapter 4, the dog will always seek approval before exercising initiative. Thus the dilemma of the 'dog-training model' of classroom control is that children who respond to this treatment become reluctant to engage in independent learning, while pupils who respond to challenging situations may react badly when teachers use power to control their behaviour. An alternative strategy is therefore required, one that allows teachers to perform their duties under reasonable conditions but also allows pupils to take responsibility for their behaviour in the same way that they are expected to exercise responsibility for their learning.

From the teacher's point of view, abandoning the exercise of control through authority appears to be a high-risk strategy, with the likelihood that one will be seen as weak by the pupils. Part of the reason for this concern stems from the lack of a clear practical alternative. In the past, the exemplars of good progressive practice have been drawn from outside the state system, where, presumably because parents were paying for their children's education, they were in agreement with the principles on which the school was run. Thus, in A. S. Neill's Summerhill school, there was consistency in the way that the children's learning and behaviour problems were dealt with. If a child stole money from Neill's desk, the coins were replaced until the pupil, wearied, perplexed or disturbed by the lack of an authoritarian response, eventually came to terms with the problem. In the same way, pupils who refused to participate in mathematics lessons were allowed to opt out until they wearied of this course of action. These descriptions, however, would appear to a teacher within the state system to border on anarchy when faced with the kinds of parental pressure that would result when it was discovered that one child's dinner money had been stolen and that the teacher was doing nothing about it.

Thus we require a system of class management that is neither authoritarian nor permissive. Within this classroom environment:

(a) Teachers should feel relaxed and in control.
(b) Pupils should be able to respond to the teacher in the same way that the children responded to 'naughty teddy' in the number conservation experiment – without fear or failure of loss of self-esteem.
(c) There must be a secure structure that takes into account, as far as possible, the needs of the teacher and the children.
(d) The rules and routines – Pollard's (1987) 'working consensus' – that form this secure structure should be negotiated openly rather than, as at present, by means of subtle 'exchange bargains'.

In the United States there are programmes that attempt to develop this 'negotiated model' of behaviour. One of these, called 'Teacher Effectiveness Training', is of particular interest because it has been used extensively in Dutch schools, which have lately been commented upon favourably by HMI. In the late 1970s the Dutch educational authorities paid a number of visits to Britain to study progressive methods in action, prior to setting up their Primary Reform Programme (CDCC, 1985). The Dutch educationalists appear to have been favourably impressed by the general atmosphere of the British informal primary classroom, but to have been concerned with the extent to which the children continued to be heavily dependent on the teacher for instruction. This, as we have seen, led the teacher to spend less time supporting children's learning and more time on routine organisational activities. The Dutch authorities therefore sought to combine the organisation of the British primary classroom with a pedagogy that maximised the time teachers spent in interaction with the pupils about tasks. Thomas Gordon's Teacher Effectiveness Training Programme was chosen, in part, because it emphasised the analysis of teaching time as the starting point for attempts to reconceptualise teachers' thinking about classroom practice.

Gordon describes existing teacher–pupil relationships as being concerned with winning and losing. He argues that both the authoritarian and the permissive approaches are essentially

> win–lose approaches and power based philosphies. Those who advocate strictness, strong authority, regimentation and so on want adults to direct and control youngsters by using the power and authority that adults possess. Those who advocate permissiveness and freedom for kids in schools unwittingly are opting for conditions in which students are permitted to use their power and to make life miserable for their teachers. Whichever one of these schools of thought prevails somebody is bound to lose.
>
> (Gordon, 1974, p. 18)

One of the reasons that teachers continue to use power in the classroom to maintain control stems from the high standards that are expected of the profession. Gordon names a number of myths that are generally thought to be characteristic of good teachers: good teachers are calm and always even tempered, have no biases, hide their real feelings, do not have favourites, provide a stimulating learning environment that is at the same time quiet and orderly, are consistent, do not show partiality, know all the answers and support each other regardless of personal feelings. However, as Gordon remarks, this implies that

> good teachers must be better, more understanding, more knowledgeable, more perfect than average people. To those who accept these myths, teaching means they must rise against human fraility, . . . they must be, in a word, virtuous . . .
>
> The essential fallacy here is basic: these myths ask teachers to deny their humanity.
>
> (Gordon, 1974, p. 22)

By way of illustrating this point, Gordon quotes one teacher with twenty-five years' experience who struggled to come to terms with this 'good teacher' model:

> 'For most of my teaching career I saddled myself with the role of super-teacher. My intentions were seemingly reasonable. I wanted to be the best teacher I could be. From time to time, out of frustration or weariness, I would

drop my role and be just me, a person. When this happened
the relationship between me and the students changed,
became closer, more intimate, more real. This frightened
me since I had been taught to keep 'distance' between me
and my students, warned that 'familiarity breeds con-
tempt' and I would 'lose control' of the situation if the
students really got to know me . . . Sometimes during these
periods of realness students did or said things I didn't like.
At these times I reverted to my teacher role to maintain
control, restore order or express my displeasure.

I spent years vaccillating between the real me when I
could teach and the role of the teacher when I could
maintain order.'

(Gordon, 1974, p. 23)

This again illustrates the dilemma of progressive education identified
earlier in the chapter: pupils are expected to be in control of their learning while the teacher retains control of their behaviour.

In the Teacher Effectiveness model, the relationship between teacher
and pupil is divided into three zones. One zone concerns student-
owned problems, for example difficulties at home with parents.
Another zone describes teacher-owned problems, as when the pupils'
behaviour becomes unacceptable. In the third zone no problems exist
and genuine learning can therefore take place. The aim of the
programme is to create as large a 'no problems area' as possible.
Among a range of 'teacher-owned problems' are lateness, leaving
desks untidy, calling out, and various forms of time wasting. Such
behaviour cannot be handled in the same way as a 'pupil-owned
problem'. When the pupil owns the problem, the child will generally
initiate the communication, although it may require considerable skill
on the part of the teacher to understand the underlying messages that a
routine conversation might contain. In this situation the teacher acts as
a listener and a counsellor, taking a passive role and encouraging the
pupil to offer a solution. When, however, the teacher owns the
problem, they must initiate the communication. The teacher is
primarily interested in their own needs (in many cases survival). In
such cases, adopting the counsellor posture is inappropriate, since
accepting the pupil's solution will not take the teacher's needs into
account.

This leaves the teacher with three alternatives when attempting to
change pupils' unacceptable behaviour. Either the teacher can try to

change the pupil, or they can attempt to change the environment so as to remove the problem, or they can attempt to change their own behaviour. For example, a teacher may be annoyed because pupils come out and interrupt when they are hearing other children read. Either the pupils must learn to be less dependent on the teacher for help, or the teacher can provide pupils with routine, less-demanding tasks when hearing others read, or they can learn to live with the interruptions on the grounds that these particular pupils need more attention than others.

Sending the Right Messages

In attempting to change a pupil's behaviour the teacher first needs to confront the individual by sending a message indicating that the behaviour is unacceptable. Confrontation, here, does not carry its usual meaning of forcing the other person to 'back down'. In the sense that Gordon uses the word it refers to the act of 'facing up to one's own needs' and 'having the courage to expose to one's pupils what could be seen as a weakness, given that pupils too have been indoctrinated with the notion of "super-teachers" ' (Gordon, 1974, p. 129). In order to confront students with their problems in this manner, a teacher needs to send what Gordon calls an 'I' message. Such messages contain three parts – a non-judgemental description of the behaviour that is objected to, an observable concrete effect of that behaviour upon the teacher, and an indication of the feelings that these effects have. Gordon offers, by way of an example, a situation where pupils will not sit straight but leave their feet in the aisle. The teacher might say, 'When you have your feet in the aisle [description of behaviour] I am apt to trip over them [concrete effect] and I'm afraid I'll fall and get hurt [feeling]'.

The initial non-judgemental description is most important. Consider, for example, the impact on pupils of the following alternatives:

'When I find papers left on the floor . . . '

and

'When you are sloppy and leave messes on the floor . . . '

or

'When you push Johnny on the playground . . . '

and

'when you act like a bully in the playground . . . '

Gordon claims that these 'I' messages produce less defensiveness from pupils than the more usual 'You' messages. The latter often feature in class discussions, as in the early example where the children were told 'You are behaving like infants'. Some kinds of 'I' messages, which impose solutions, are really 'You' messages in disguise. For example, the teacher who said 'I never have liked noise and I never will' on the first day of the 9-year-old pupils' first term in the middle school is adopting the kind of approach used by the sergeant major with new army recruits. The message in effect is 'If you are prepared to play the game according to my rules then you will not find me such a bad person, but if you break my rules then watch out!' Discipline of this kind, it was argued, developed unquestioned obedience on the part of the soldier under extreme conditions of danger. The approach, even if not so harshly implemented, hardly seems appropriate for the primary classroom.

In his book, Gordon describes one teacher's experience in using 'I' messages in her classroom for the first time.

'I was reluctant to try an "I" message with the kids I have. They are all so hard to manage. Finally, I screwed up my courage and sent a strong message to a group of children who were making a mess with water paints at the back of the room by the sink. I said, "When you mix paints and spill them all over the sink and the table, I have to scrub them up later or get yelled at by the caretaker. I am sick of cleaning up after you and I feel helpless to prevent it from happening." I just stopped then and waited to see what they would do. I really expected them to laugh at me and take that "I don't care" attitude they'd had all year. But they didn't! They stood there looking at me for a minute like they were amazed to find out I was upset and then one of them said, "Come on, let's clean it up." I was floored. You know, they haven't turned into models of perfection, but now they clean up the sink and tables everyday whether they spill paint on them or not.'

(Gordon, 1974, p. 140)

Another teacher commented, after trying such messages for the first time, that part of the problem lay in her persistent attempts to maintain a calm unruffled image even if the pupils' behaviour had, in reality, put her under stress.

'One afternoon last week it was hot. I was tired and had a headache. I realised my face was hurting from a smile on it and that the noise the kids were making was really "below my line". I decided to stop smiling and tell them how I was feeling. I said, "I'm tired, my head hurts and I'm sick of smiling and pretending that all the noise you are making doesn't bother me. It does. I don't think I can stand it any more." I was amazed. The children quietened down right away and one of them even brought me a glass of water! I guess I shouldn't have been so surprised. After all, they didn't know how I felt until I'd told them. I had been smiling and acting as if I had been feeling good until then.'

(Gordon, 1974, p. 37)

It is clear that teachers in Nias's (1988) study, referred to earlier, also found that this kind of relationship fostered a high degree of respect, trust and shared concern, which extended into learning. One of the teachers asked by Nias to provide an account of informal learning in her classroom, in talking about the relationship responded by saying, 'I expect it to be a two-way thing, for example, if I'd been away ill, I want them to ask how I am.' This teacher continued:

'What teaching this way means for me is that I am happy I feel cared for. I don't feel as if I am acting. I don't feel stressed or bored, I never look at the clock, I don't have to fight for control and I have the satisfaction of knowing that I do the job better. That I am a better teacher.'

(Nias, 1988, p. 135).

Organising the Classroom Together

Another possibility, as indicated earlier, is for the teacher, together with the pupils, to change the environment so that the cause of the behaviour problem is removed. Most primary schools place a great deal of emphasis on this aspect of control by providing quiet carpeted areas and by trying to stimulate the children's interest in legitimate activity through the use of colour and display. Usually, however, such arrangements are determined by the teacher without the pupils' direct participation. This is because teachers are trained to regard the management of time and space in the classroom as one of their major responsibilities.

Gordon regards the distribution of time, in particular, as a major component in the cause of teacher and student conflicts. He points out that, even when effective teaching is taking place, the atmosphere of a typical primary classroom is one where time is 'diffused'. Both pupils and teachers are flooded with incoming stimuli. Children are carrying out a variety of tasks and moving around the room on routine activities, such as borrowing pencils or rubbers. In the process chairs are moved, articles knocked from tables and conversation levels rise. In recent years, schools have been built as economically as possible so that space is often severely restricted. As Gordon observes, 'Seating is usually so uncomfortable as to be unthinkable for use in a home or in a modern business office. Hard surfaces and parallel walls often cause acoustical problems. Storage is inevitably a problem: it is either inadequate, inconvenient, or both' (Gordon, 1974, p. 157). Over a period of time both pupils and the teacher become accustomed to this workplace and adapt to it. They are able to block out most of these incoming stimuli so that they can concentrate on one particular activity. This screening process, however, requires an expenditure of energy. As this energy level becomes depleted during the day, the pupils find it harder and harder to relate to each other without tension.

To remedy this, Gordon proposes that the work programmes should, as far as possible, be planned jointly with the children, to provide opportunities for both 'individual time' and 'optimum time'. Individual time allows children to work quietly, on their own, out of the way of other children, while 'optimum' time provides pupils with opportunities to spend an extended period alone with the teacher. In the follow-up to the ORACLE study, 'Effective Group Work in the Primary Classroom', one teacher successfully negotiated a system of sharing out 'optimum time' between the twenty-eight pupils in her junior class of 9 year olds. She began by posing her problem to the children. After one particularly difficult afternoon, when the children all seemed to want her attention, she sent the following message to her class:

'When you all come out like this, I don't know what to do and feel very frustrated. I know you want my help and I'm really interested in what you're doing. I want to talk about your work with you but all the time I keep on thinking of the others who are waiting and this makes me try to get

through with you as quickly as possible so that I can start
on the next one. Can you help me solve my problem?'

After some discussion the children decided to keep a record of the
reason why they came out to see the teacher. Some pupils were
amazingly frank and said, 'I felt bored'. In most cases the reasons had
to do with a need to obtain information, to check answers, to receive
permission or to spend time talking over their ideas. From there the
class went on to decide priorities and to look for alternative solutions
for some of these needs. Certain permissions were dealt with by an
agreed set of rules, for example going to the lavatory. Children could
now go to the lavatory without permission, but if more than three
others were waiting to see the teacher then the pupil would come back
and carry on until the numbers in the queue were reduced. Information should, whenever possible, be obtained from a neighbour, and
answers should be looked up in the teacher's workbook.

The pupils, together with the teacher, decided it was most important
to provide an extended period of time when pupils could talk over their
ideas about their writing or their painting with the teacher. A booking
system was therefore arranged for a limited time each day and it was
agreed that each pupil could have 5 minutes of extended time per week.
Other pupils needing assistance, if they couldn't get help from a neighbour, would get on with something else until the extended time was
over. The system worked well. Observations in this classroom showed
there was less *intermittent working* and less *easy riding* once the
schedule had been put into operation. The schedule was flexible and,
with the agreement of the class, the teacher could increase this time for
some pupils on particular occasions.

A colleague of this teacher, with a 6-year-old class, decided to try the
same thing with her pupils. She drew up a checklist of activities with
which the pupils commonly needed her help, but used pictures instead
of words to represent each activity. Thus the checklist depicted a book
to indicate that a child was reading to the teacher. Children took it in
turns to record with a tick what the teacher was doing at regular time
intervals (the teacher borrowed an ORACLE audio-tape with a 1
minute pulse). Some children dispensed with ticks and put faces
instead. The teacher was quite surprised to see how often they drew the
face with her mouth turned down in a sad or stressful look! In the same
way as in the junior class, these pupils and their teacher invented the
notion of 'big time' when other children left you alone with the
teacher. Again, rules were agreed on how children should conduct

themselves when it was someone else's turn for 'big time'. Observations in this classroom confirmed that the children took their responsibility for maintaining this environment seriously. Work levels improved.

Dutch schools that have taken part in Gordon's Teacher Effectiveness programme have used a different approach. In one school, for example, with 268 children aged from 4 to 12, much use has been made of tape recorders and computers to reduce the time teachers spend on routine tasks and to provide pupils with more 'optimum' time. For example, spelling and grammar exercises were put on tape so that children could listen in a quiet area with the earphones shutting out the noise in the class. All children were expected to do a certain number of these exercises each month. In the same way, using a friendly parent to programme the computer, most of the computation exercises were transferred from worksheets to disc. Each pupil had a password and could set the time interval for completing each question at a point somewhere between 15 seconds and 1 minute. Failure rates were stored on a personal record of achievement and presented to the teacher during periods of 'optimum time'.

This method appears not only to have the advantage of cutting down the routine marking that can occupy such a large proportion of a teacher's day; it also avoids frequent debates with parents and administrators about the value of teaching grammar and spelling. Many teachers, while not opposed to direct instruction in these skills, are often concerned about the amount of time such activities can take up in relation to other parts of the curriculum. Limiting the time given to such things as spelling tests tends to be seen by parents as a sign that the teacher doesn't care about the 3Rs. Teachers in the Dutch schools are able to demonstrate to such parents that this is not the case.

Moving in and out of the Classroom

Another area where conflict can arise involves movement in and around the school. Many schools that claim to subscribe to the principles of informal education and to promote independence in their children still insist on marching in and out of school from the playground, often using whistles and bells to initiate the exercise. At other times, indirect messages are given to reinforce such rules – in one case during the ORACLE study, the teacher told the children that they mustn't steal another teacher's space when they were standing out in the corridor (i.e. the pupils should line up on the right-hand side of the

door). Often these decisions are justified in terms of safety or the fear
that smaller children will be trampled underfoot if movement is not
controlled by the teacher. The assumption behind this reasoning is
clearly that, unless there is close teacher supervision, the situation will
degenerate into chaos. The alternatives appear to be either having rules
or having no rules. The approach advocated by Gordon and his colleagues, however, insists on rules but argues that these rules can be
agreed jointly by pupils and teachers. One teacher relates an incident
where:

> 'They were always lining up and I'd have to go out and
> yell at them to line up. By the time they'd all got there and lined
> up we'd wasted at least ten minutes. When we got into the
> room I'd say, ''When the bell rings do we continue to play,
> class?'' and they'd say, ''No.'' Then I'd say, ''What do we
> do when the bell rings, class?'' and they'd chant ''Line
> up.'' And then I'd say, ''From now on I won't have to yell at
> you to line up, right?'' And they'd say, ''Right.'' And the
> next day, there I'd be, yelling at them to line up.
>
> Well this week I sent an ''I'' message instead of asking
> my usual questions. I told them how tired I was of yelling at
> them to line up and how worried I was that the Head-
> teacher was going to give me a poor rating because of all
> the time we had wasted. Then I listened to them.
>
> I couldn't believe my ears. They said they were sick of
> standing out there waiting for me and asking why they had
> to line up anyway. They couldn't understand why they
> couldn't come into the room when the bell rang.
>
> I said we'd always lined up and they asked why? I
> thought about it for a while and then I said I couldn't think
> of any reason why students had to line up except that it
> was just the way things were done.
>
> They didn't buy that. So we decided to define our needs.
> Mine were to have them get in from the playground to the
> classroom in an orderly manner in as short a time as pos-
> sible. Theirs was to avoid standing in a line for five or more
> minutes waiting for me to arrive to escort them and then
> having to march like soldiers.
>
> We decided on a solution, suggested by one of the kids,
> when the bell rang they were to walk to the room from the
> playground and I was to walk from the staff room and we'd

go in. We've been trying it for three days now and it's working beautifully. We save ten minutes a day in the round-ups and in the time that I used to spend lecturing them on lining up and marching quietly. But, the biggest difference is about how we feel about each other when we get to the room. Everybody used to be mad by the time we'd lined up. Now we go into the room feeling good and that sometimes saves the whole afternoon.'

(Gordon, 1974, p. 243)

This long extract in many ways typifies the approach of teachers who are trying to face up to the essential dilemma of progressive teaching. Teachers who wish children to engage in independent learning require pupils who are unafraid, self-reliant and self-disciplined, but it is precisely pupils with these kinds of qualities who are likely to react badly to the teacher's imposition of control over their behaviour. If the teacher continually exercises power, particularly when conflicts occur over matters of behaviour, pupils will conform either out of fear of embarrassment or fear that they will lose status and therefore self-esteem. This strategy of avoidance requires them to be dependent upon the teacher for clues about what constitutes acceptable behaviour and this dependency transmits itself to their work.

Sharing Responsibility for the Teacher's Needs

The alternative approach involves, whenever necessary, shared decision-making, with consideration given to both the teacher's and pupils' needs. This differs from the behaviour modification process where the emphasis is on the teacher's wants. Initially, this negotiated approach requires teachers to face their pupils with explanations of their needs so that the children can accept their share of responsibility. Thus teachers try to say not 'I want quiet' but 'I need quiet because I can't give out these instructions'.

It cannot be said too often that the negotiated approach does not hand over control to the children. Children need to exercise their freedoms within a framework, so they need to know which solutions to problems that they suggest are unacceptable to the teacher because they do not meet the teacher's needs. Nor does the approach mean that teachers should never tell children what to do. Telling a class to sit down or to work quietly only becomes a problem if the children decide to exert their power by reason of their numbers and refuse to comply.

It is at this juncture that the non-evaluative 'I' messages are required.

Over the years a number of schools in the various ORACLE studies have developed procedures that make use of these principles. One teacher devotes Friday afternoons to 'an open discussion' in which issues of rules and procedures are debated. Another school constructed a paper brick wall with a face appearing over the top and the caption 'It isn't fair'. Both children and teachers could take a yellow paper brick and write about something that wasn't fair and place it on the wall. Each week the yellow bricks would be collected and form part of class discussion.

When teachers use their authority to control the class and are unable to resolve the conflict at their first attempt the only recourse is to increase the power. This process can be stressful because the individual is on trial, in the eyes of both the pupils and the other teachers. Negotiating rules of behaviour has one great advantage. Although it may take time to agree the rules, the rules are everybody's so that if they are broken it is no longer a defeat, in personal terms, for the teacher. One teacher described this reduction in stress after she had undergone Gordon's programme:

> 'I was ready to quit teaching because of the constant need to be a disciplinarian. The course showed me that the real problem was my rules. I made them and I had to enforce them. That's all I accomplished most of the time. When I let the class set the rules this changed. I have time to teach now and the students like me more because I am a teacher instead of a disciplinarian. I don't know if they learn any more but we have a lot more fun learning it.'

> (Gordon, 1974, p. 272)

What is lacking at present, however, is a sustained effort on the part of teachers who use the negotiated approach successfully to reflect on the process, particularly the first encounters. This is needed for two reasons. First, an alternative is needed to the prevalent methodology of the 'don't smile until Christmas' paradigm and its various 'softer' guises where the children are first controlled by power and then the power is gradually relaxed. The second reason concerns the methods used in teacher training. Teachers in Nias's (1988) study all echoed the familiar claim that they spent the first five years building up their confidence before they were ready to experiment more fully with informal learning approaches. One suspects, however, that many teachers never build up sufficient confidence to take this step and that their training encouraged them in the belief that to abandon traditional methods of control would be too great a risk. The question of training is therefore addressed in the final chapter.

CHAPTER 9

Personal Postscript and the Dilemmas of the Teacher Trainer

Writing this last chapter constitutes a risk, in that it makes an attempt to relate my own experience of going back to the classroom to that of students who are training to enter the profession. Rereading my field notes, which were written up after each school day (a possible reason why my preparation sometimes lacked thoroughness), I am struck by their schizophrenic quality. I now understand why the headteacher, when he read them, described my account as 'self-indulgent'. At the same time, they do convey something of the nature of the activity that is primary teaching – the total absorption, the interest, the rewards when children begin to expand their ideas, the disappointment and frustration described by the teacher in the previous chapter when things go wrong and when one is at loggerheads with the class. Above all, there is the comradeship and support of colleagues who may laugh at one's mistakes but, providing that one can demonstrate care and concern about children, will give unstintingly of their time and support.

I was lucky enough to spend time in a school where teachers exhibited these qualities. Yet, when I brought other teachers to the school, as I sometimes did as part of my courses at the university, they usually said, 'I don't see anything special here'. This only suggests to me that there are many such schools up and down the country and many such teachers.

When I worked in this particular school, every teacher was there by 8.30 a.m. and many arrived at 8.00 a.m. Few left before 5.00 p.m. – until the teacher's action, that is. As the staff withdrew their goodwill, one could see the effects working through the school in terms of the relationships between the pupils and the teachers. A degree of 'authoritarianism' that I had never before witnessed began to creep into the system in order to deal with problems that occurred in the playground during school dinners. I mention this to provide the context for some of the incidents that I wish to describe. At the same time, I hope it makes the point that those who thought it necessary to 'take on' the teachers and impose strict contractual obligations have paid a high price for their victory.

Another reason for risking a personal account concerns the current state of primary teacher training. As long ago as the late 1960s, William Taylor described the world of teacher training as one of 'social and literary romanticism' in which there was 'suspicion of the intellect and the intellectual: a lack of interest in political and structural change: a stress upon the intuitive and the tangible, upon spontaneity and creativity . . . and a flight from rationality ' (Taylor, 1969, p. 12). Little appears to have changed. As I have written elsewhere (Galton, in press), training programmes can be characterised by their variety, their ineffectiveness, the anti-intellectual stance taken by many of the practitioners and, as Simon (1981) has cogently argued of primary teaching in general, a lack of pedagogic theory to inform practice. I believe that in the next few years these problems will need to be acknowledged and faced.

There is little evidence to suggest that primary training is effective in overcoming the weaknesses in practice described in this book. Lacking a firm theoretical foundation there are as many variations of courses as there are institutions and, as an external examiner, I see very little difference in the performance of the majority of students as I go from institution to institution. Training, as Alexander (1984b) points out, has exhausted a number of models, the latest of which is that of the 'reflective teacher' (Pollard and Tann, 1987). While the notion of reflection is itself important, it is also problematic (Calderhead, 1988). The role of the tutor is clearly critical, but in the reflective model it is defined to allow individuals to interpret their roles in a variety of ways. As the IT-INSET (Initial & In-Service Training) project evaluation has shown, by taking certain roles, the tutors can nullify the objectives of the enterprise (Ashton and Peacock, 1988). When tutors are faced with an innovation, the cry 'But we've always done this!' is heard as frequently among college and university trainers as it is in schools.

The current educational climate suggests that, if we cannot demonstrate clearly the importance of pedagogy within a training programme so that we bring an intellectual rigour to the process of learning to teach, and if we cannot show that the students are very different as a result of this experience, then questions will increasingly be raised about value for money. As part of a tidying up process for people who have 'special' qualities, such as experience of industry or teaching abroad, the government is proposing to 'license teachers' by apprentising them in schools. There are bound to be some who will say 'if this works for these few individuals why not with all new teachers?' The following account is therefore offered, not as a set of solutions to these problems, but to highlight some of the dilemmas to which those of us who are involved in primary training need to give our serious attention.

Practising Different Teaching Strategies

The first incident concerns the contrasts between working in a direct manner and creating a situation where the children come to feel that they have, at least, joint ownership of the learning.

The children are playing a series of games from a book on mathematics, which is designed to help them overcome various weaknesses. The games concern factors, multiplication, subtraction and place value. My rough field notes record the following events:

> The slowest group is playing a game whereby a pupil throws the dice and moves his counter the equivalent number of places along a board marked one to a hundred. Whenever he lands on a five or a multiple of five he advances five spaces (e.g. if he lands on five he moves to ten, if he is on ten he moves to fifteen). Landing on a seven or a multiple of seven has him moving back seven places (e.g. from fourteen to seven, etc.).
>
> I watch the children play and it is clear that they are only interested in getting to a hundred and winning. In some cases they move up five but never back seven. I join them and explain the purpose of the game again and also make a list of all the fives and all the sevens on the board, thereby inventing a rule for thirty-five and seventy. But I see boredom (and slight hostility) in their faces. Who is this person spoiling our game? Why can't we just move the counters on as we want and win? From the teacher's point of view there isn't much point in playing unless the children are doing more than counting. When I'm there it makes them focus on the seven times table (which presumably is the point of the game) but it is counterproductive in terms of their motivation and interest. None of the children understood the purpose of the game and the class teacher has

not explained to them why they were playing it. I asked the children why they were playing and they simply said, 'It's just a game.'

Later, I join another group of children playing another game where they had to imagine that one of them was standing at the centre of eight posts at the corners and mid-points of a three by three square. The children had to draw a five by five square outside the first one, draw in more posts and then work out how many they couldn't see. They then had to repeat it for a seven by seven square and see if they could discover a rule relating the size of the square to the number of posts they couldn't see. I had the bright idea of getting a piece of square paper and using coloured counters to represent the posts. This worked really well and it appeared that the rule was simple, namely, as one moved to the next square one doubled the number of posts one could see. Rashly, thinking that this was an opportunity to show the value of a rule in mathematics, I asked them to predict what would happen in a nine by nine square. Each child gave a different answer.

I suggested they should construct a nine by nine square with counters and check. None of the children's solutions worked although two of them were valid deductions from the previous data. Thinking that the rule was more complicated, I suggested they might try an eleven by eleven square but again no pattern emerged, so they went on to do thirteen by thirteen. The children grew very interested and by this time other pupils had joined but, alas, I was unable to find the rule and had to promise to go away that evening and work it out. Throughout the rest of the afternoon the children kept coming up to me with different solutions. They seemed to like the fact that I couldn't work it out either and, whereas with the game of sevens the children had been very reluctant to offer answers, here they were prepared to risk all sorts of suggestions without any feelings of apparent embarrassment.

This was but one of the many dilemmas raised in mathematics classes. I witnessed many instances illustrating children's fears of getting things wrong during straightforward practice sessions. One child actually put her hand over the book to prevent the answer from being seen (this happened with several other teachers). Other pupils were genuinely amazed when allowed to check their own answers. The counting fives and sevens game had a high degree of risk attached to it unless one had mastered one's tables. Some children therefore ignored the rule about sevens, thus reducing the game to a simple counting exercise. Paradoxically, the group that had the most difficult problem – the one with the posts – required least attention, getting on and organising each stage of the activity for themselves.

The question, however, is how such an incident might have been interpreted by many tutors. Would I have been criticised for confusing children by giving them a problem that I had not checked out beforehand? What should I have done about the children who ended up simply counting up to a hundred? In this situation, the advice that tutors give to the students seems to emphasise what might be termed 'entry strategies'. The trouble could have been avoided with better preparation, better anticipation, etc. My own experience and my observations of other teachers suggest that we often do things on the spur of the moment, like extending the problem of the posts, and what students need are 'exiting' strategies that allow them to cope with these uncertainties and make the best of the situation.

In many cases, the role of the trainer appears not dissimilar to that of the professional golf coach of the traditional kind, as I have argued elsewhere (Galton, in press). The problem incident is broken down into component parts in the same way as a golf swing is analysed. Then each step is rehearsed. In golf, if a mistake is made the ball is simply replaced and the learner tries again. Teaching, however, is not like golf. No two incidents are ever that similar. In school, conditions are always varying. There may be interruptions by visitors, unexpected opportunities for outings, rearrangement of space, and so on. The situation is more like the actual golf round where the ball has to be played where it lies and we have to apply the method to a novel situation. It's then that the coaching technique lets us down and we begin to play safe by working on the assumption that we will not play our best shot; we therefore take an easier club to make certain of some progress. Too much teaching practice sees students playing safe in this way.

The New Teacher and Classroom Control

However, the major dilemmas in training concern behaviour. Here serious questions have to be addressed concerning the model that we propose to use in order that students can achieve a reasonable level of control in the classroom by the time that teaching practice has ended. If we accept the argument in this book that children will only risk taking responsibility for their own learning if they are also encouraged to take responsibility for their behaviour, then what should we demand of students, particularly in classrooms where such a system does not operate? Many tutors argue that it is unreasonable to ask a student, in so short a time, to try to change the existing system. Students are therefore encouraged to be firm, as a temporary expedient even to shout, and, particularly in the reception class, to use tricks (hands on head, finger on lips, etc.) that I have argued are very reminiscent of dog-training strategies. As tutors we comfort ourselves that during their first year of employment, as the students gain more confidence and have their own class, they will put our theories into practice. There is little evidence from the research to suggest that this happens in the majority of cases. If we decide, however, that students must impose the rules of behaviour then we should ask ourselves why we encourage them to offer a range of challenging activities knowing that inevitably these will end up being 'heavily' guided by the student. In promoting the ideas of independent learning among students, while at the same time telling them to 'crack down' on the pupils until they are in firm control, we may unwittingly be providing messages for the future that this strategy is reasonable and effective.

What is it like to be a student in these circumstances? Here is my account of the first time I took a class on my own. We had been doing a project in the local woods with the children choosing to investigate soil samples, leaves and bark of trees, twigs, etc.

> We got started on our topic. Some things just didn't work. Some of the children were using lamps to shine on the samples of leaf debris to see if there were any creatures that would be forced out into the darkened beaker below (as in the book). But the lamps kept on playing up and someone (allegedly the Headteacher) had forgotten to order the spares. Some of the children were planting out seeds into the soil, but most of my attention was given to a group who were sieving the various soils. I tried to get them to think about 'fairness' by weighing the amounts of materials which had not passed through the sieve, but they needed a lot of help in order to work out the mathematics of the weighing exercise. Consequently I was rushing to get round to some of the others.

The children then begin writing up their accounts of the experiments, but there are lots of requests for help with various words. They want to know whether to use 'were' or 'where', 'there' or 'their'. If I have time I shall make a small dictionary of these most obvious mistakes and title it 'Which Word Do You Want to Use?' Each page would have two sentences, one with each word of the pair, because whenever I ask the children to select the most appropriate word after hearing the sentence with the word in it they can do it.

After a while it becomes clear that we need to sit down together and talk more about what the children have done before writing up the experiments. I stop them from writing and agree to their request to continue sewing (they have traced out various creatures on hessian and are sewing them in bright woollen colours as part of a large display). This is the moment for baiting Mr. Galton in order to see 'How far can we go?' I think it was Clare who starts it by coming up to me and saying 'You don't get cross like some teachers here, Mr. Galton. Do you?' Impossible not to feel a warm glow of pride. At that time I had not yet realised what was coming. What they were really asking, of course, was 'What do we have to do to get you cross like other teachers?' From then on, most of the children show total learned helplessness. They can't find things, they can't do things, although I have seen them perform the same tasks several times with other teachers. They all want to go to the lavatory. Clearing up takes ages and there are grumbles that it is other people's mess not theirs. By now I am trying not to show my annoyance which is, of course, what they are trying to make me do. In the end, I take the four silliest girls and tell them that they have made it difficult for us to work. I ask them to stay behind for one minute, reading calmly to show me that they can do it. There are protests, more giggles, threats to go, but I sit there and read quietly with them, looking occasionally at my watch, and, wonder of wonder, things settle down.

This account was written immediately after the lesson. No doubt many tutors would argue that poor organisation and lack of preparation contributed to my problems. There may have been better ways of handling the pupils' dependency. I could, for example, have confronted the children with their behaviour. But that is not the point of describing the incident. My recollection of events as written here was that, although being tested, I remained calm and came out of the situation reasonably well. I imagine that a student might write in his evaluations,

> 'The class was a bit noisy but eventually the children settled. I had to keep one or two of the girls back at the end for a short period to show that I meant business when I asked for quiet.'

However, when the teacher from the adjoining base area came in next morning the first thing she laughingly greeted me with was 'Hello Hitler'! To my amazement she went on to describe the several occasions when she had walked through the base and heard me being authoritative, once telling a child 'Don't put your fingers in the soil' (a reference to an incident when one of the girls had put her fingers in messy, sludgy water and soil and was trying to wipe it on her neighbour). More importantly, I had shouted at the end of the afternoon saying, 'I gave you out ten needles and I want ten back. Where are my needles?'

This seemed to me at the time, and still does, a remarkable illustration of the perception gap in teaching. Until I was told about the incident and until I got the children to confirm it later, I had no recollection of asking for the needles. It also illustrates, most vividly, the difference between 'coping' and 'expressive' behaviour and the way we suppress feelings that we do not wish to acknowledge. Just before my co-teacher left for the day she had reminded me, quite offhandedly, about the needles. Because they were using wool, the children needed needles with large eyes and these were in short supply. It was essential, therefore, for future occasions that I got them all back. It seems clear that, even if unconsciously, this fact registered with me as one of great significance. This was my first day alone with the class and naturally I hoped to prove myself to my co-teacher. What better way than by saying to her next day, 'You gave me ten needles and here are your ten needles back'? In my head, being a good teacher was about not losing control, trying to avoid conflict, recognising that the children would test me out, and so on. In my heart, being a good teacher was about getting ten needles back from the children. It appears that it was the heart that ruled the head in these classroom exchanges.

Every year I read a large number of diaries and files when I visit students on teaching practice. I would guess that many of these student teachers experience initiations of a similar kind to mine. I have never yet seen any accounts of such experiences that describe such feelings and tensions.

Indeed, I recently visited a student, as an external examiner, and read the following evaluation in her teaching practice file.

> I missed Su [the class teacher] today. The children were restless and didn't seem to want to settle. I had to get quite cross with Vincent on several occasions.
>
> Games in the afternoon were better. The children enjoyed practising 'starts' for the sports day races, although one or two were a little silly.
>
> Oh God! What a day.

It transpired, when talking to the class teacher, that the student had at one point rushed out of the classroom in tears. When I asked this student why she had left out all mention of what had obviously been a traumatic experience in her evaluation, she replied 'I didn't think it would go down well with my tutor'.

This remark would appear to reinforce Gordon's view that the myth of the 'super-teacher' hinders our professional development because it causes us to exclude any mention of our feelings when describing classroom incidents (see Chapter 8). My argument, however, is that teacher training courses actually help to perpetuate this situation. Having examined in some dozen different institutions I have rarely met a student who felt it was legitimate to express their feelings within their evaluation. Objectivity – triangulating one's assessment of what pupils learned – seems to be what is required.

The students take their cue from their tutors and tutors seem reluctant to offer themselves as models. This certainly appears to be the case in the accounts collected by the Teacher Education Study Group of the Society for Research into Higher Education concerning their members' 'recent and relevant experience'. There is little in these accounts that indicates the passion of teaching, the stress coupled with the wonderful moments when pupils will trust you enough to confide precious secrets, as in my own case when Debbie was helping me to sew my creature.

> DEBBIE: Bevan's going out with Michelle.
> ME: What does going out mean?

DEBBIE: Going to the park and kissing. Michelle was shy
so we had to write a note to Bevan saying she
fancied him.

Instead, the author of one report from the Teacher Education Study
Group evaluates his experience as follows:

Subsequently, it has been suggested that I comment on
how others see me. In one sense I must answer that I don't
know, for whoever sees himself or takes others' comments
at face value? In another sense I can offer a few observations.

My teaching colleagues were generous in their gifts of
the currency of the classroom – yoghurt pots and toilet
rolls – when I was needy. They gave information and
advice and saved me from my scrawled labelling with their
practised and bold scripts. They also pulled me up for
breaking with unimagined customs and, had I been a
permanent member of staff, this would have led to friction.
As a guest, like a student, I acquiesced. The Head too
generally took me as a colleague, although sometimes he
talked to me as an outsider with whom problems might be
shared.

The children – sensibly, I think – treated me as a short-
stay guest. While all accepted me, there were degrees of
enthusiasm and in general their regular teacher was preferred. And as a teacher myself I'd have worried had a student
built better relations with my class than I had. Similarly,
parents preferred to talk to the class teacher.

(Mills, 1985, p. 16)

Not surprisingly, the author concludes that a tutor's 'recent and
relevant' school experience has 'little direct and practical value in
terms of keeping one's hand in – keeping a grasp of reality'. He goes
on,

If this sort of updating will not for most tutors enlighten
through an encounter with reality what is the point of
returning to yesterday's job?

This conclusion seems, to me, to miss the whole point of the
experience. This is that it allows the tutor to research the classroom
alongside the experienced teacher in ways that explore the tensions

between theory and practice. Equally important, the experience allows the tutors to say to the student, 'Let me tell you how I felt so you will be encouraged to tell me how you felt'. The writer of the report, however, does not see this as a positive benefit.

> In short, I was like a student teacher. I kept, religiously, a file. An *unexpected* outcome was that I became more sympathetic to students on teaching practice: perhaps my standards were somewhat lowered even?
>
> (Mills, 1985, p. 16)

Again, this surely misses the point. If we wish more students to try out negotiated models of learning, or at least to explore the personal problems involved when using more authoritarian approaches, then we need to begin by sharing common experiences with our students. A central theme of primary training is that children learn best through experience and activity. Why should we reject this model in our own dealings with students?

The New Teacher and the Art of Negotiation

My third and final incident therefore concerns another failure of control, this time more calculated in that it was an attempt to re-negotiate the arrangements for 'quiet reading'. This reading was done in a gallery which was open to the gymnasium. Most of the staff used only one-third of this space because all children were then in the teacher's sight. This meant, however, that they were very cramped. I therefore decided to bargain with the class so that they could spread themselves out, provided they remained quiet. My field notes recorded the following experience:

> As we get ready to go up the stairs, Ian is involved in a scuffle with Lee. The other children complain that he has pushed in front because he wants to get the bean bag. I say to him, 'Do you want the bean bag, Ian?' and he replies, 'No', so I then say, 'You don't need to rush up the queue then, do you?'
>
> I stay at the bottom of the stairs seeing everyone through. By the time I come up, Ian is sitting on the bean bag. Just how he got it I don't know, but I suspect he pushed someone else off. I decide not to tackle the issue but to leave well alone. The children won't settle so I have

to stop them and put the case once more for letting me hear people read, allowing them to sit comfortably and getting on quietly. I still have to go round to sort out various niggles, with two children trying to push against the bean bag. Eventually, everyone settles except Ian. He just won't stop. He talks, he pushes, he does everything to annoy me. His restlessness communicates itself to some of the other boys and I find myself constantly having to reason with him to settle down. Eventually, the noise drops to a reasonable level but then, just as two prospective parents arrive to view the library area with the Deputy, Carl is involved in a scuffle with Jason over where they are sitting. I ask Carl to come out and see me, pointing out, as reasonably as I can, what his behaviour must have looked like to the people coming up the stairs. In fact they probably didn't see him because there is a wall obscuring the way, but the thought seems to sober him down and peace is restored until Ian starts again. I turn to him and in the most reasonable voice I can muster, despite my irritation, say,

'Look Ian. When you go on like this I can't hear people read. People who need some practice can't do it because everytime I settle down to listen I have to look up and stop you from fooling around. Why are you doing this? Is it because you want to make me lose my temper? I suppose if you want me to shout I can but it won't do me or you any good will it?'

It seems to work. I suppose he was trying to get my attention because I haven't picked him out to read which I usually do when I join his group but I am trying a new strategy of reinforcing his good rather than his poor behaviour. However, he now settles, but sitting next to him is a small boy called Michael and he starts talking to him. And then, quite unfairly, I let this get to me. It's Michael's first offence but I treat it as if he is responsible for Ian's misdemeanours. I get up and go across to Michael and pull him away from Ian, making him sit in front of me on the floor. I then have a go at him.

'Now why, Michael, why? You heard me ask Ian for quiet didn't you? I thought we had a bargain. Why are you doing this to me?'

He is silent and resentful. I suppose he is thinking that

this is the first time he has done anything and here I am going on at him so. So I soften my voice a lot and I ask him whether he thinks it's right to do what he did. At last he responds with a small 'No' and for a moment I thought he was going to cry. However, he settles down and reads quietly and after my outburst the class is very silent.

At the end of the session I ask Michael to stay behind. I have seen him rubbing his arm where I must have grabbed him too hard. I see the headlines – Professor assaults nine year old – parents complain. I say to him 'You weren't very happy then were you?' He says, 'No. It wasn't fair. Ian talked lots of times and you didn't do him for it. I only talked once.' I try to explain saying, 'I'm sorry, Michael.' I then go on to explain about my stress in trying to get Ian settled and then his talking started Ian off again, particularly after the two parents came up. As we go down the stairs I put my arm round his shoulder and say to him 'I'm sorry. You got it really because of Ian. I hope there are no hard feelings', and he now rewards me with an angelic smile and says 'No'.

At the time I had not read Thomas Gordon's book, *Teacher Effectiveness Training* (1974), but in it he readily acknowledges that first encounters with 'I messages' are likely to be extremely stressful and that inevitably teachers will publicly resort once again to using power, as I did with Michael. Gordon concedes that the use of authority may be worth the price in circumstances where there is clear and obvious danger to others, where the child cannot stand the logic of the teacher's position, or where there is time pressure. However, he points out that in such situations teachers can take steps, afterwards, to prevent permanent damage to the relationship by explaining to the student why they used their authority, saying they are sorry, actively listening to the student's feelings, offering to make up in some way acceptable to the student, and initiating some planning with the pupil to avoid getting into a similar situation in the future.

Later I came to see that this incident was the turning point. The next day I was able to discuss with the group what I had felt like in the situation and this, in turn, caused them to express their anxieties about reading aloud – 'You're scared you make a mistake'. We agreed on ways in which we could signal to each other more openly about these anxieties and problems. Like the teacher quoted in the previous chapter, I do not claim that it solved all my problems, but it marked the beginning of a change in the relationship with the class, which was reflected in the work that the children began to do. In retrospect, the incident in the library developed badly because I began it badly. Before going up to the balcony, I sent too many 'You' messages. I didn't ask them whether they would like to spread themselves out, I simply told them that that was what they were going to do. I told them what I expected of them without saying why. The problem was therefore my problem rather than a jointly owned one.

Teaching Practice: Experimentation or Virility Test

Clearly the situation was a stressful one, with the usual questions of 'How far can I let them go before I really lose control?' filling my mind. This communicated itself to me in my reaction to Michael. But how would we as trainers handle this if I had been a student? Would we simply say that the attempt was too ambitious or can we create conditions that enable the student to try out these strategies?

One method I have used myself is to negotiate on the student's behalf by asking the children to put themselves in the position of the student teacher and asking, 'How can we make things better?' Many tutors and teachers that I have spoken to about my intervention are against this practice, arguing that it undermines the student's authority with the pupils. But this judgement surely arises from a view of teacher training as a kind of 'virility test' in which the student has to prove himself to be as competent as the class teacher; this is perhaps why so many students adopt the actual practices of their mentors. If we wish to encourage students to see teaching practice as a period of experimentation, we need to get the classroom teacher to negotiate suitable conditions for the student. In this way the rules are clearly understood before the practice begins and the whole period of testing out the student is minimised. If we wish students to adopt negotiation as a strategy in the classroom, then students must, as Joyce and Showers (1983) argue, enjoy at least some limited success.

My final comment, therefore, is a reflection on my whole experience of going back to the classroom. This was written after I returned to the university. In some ways, I believe, it provides an agenda for an attempt to develop an effective pedagogy for the primary classroom as we move towards the end of the twentieth century.

I asked myself, was it wrong for me to try to go into a class and operate in a slightly different way from the more

familiar teacher when I hadn't built up the same relationship? At times, clearly, the strain told because I am sure my
voice took on a tense note and the other staff discerned
this. It would be the same for any student. But the whole
experience has convinced me that the analysis is right. You
can have control but you get dependency in work. It may
not be so open as in my own case where the children, to try
me out, were continually coming and asking for help at
first, but there is no doubt that underneath the friendliness
the children have insecurity which comes from worrying in
case they don't get the right answers, which in many cases
they define as being the answer the teacher wants.
Children in the first year base were very dependent or, as
most of the teachers said, 'fussy'. The question is how one
gets a whole school policy whereby staff can agree to
operate in a certain way and then translate that policy to fit
in with their own particular values, beliefs and strengths.
The four of us in the second year base area were unable to
plan a coherent strategy for doing an exercise in estimation
and measurement and yet here I am suggesting that a
much more difficult kind of continuity should be developed
across different base areas.

This school is outstanding in many ways and I have
learnt this in the short time that I have been here. The staff
support each other, witness the help they gave me and the
support they gave other teachers when they were having
similar difficulties because of temporary supply cover.
They are prepared to work long hours in trying to develop
interesting and varied curriculum activities for the children,
and the concern for their pupils' welfare is outstanding. Yet
all of us continually started things we couldn't finish
because either the necessary base areas were required by
someone else and trade-offs couldn't take place or
because we needed to fit in other things such as completing sports heats or carrying out sponsorship exercises.
We were all continually frustrated by events.

Yet in spite of all these difficulties I think there is no other
way to proceed but to try to shift more responsibility onto
the children for both the management of their learning and
the management of their classroom environment so that
they do not need constant teacher direction. To work this

system well you have to be wonderfully skilful and naturally gifted like some of the teachers here. It is harder for the rest of us who can't diffuse a crisis situation so easily or lack the easy humour to joke children away from confrontations. In the end, you probably have to be prepared to give yourself totally because the children can rapidly identify a false sense of openness in negotiation. I suppose the next stage is to get those teachers who seem to do these things naturally to reflect critically on their own practice. At the moment, someone who is a master of the craft can sometimes be seen as a potential threat by the rest of us because we don't think we can match up to their expectations. Because no-one is in a position to offer evidence to support their success at negotiation, it is possible for the rest of us to say, 'I still believe that you need to be firm at first, etc.' We need to be able to put these different views to empirical testing with teachers observing each other's practice critically. This school is further down the road than many others I have visited in this respect. The fact that they still have a long way to go (as the staff would acknowledge) only makes the task of trying to change some other schools, which are much less responsive to such issues, a very daunting one. But we must try if we are to tackle the problems which are endemic to teaching at the moment and which exhaust teachers so much that they have little energy to rethink and re-evaluate their practice. I relished those calmer periods during my time in the school when we were involved in modelling clay or sewing and I hated the times under pressure when the children, with little confidence in their work, were continually 'at me' for help and support. Like my students here at the University, I wanted sometimes to say to the pupils, 'You can't be enjoying this and neither am I. Let's find a better way.'

Many of the students I teach already possess those natural gifts of seemingly easy rapport with young children that are characteristic of the best primary teachers. If someone less talented can enjoy a limited success during a six-week period in the search for 'a better way', then so too can they.

References

Aitken, M., Bennett, S. N. and Heskett, J. (1981) 'Teaching styles and pupil progress: A reanalysis'. *British Journal of Educational Psychology*, **51**: 170–86

Alexander, R. (1984a) *Primary teaching*. London: Holt, Rinehart & Winston

Alexander, R. (1984b) 'Innovation and continuity in the initial teacher education curriculum'. In R. Alexander, M. Craft, and J. Lynch (eds) *Change in teacher education*. London: Holt, Rinehart & Winston

Alexander, R. (1988) 'Garden or jungle: Teachers' development and informal primary education'. In A. Blyth (ed.) *Informal primary education today: Essays and studies*. Lewes: Falmer Press

Allport, G. W. (1966) 'Expressive behaviour'. In B. Semeonoff (ed.) *Personality assessment*. London: Penguin Books

Anderson, H. H. (1939) 'The measurement of domination and of socially integrative behaviour in teachers' contacts with children'. *Child Development*, **10**: 73–89

Anderson, L., Evertson, C. and Brophy, J. (1979) 'An experimental study of effective teaching in first-grade reading groups'. *Elementary School Journal*, **79**: 193–223

Anthony, W. S. (1979) 'Progressive learning theories: The evidence'. In G. Bernbaum (ed.) *Schooling in decline*. London: Macmillan

Anthony, W. S. (1982) 'Research on progressive teaching'. *British Journal of Educational Psychology*, **52**: 381–5

Armstrong, M. (1980) *Closely observed children*. London: Writers and Readers Co-operative and Chameleon Press

Armstrong, M. (1981) 'The case of Louise and the painting of landscape'. In J. Nixon (ed.) *A teachers' guide to action research*. London: Grant McIntyre

Ashton, P. (1981) 'Primary teachers' approaches to personal and social behaviour'. In B. Simon and J. Willcocks (eds) *Research and practice in the primary classroom*. London: Routledge & Kegan Paul

Ashton, P. and Peacock, A. (1988) Centre for Evaluation and Development in Teacher Education, *Final Report*, University of Leicester

Auld, R. (1976) *The William Tyndale junior and infants schools*, A report of the Public Inquiry. London: ILEA

Ausubel, D. (1978) 'In defense of advanced organisers: A reply to the critics'. *Review of Educational Research*, **48**: 251–7

Bandura, A. (1986) *Social foundations of thought and action*. Englewood Cliffs, NJ: Prentice Hall

Barker-Lunn, J. (1970) *Streaming in the primary school*. Slough: NFER

Barker-Lunn, J. (1984) 'Junior school teachers: Their methods and practices'. *Educational Research*, **26**: 178–87

Barr, A. S. (1935) 'The validity of certain instruments employed in the measurement of teaching ability'. In H. Walker (ed.) *The measurement of teaching efficiency*. New York: Macmillan

Barrett, G. (1986) *Starting school: An evaluation of the experience*, Final Report to the AMMA (Assistant Masters and Mistresses Association) CARE (Centre for Applied Research in Education), University of East Anglia

Barrow, R. (1984) *Giving teaching back to teachers*. Brighton: Wheatsheaf

Bassey, M. (1978) *Nine hundred primary school teachers*. Slough: NFER

Bealing, D. (1972) 'Organization of junior school classrooms'. *Educational Research*, **14**: 231–5

Becker, H. S., Geer, B. and Hughes, E. (1968) *Making the grade: The academic side of college life*. New York: John Wiley

Beckman, L. (1976) 'Causal attributions of teachers and parents regarding children's performance', *Psychology in Schools*. **13**: 212–18

Bennett, N. (1976) *Teaching styles and pupil progress*. London: Open Books

Bennett, N. (1978) 'Recent research on teaching: A dream, a belief and a model', *British Journal of Educational Psychology*, **48**: 127–47

Bennett, N. (1987) 'The search for the effective primary teacher'. In S. Delamont (ed.) *The primary school teacher*. London: Falmer Press

Bennett, N. and McNamara, D. (eds) (1979) *Focus on teaching*. London: Longman

Bennett, N., Andreae, J., Hegarty, P. and Wade, B. (1980) *Open plan schools*. Slough: NFER

Bennett, N., Desforges, C., Cockburn, A. and Wilkinson, B. (1984) *The quality of pupil learning experiences*. London: Lawrence Erlbaum

Berliner, D (1979) 'Tempus educare'. In P. Peterson and H. Walberg (eds) *Research on teaching: Concepts, findings and implications*. Berkeley, Calif.: McCutchan

Bernbaum, G. (1976) 'Education: The desert of the mind', an inaugural lecture. University of Leicester, mimeo

Bernbaum, G. (1979) *Schooling in decline*. London: Macmillan

Block, J. (1971) *Mastery learning: Theory and practice*. New York: Holt, Rinehart & Winston

Bloom, B. S. (1971) 'Learning for mastery'. In B. S. Bloom, J. T. Hastings and G. F. Madaus (eds) *Handbook of formative and summative evaluation of student learning*. New York: McGraw-Hill

Blyth, A. (1984) *Development, experience and curriculum in primary education*. London: Croom Helm

Borg, W. R. (1980) 'Time and school learning'. In C. Denham and A. Lieberman (eds) *Time to learn*. Washington DC: Department of Education and Welfare, National Institute of Education

Boydell, D. (1974) 'Teacher–pupil contact in junior classrooms'. *British Journal of Educational Psychology.* **44**: 313–18

Boydell, D. (1975) 'Pupil behaviour in junior classrooms'. *British Journal of Educational Psychology.* **45**: 122–9

Brophy, J. (1979) 'Teacher behaviour and its effects'. *Journal of Educational Psychology*, **71**: 733–50

Brown, I. and Inouye, D. (1978) 'Learned helplessness through modelling: The role of perceived similarity in competence'. *Journal of Personality and Social Psychology*, **36**: 900–8

Bruner, J. (1966) *Towards a theory of instruction.* Cambridge, Mass.: Harvard University Press

Bruner, J., Goodnow, J. and Austin, A. (1977) *A study of thinking.* New York: John Wiley

Burke, E. and Lewis, D. G. (1975) 'Standards of reading: a critical review of some recent studies'. *Educational Research.* **17**: 163–74

Burns, R. (1982) *Self-concept, development and education* London: Holt, Rinehart & Winston

Burstall, C. (1979) 'Minding the nets: A commentary on class size research'. *Trends in Education*, **3**: 27–33

Bussis, A. M. and Chittenden, E. A. (1970) *Analysis of an approach to open education*, Interim Report. Princeton, NJ: Educational Testing Service

Calderhead, J. (ed.) (1987) *Exploring teachers' thinking.* London: Cassell

Calderhead, J. (1988) 'Reflective teaching and teacher education', Proceedings American Educational Research Association Annual Meeting, New Orleans 1988

Callaghan, J. (1976) 'Towards a national debate – The Prime Minister's Ruskin speech'. *Education*, 22 October, pp. 332–3

Carroll, J. (1963) 'A model of school learning'. *Teachers' College Record*, **64**. 723–33

Cazden, C. (1969) *Infant school.* Newton, Mass.: Education Development Centre

CDCC (1985) 'Evaluation visit to the Dutch contact school "H. K. Van Duigvenvoorde" at Oost-Souberg (Zeeland)'. Council of Europe Project No. 8 *Innovation in Primary Education*, DECS/EGT, 85, 6. Strasbourg

Child Education (1986) Project file: Attitudes – how teachers deal with some of those tricky moments. **63**(6): 15–22

Coe, J. (1966) 'The junior school: approaches to non-streaming'. *Forum*, **8**: 76–9.

Cohen, A. and Cohen, L. (eds) (1986) *Primary education: A sourcebook for teachers.* London: Harper & Row

Coker, M., Medley, D. and Soar, R. (1980) 'How valid are expert opinions about effective teaching?' *Phi Delta Kappa*, **62**: 131–4

Cole, J. and Lunzer, E. (1978) 'Reading for homework'. University of Nottingham, mimeo

Coulter, F. (1981) *Secondary school students*, Cooperative Research Series No. 7. Perth, Western Australia: Education Department.

Cowie, M. (1989) 'Children as writers'. In D. Hargreaves (ed.) *Children and the arts.* Milton Keynes: Open University Press

Cowie, M. and Hanrott, M. (1984) 'The writing community: A case study of one junior school class'. In M. Cowie (ed.) *The development of children's imaginative writing*. London: Croom Helm

Cox, C. B. and Dyson, A. E. (eds) (1969a) 'Fight for education: A Black Paper'. *Critical Quarterly Society* (London)

Cox, C. and Dyson, A. (eds) (1969b) 'Black Paper Two: The Crisis in Education'. *Critical Quarterly Society* (London)

Croll, P. (1986) *Systematic classroom observation*. London: Falmer Press

Croll, P. and Moses, D. (1985) *One in five: The assessment and incidence of special educational needs*. London: Routledge & Kegan Paul

Croll, P. and Galton, M. (1986) 'A comment on "Questioning ORACLE" by John Scarth and Martyn Hammersley'. *Educational Research*, **28**(3): 185–9

Cuban, L. (1984) *How teachers taught: Constancy and change in American classrooms, 1890–1980*. New York: Longman

Dearden, R. (1976) *Problems in primary education*. London: Routledge & Kegan Paul

Delamont, S. (1983) *Interaction in the classroom*, 2nd edn. London: Methuen

Delamont, S. and Galton, M. (1986) *Inside the secondary classroom*. London: Routledge & Kegan Paul

Denham, C. and Lieberman, A. (eds) (1980) *Time to learn*. Washington DC: Department of Health, Education and Welfare, National Institute of Education

Dennison, W. (1978) 'The Assessment of Performance Unit: Where is it leading?' *Durham and Newcastle Review*, **40**: 31–6

Department of Education and Science (1977) *Education in schools: A consultative document* (Green Paper) Cmnd 6869. London: HMSO

Department of Education and Science (1985) *Better Schools*, Cmnd 9469. London: HMSO

Dillon, J. (1982) 'The multidisciplinary study of questioning'. *Journal of Educational Psychology*, **74**: 147–65

Doyle, W. (1979) 'Classroom tasks and student abilities'. In P. Peterson and H. J. Walberg (eds) *Research on teaching: Concepts, findings and implications*. Berkeley, Calif.: McCutchan

Doyle, W. (1983) 'Academic work'. *Review of Educational Research*, **53**(2): 159–99

Doyle, W. (1986) 'Classroom organisation and management'. In M. Wittrock (ed.) *3rd handbook of research on teaching*. New York: Macmillan

Duckworth, E. (1979) 'Either we're too early and they can't learn it or we're too late and they know it already: The dilemma of "Applying Piaget" '. *Harvard Educational Review*. **49**(3): 297–312

Dunkin, M. J. and Biddle, B. J. (1974) *The study of teaching*. New York: Holt, Rinehart & Winston

Dweck, C. (1975) 'The role of expectation and attributions in the alleviation of learned helplessness'. *Journal of Personality and Social Psychology*, **31**: 674–85

Edwards, A. and Westgate, D. (1987) *Investigating classroom talk*. Lewes: Falmer Press

Egan, K. (1983) *Education and psychology*. New York: Teachers' College Press

Eggleston, J., Galton, M. and Jones, M. (1975) *A science teaching observation schedule*, Schools Council Research Series. London: Macmillan Educational

Eggleston, J., Galton, M. and Jones, M. (1976) *Processes and products of science teaching*, Schools Council Research Series. London: Macmillan Educational

Eisner, E. (1977) 'On the uses of educational connoisseurship and criticism for evaluating classroom life'. *Teachers' College Record*, **78**: 345–58

Elliott, J. (1976a) *Developing hypotheses about classrooms from teachers' practical constructs – An account of the work of the Ford Teaching Project*. University of North Dakota: North Dakota Study Group on Evaluation

Elliott, J. (1976b) 'Preparing teachers for classroom accountability'. *Education for Teaching*, **100**: 49–71

Evertson, C. and Emmer, E. (1982) 'Effective management at the beginning of the school year in junior high classes'. *Journal of Educational Psychology*, **74**: 485–98

Featherstone, J. (1971) *Schools where children learn*. New York: Liveright

Fisher, C. *et al.* (1980) 'Teaching behaviors, academic learning time and student achievement: An overview'. In C. Denham and A. Lieberman (eds) *Time to learn*. Washington DC: Department of Health, Education and Welfare, National Institute of Education

Flanders, N. A. (1964) 'Some relationships among teachers' influence, pupils' attitudes and achievement'. In J. Biddle and W. J. Ellena (eds) *Contemporary research on teacher effectiveness*. New York: Holt, Rinehart & Winston

Forum Observer (1966) 'The junior school: Anatomy of the non-streamed classroom'. *Forum*, **8**: 79–85

France, N. and Fraser, I. (1975) *Richmond tests of basic skills*. London: Nelson

Gage, N. (1964) 'Theories of teaching'. In E. Hilgard (ed.) *Theories of learning and instruction*, Yearbook No. 63. University of Chicago, Ill.: National Society for the Study of Education

Gage, N. (1978) *The scientific basis of the art of teaching*. New York: Teachers' College Press

Gage, N. (1985) *Hard gains in the soft sciences: The case of pedagogy*, CEOR Monograph. Bloomington, Ind.: Phi Delta Kappa

Gage, N. and Berliner, D. (1988) *Educational psychology*, paperback edition. Boston: Houghton Mifflin

Gallagher, J. J. (1970) 'Three studies of the classroom'. In J. Gallagher, G. Nuthall and B. Rosenslinde (eds) *Classroom observation*. Mimeograph No. 6, AERA Series: Curriculum Evaluation, pp. 74–108. Chicago: Rand McNally

Galton, M. (1979) 'Systematic classroom observation: British research'. *Educational Research*, **21**(2): 109–15

Galton, M. (1981) 'Teaching groups in the junior school. A neglected art'. *Schools Organisation*, **1**(2): 175–81

Galton, M. (1987) 'An ORACLE chronicle: A decade of classroom research'. *Teaching and Teacher Education*, **3**(4): 299–314

Galton, M. J. (1988) 'The nature of learning in the primary classroom'. In A. Blyth (ed.) *Informal primary education today*. London: Falmer Press

Galton, M. (in press) 'Primary teacher training: Practice in search of a pedagogy'. In A. McClelland and V. Varma (eds) *Advances in teacher education*. London: Hodder & Stoughton

Galton, M. and Delamont, S. (1985) 'Speaking with forked tongue? Two styles of observation in the ORACLE Project'. In R. Burgess (ed.) *Field methods in the study of education*. Lewes: Falmer Press

Galton, M. and Simon, B. (eds) (1980) *Progress and performance in the primary classroom*. London: Routledge & Kegan Paul

Galton, M. and Willcocks, J. (eds) (1983) *Moving from the primary classroom*. London: Routledge & Kegan Paul

Galton, M., Patrick, H., Appleyard, R., Hargreaves, L. and Bernbaum, G. (1987) 'Curriculum provision in small schools: The PRISMS Project', *Final Report*. University of Leicester, mimeo

Galton, M., Simon, B. and Croll, P. (1980) *Inside the primary classroom*. London: Routledge & Kegan Paul

Gardener, D. (1950) *Long term results of infant school methods*. London: Methuen

Gardener, D. (1966) *Experiment and tradition in primary schools*. London: Methuen

Giaconia, R. M. and Hedges, L. (1982) 'Identifying features of effective open education'. *Review of Educational Research*, **52**: 579–602

Glass, G. (1982) 'Meta analysis: An approach to a synthesis of research results'. *Journal of Research in Science Teaching*, **19**(2): 98–112

Good, T. and Brophy, J. (1986) 'Teacher behavior and student achievement'. In M. Wittrock (ed.) *Handbook of research on teaching*, 3rd edn. New York: Macmillan

Good, T. and Grouws, D. A. (1979) 'The Missouri Mathematics Effectiveness Project: An experimental study of fourth grade classrooms'. *Journal of Educational Psychology*, **71**(3): 355–62

Good, T., Grouws, D. and Beckerman, T. (1978) 'Curriculum pacing: Some empirical data in mathematics'. *Journal of Curriculum Studies*, **10**: 75–81

Gordon, T. (1974) *T.E.T. Teacher Effectiveness Training*. New York: Peter Wyden

Graves, D. (1983) *Writing: Teachers and children at work*. Exeter, NH: Heinemann

Gray, J. and Satterly, D. (1976) 'A chapter of errors: Teaching styles and pupil progress in retrospect'. *Educational Research*, **19**(1): 45–56

Gray, J. and Satterly, D. (1981) 'Formal and informal? A reassessment of the British evidence'. *British Journal of Educational Psychology*, **51**: 187–96

Gretton, J. and Jackson, M. (1976) *William Tyndale*. London: Allen & Unwin

Hadow Report (1931) *Report of the Consultative Committee on the Primary School*. London: HMSO

Hamilton, D. and Delamont, S. (1974) 'Classroom research: A cautionary tale'. *Research in Education*, **11**: 1–15

Hargreaves, A. (1978) 'The significance of classroom coping strategies'. In L. Barton and R. Meighan (eds) *Sociological interpretations of schooling and classroom. A re-appraisal*. Driffield: Nafferton Books

Hargreaves, A. (1979) 'Strategies, decision and control: Interaction in a middle school classroom'. In J. Eggleston (ed.) *Teacher decision-making in the classroom*. London: Routledge & Kegan Paul

Hargreaves, D., Molloy, C. and Pratt, A. (1982) 'Social factors in conservation'. *British Journal of Psychology*, **73**: 231-4

Harnischfeger, A. and Wiley, D. (1978) 'Conceptual issues in models of school learning'. *Curriculum Studies*, **10**(3): 215-31

Highet, G. (1963) *The Art of teaching*, paperback edition. London: Methuen

HMI (1978) Department of Education and Science, *Primary education in England: A survey by HM Inspectors of Schools*. London: HMSO

HMI (1983) *9-13 middle schools: An illustrative survey*. London: HMSO

HMI (1985) *Education 8-12 in combined and middle schools*. London: HMSO

Hoggart, R. (1980) 'The uncertain criteria of deprivation'. In A. V. Kelly (ed.) *Curriculum context*. London: Harper & Row

Holt, J. (1984) *How children fail*, revised edition. Harmondsworth, Middx: Penguin

Hull, W. (1971) 'Leicestershire revisited'. In C. Rathbone (ed.) *Open education: The informal classroom*. New York: Scholarly Book Service

Husen, T. (ed.) (1967) *International study of achievement in mathematics*. New York: Wiley

Isaacs, N. (1955) *Piaget and progressive education*. London: National Froebel Foundation

Jones, D. (1987) 'Planning for progressivism: The changing primary school in the Leicestershire authority during the Mason era 1947-71'. In R. Lowe (ed.) *The changing primary school*. London: Falmer

Joyce, B. and Showers, B. (1983) 'Transfer of training: the contribution of coaching'. *Journal of Education*, **163**(2): 163-72

Joyce, B. and Weil, M. (1980) *Models of teaching*, 2nd edn. New Jersey: Prentice Hall

Kelly, V. (1982) *The curriculum theory and practice*, 2nd edn. London: Harper & Row

Kelly, V. (1983) 'Research in the primary curriculum'. In G. Blenkin and V. Kelly (eds) *The primary curriculum in action*. London: Harper & Row

Kelly, V. (1986) *Knowledge and curriculum planning*. London: Harper & Row

Kemp, L. (1955) 'Environmental and other characteristics determining attainment in primary schools'. *British Journal of Educational Psychology*, **25**: 67-77

Kliebard, H. (1986) *The struggle for the American curriculum 1893-1958*. New York: Methuen

Kounin, J. (1970) *Discipline and group management in classrooms*. New York: Holt, Rinehart & Winston

Kutnick, P. (1988) *Relationships in the primary school classroom*. London: Paul Chapman

Laslett, R. and Smith, C. (1984) *Effective classroom management*. London: Croom Helm

Lovell, K. (1961) *The truth of basic mathematical and scientific concepts in children*. London: University of London Press

McClelland, D.C. (1963) 'On the psychodynamics of creative physical scientists'. In M. Gruber *et al.* (eds) *Contemporary Approaches to Creative Thinking*. New York: Atherton

McGarrigle, J. and Donaldson, M. (1975) 'Conservation accidents'. *Cognition* 3: 314–50

McIntyre, D. I. (1980) 'Systematic observation of classroom activities'. *Educational Analysis*, 2(2): 3–30

McIntyre, D. and MacLeod, G. (1978) 'The characteristics and uses of systematic classroom observation'. In R. McAleese and D. Hamilton (eds) *Understanding classroom life*. Slough: NFER

Manning, D. (1977) 'The influence of key individuals on student teachers in urban and suburban settings'. *Teaching and Teacher Education*. 13(2): 2–8

Meadows, S. (1986) *Understanding child development*. London: Hutchinson

Measor, L. and Woods, P. (1984) *Changing schools: Pupil perspectives on transfer to a comprehensive*. Milton Keynes: Open University Press

Medley, D. M., Quirk, T. J., Schluck, C. G. and Ames, N. P. (1973) 'The Personal Record of School Experience' (PROSE). In E. G. Boyer, A. Simon and G. Karafin (eds) *Measures of maturation: An anthology of early childhood observation instruments*, vol. II, Philadelphia: Research for Better Schools Incorporated

Mills, C. (ed.) (1985) *The impact of cate*. Report of a one-day conference of the Teacher Education Study Group (TESG) of the Society for Research into Higher Education, 26 October

Mortimore, P., Sammons, P., Stoll, L., Lewis, D. and Ecob, R. (1987) *School matters: The junior years*. London: Open Books

Neave, G. (1987) 'Challenges met: Trends in teacher education 1975–1985'. In *New Challenges for Teachers and their Education*, M.Ed. 15–4. Strasbourg: LDCC

Nias, J. (1984) 'The definition and maintenance of self in primary teaching'. *British Journal of Sociology of Education*, 5(3): 267–80

Nias, J. (1985) 'Reference groups in primary teaching: Talking, listening and identity'. In S. Ball and I. Goodson (eds) *Teachers' lives and careers*. Lewes: Falmer Press

Nias, J. (1988) 'Informal education in action: Teachers' accounts'. In A. Blyth (ed.) *Informal primary education today*. London: Falmer Press

Norman, D. (1978) 'Notes towards a complex theory of learning'. In J. Pellegrino, S. Fokkena, *et al.* (eds) *Cognitive psychology and instruction*, NATO Conference Proceedings, 13–17 June 1977, Free University of Amsterdam. New York: Plenum Press

Olson, W. C. (1929) 'The measurement of habits in normal children'. *Institute of Child Welfare*, monograph 3

Plowden Report (1967) *Children and their primary schools*, 2 vols, Report of the Central Advisory Council for Education in England. London; HMSO

Plowden, Lady B. (1987) ' "Plowden" twenty years on'. *Oxford Review of Education*, 13(1): 119–25

Pollard, A. (1985) *The social world of the primary school*. London: Holt, Rinehart & Winston

Pollard, A. (ed.) (1987) *Children and their primary schools*. London: Falmer Press

Pollard, A. and Tann, S. (1987) *Reflective teaching in the primary classroom*. London: Cassell

Richards, C. (1975) 'Primary teachers' perceptions of discovery learning'. In P. Taylor (ed.) *Aims, influence and change in the primary curriculum*. Slough: NFER

Richards, C. (1982) 'Primary education 1974–80'. In C. Richards (ed.) *New directions in primary education*. Lewes: Falmer Press

Rogers, V. (1970) *Teaching in the British primary school*. London: Collier Macmillan

Rosenshine, B. (1979) 'Content, time and direct instruction'. In P. Peterson and H. Walberg (eds) *Research on teaching: concepts, findings and implications*. Berkeley, Calif.: McCutchan

Rosenshine, B. (1980) 'How time is spent in elementary classrooms'. In C. Denham and A. Lieberman (eds) *Time to learn*. Washington DC: Department of Health, Education and Welfare, National Institute of Education

Rosenshine, B. (1987) 'Direct instruction'. In M. Dunkin (ed.) *Teaching and teacher education*. Oxford: Pergamon Press

Rowe, M. B. (1974) 'Wait-time and rewards as instructional variables, their influence on language, logic and fate control'. *Journal of Research in Science Teaching*, **11**: 81–94

Rowland, S. (1984) *The enquiring classroom*. Lewes: Falmer Press

Rowland, S. (1987) 'An interpretative model of teaching and learning'. In A. Pollard (ed.) *Children and their primary schools*. London: Falmer Press

Scarth, J. and Hammersley, M. (1986) 'Questioning ORACLE: An assessment of ORACLE's analysis of teachers' questions'. *Educational Research*, **28**(3): 174–84

Scarth, J. and Hammersley, M. (1987) 'More questioning of ORACLE: A reply to Croll and Galton'. *Educational Research*, **29**(1): 37–46

Schools Council (1978) *Impact and take up project*, 1st Interim Report. London: Schools Council

Schools Council (1980) *Impact and take up project*, 2nd Interim Report. London: Schools Council

Schools Council (1983) *Primary practice: A sequel to 'The practical curriculum'*, Working Paper 75. London: Methuen

Selleck, R. J. W. (1972) *English primary education and the progressives 1914–1939*. London: Routledge & Kegan Paul

Sharp, R. and Green, A. (1975) *Education and social control: A study in progressive primary education*. London: Routledge & Kegan Paul

Silberman, C. E. (1970) *Crisis in the classroom: The remaking of American education*. New York: Random House

Silberman, C. E. (ed.) (1973) *The open classroom reader*. New York: Vintage Books

Simon, B. (1953) 'Intelligence testing and the comprehensive school'; reprinted in B. Simon (1971) *Intelligence, psychology and education*. London: Lawrence and Wishart

Simon, B. (1981) 'Why no pedagogy in England?' In B. Simon and W. Taylor (eds) *Education in the eighties*. London: Batsford Educational

Simon, B. and Willcocks, J. (eds) (1981) *Research and practice in the primary classroom*. London: Routledge & Kegan Paul

Soar, R. (1977) 'An integration of findings from four studies of teacher effectiveness'. In G. Borich and K. Fenton (eds) *The appraisal of teaching: concepts and process*. Reading, Mass.: Addison Wesley

Soar, R. S. and Soar, R. M. (1972) 'An empirical analysis of selected follow through programs: An example of a process approach to evaluation'. In I. J. Gordon (ed.) *Early childhood education*. Chicago: National Society for the Study of Education

Southgate, V., Arnold, H. and Johnson, S. (1981) *Extending beginning reading*. London: Heinemann (for the Schools Council)

Spooner, R. T. (1980) ' "Teacher Craft" a review of *Focus on Teaching*' N. Bennett and D. McNamara (eds). *Education*, 27 June

Stallings, J. (1980) 'Allocated academic learning time revisited or beyond time on task'. *Educational Research*, **8**(11): 11–16

Start, K. B. and Wells, B. K. (1972) *The trend of reading standards*. Slough: NFER

Sternberg, R. (1982) 'Reasoning, problem solving and intelligence'. In R. Sternberg (ed.) *Handbook of human intelligence*. Cambridge: Cambridge University Press

Taba, H. (1966) *Teaching strategies and cognitive functioning in elementary school children*, United States Office of Education (USOE), Co-operative Research Project No. 1574. San Francisco State College

Taba, H. and Elzey, F. F. (1964) 'Teaching strategies and thought processes'. *Teacher College Record*, **65**: 524–34

Taylor, W. (1969) *Society and the education of teachers*. London: Faber

Tizard, B., Blatchford, D., Burke, J., Farquhar, C. and Plewis, I. (1988) *Young children at school in the inner city*. Hove and London: Lawrence Erlbaum

Warburton, F. (1964) 'Attainment in the school environment'. Ch VI in S. Wiseman, *Education and the environment*. Manchester: Manchester University Press

Warnock Report (1978) *Report of the Committee of Enquiry on the Education of Handicapped Children and Young People*. London: HMSO

Weiner, B. (1986) *Attributional theory of motivation and emotion*. New York: Springer-Verlag

Whitbread, N. (1972) *The evolution of the nursery–infant school 1800–1970*. London: Routledge & Kegan Paul

Whiteley, B. and Friele, I. (1985) 'Children's causal attributions for success and failure in achievement settings'. *Journal of Educational Psychology*, **5**: 608–16

Wilkinson, M. (1977) *Lessons from Europe: A comparison of British and Western European schooling*. London: Centre for Policy Studies

Wittrock, M. (1963) 'Verbal stimuli in concept formation: Learning by discovery'. *Journal of Educational Psychology*, **54**: 183–90

Woods, P. (1977) 'Teaching for survival'. In P. Woods and M. Hammersley (eds) *School Experience*. London: Croom Helm

Woods, P. (1980) *Pupil strategies*. London: Croom Helm

Wragg, E. C. (1978) 'A suitable case for imitation'. *The Times Educational Supplement*, 15 September, p.18

Index